W9-CFT-449

MORE PRAISE FOR *THE CONVERT*

"[A] stellar biography that doubles as a meditation on the fraught relationship between America and the Muslim world. . . . A cogent, thought-provoking look at a radical life and its rippling consequences."
— *Publishers Weekly* (starred review)

"Spellbinding. . . . Baker's investigation of [Maryam] Jameelah yields mysteries and surprises galore. A significant contemporary figure in Islamic-Western relations becomes human, with all the foibles and angst that word implies." — *Library Journal* (starred review)

"[Baker] opens the door to the vital questions of how radical Islam has impacted the world, and what part converts such as [Maryam] Jameelah have played. . . . An important, searing, highly readable and timely narrative."
— *Kirkus Reviews* (starred review)

"[*The Convert*] is more than a biography; it gets at the heart of the ongoing conflict between Islam and the West." — *Marie Claire*

"By unpacking the boxes and piecing together [Maryam] Jameelah's complicated life, Baker untangled a nonfiction narrative as surreal as any fairy tale. . . . Engrossing." — *Star Tribune* (Minneapolis)

"This book is a beautiful illustration of a profoundly unique person, Maryam Jameelah. If you like a biography with a twist, *The Convert* is for you."— *Jewcy*

"Conversion narratives have been a staple of American writing since the Puritans arrived in New England. But if the form that stories of spiritual rebirth take is familiar to us, some journeys are longer and more fantastic than others. Surely the tale of Margaret Marcus is among the more extreme. . . . [*The Convert*] does raise fascinating questions about the relations of the West and Islam, about religion, freedom, and choice, but it's a parable as well about the quixotic search for certainty, both by Baker, who realizes its futility, and by Jameelah, who finally remains a true believer."— *Chicago Tribune*

Brown County Public Library
205 Locust Lane / PO Box 8
Nashville, IN 47448 ~~JUL~~ WITHDRAWN 2013
Ph. 812-988-2850 Fax 812-988-8119

"If you like thrillers, Deborah Baker's 'tale of exile and extremism' is a true story with a new twist at every turn of the page. If you haven't read a good biography lately, then too here's your opportunity. And this is just for starters, since *The Convert* is ample nutrition for our minds, morals and politics." —*Indian Express* (New Delhi)

"[Deborah] Baker's inquiry and investigation into the life of [Maryam] Jameelah is a nuanced and sophisticated study, in which the author grapples as much with herself and her assumptions as she does with the character whose life she is exploring. . . . The complex ways in which Baker's own voice intermeshes into the narrative is part of the sophistication and uniqueness of this search." —*India Today* (New Delhi)

"With remarkable evenhandedness, Deborah Baker reveals the terrible costs of belonging exacted by two very different, battling cultures. Sweeping books on the big wars can't do what this focused gaze on a single misfit so vividly accomplishes." —Kiran Desai

"In this unusual, sometimes funny and sometimes frightening biography Deborah Baker deftly explores the urgency and lunacy of conversion, Pakistan—and America's—romance with fundamentalism, and the necessity for a less blinkered vision of Islam." —Fatima Bhutto

BROWN COUNTY PUBLIC LIBRARY

THE CONVERT

ALSO BY DEBORAH BAKER

Making a Farm: The Life of Robert Bly
In Extremis: The Life of Laura Riding
A Blue Hand: The Beats in India

THE CONVERT

A TALE OF EXILE AND EXTREMISM

Deborah Baker

Graywolf Press

Copyright © 2011 by Deborah Baker

This publication is made possible in part by a grant provided by the Minnesota State Arts Board, through an appropriation by the Minnesota State Legislature from the Minnesota general fund and its arts and cultural heritage fund with money from the vote of the people of Minnesota on November 4, 2008, and a grant from the Wells Fargo Foundation Minnesota. Significant support has also been provided by the National Endowment for the Arts; Target; the McKnight Foundation; and other generous contributions from foundations, corporations, and individuals. To these organizations and individuals we offer our heartfelt thanks.

This book is made possible through a partnership with the College of Saint Benedict, and honors the legacy of S. Mariella Gable, a distinguished teacher at the College. Support has been provided by the Manitou Fund as part of the Warner Reading Program.

Published by Graywolf Press
250 Third Avenue North, Suite 600
Minneapolis, Minnesota 55401

All rights reserved.

www.graywolfpress.org

Published in the United States of America

ISBN 978-1-55597-582-1 (cloth)
ISBN 978-1-55597-627-9 (paper)

2 4 6 8 9 7 5 3 1
First Graywolf Paperback, 2012

Library of Congress Control Number: 2011942451

Cover design: Kimberly Glyder Design

Cover photos: Maryam Jameelah, 1962: Manuscripts and Archives Division, The New York Public Library, Astor, Lenox and Tilden Foundations (top) / George Marks, Retrofile RF, Getty Images (bottom)

Interior photos: Margaret Marcus, self-portrait, 1956: Manuscripts and Archives Division, The New York Public Library, Astor, Lenox and Tilden Foundations; Herbert and Myra Marcus, undated, from *Quest for the Truth*; Maryam Jameelah, 1962: Manuscripts and Archives Division, The New York Public Library, Astor, Lenox and Tilden Foundations

FOR MY PARENTS

Contents

"If a man passes a door which has no curtain and is not shut
and looks in, he has committed no sin."
Muhammed ibn 'Abd Allah Kahtib al-Tibrizi, Mishkat al-Masabih

"Whoever undertakes to write a biography binds himself to lying,
to concealment, to hypocrisy, to flummery. . . . Truth is not accessible."
Sigmund Freud

PART I

THE MARBLE LIBRARY

Maryam Jameelah Papers, 2.5 linear feet (9 boxes). Gift of Maryam Jameelah, April 1962, with subsequent additions. The Maryam Jameelah Papers include the correspondence, fiction, art and writings of Maryam Jameelah, née Margaret Marcus, an American Jew who converted to Islam. Her papers tell of her troubled youth, her sympathy for displaced Palestinians after the formation of modern Israel, her relationship with Maulana Sayyid Abul Ala Maudoodi, and the decision to leave America and spend the rest of her life in Pakistan.

Finding aid, Manuscripts and Archives Division, The New York Public Library, Astor, Lenox and Tilden Foundations.

al-Hijrah—The Escape

5-A Zaildar Park
Icchra
Lahore
PAKISTAN

April 18, 1962

Dear Maryam Jameelah,
Asalaam-o-aleikum wa Rahmatullah!
I am glad to know you have accepted my counsel and are ready to come to Pakistan. I pray to Allah that He may guide you to what is right and in your best interest.

I think it is advisable to mention a few things. As you must already know, our way of life and social conditions are vastly different from those in America. We lack many facilities and amenities that Americans take for granted. Therefore, the first months here will certainly prove fatiguing and taxing upon your nerves. Unless you have patience and are resolutely determined to mold your life according to ours, to live and die among your Muslim brethren, you might find it extremely difficult to reconcile yourself to our ways. Although I will try my best to look after your needs and make things easier, your steadfast cooperation is essential.

Two of my daughters are near to you in age. One is studying for an MA in English and the other a BA in economics. I hope they will make friends with you, teach you Urdu, and, in exchange, learn from you the enthusiasm of a new convert. My wife does not know English. Initially, this may hinder your intimacy with her but I hope you will pick up enough Urdu within two or three months to enable you to communicate. After you have learned Urdu, it will be relatively easy for you to learn Arabic, because these languages share vocabularies. In due course, I will also try to arrange for an Arabic teacher.

As regards marriage, I will not pressure you, but should you decide to marry, I will try to help you choose a suitable life partner. Naturally you will want to be married to a youth who lives as a good Pakistani Muslim. If you choose not to marry, I am prepared to welcome you forever as a member of my family. I am inviting you to share my hospitality in the spirit with which the early Muslim inhabitants of Medina extended their invitation to their forlorn brethren outside of Medina and I wish you to respond with a similar spirit of migration, thinking that bonds of faith are firmer and stronger than relationships of flesh and blood.

There is still another reason why you should postpone any decision about marriage. When you arrive, my wife will train you in how a Pakistani Muslim wife runs her home and manages her household affairs. This knowledge will stand you in good stead when you are facing married life. For such a marital relationship to achieve success, it is essential to learn the social etiquette of Muslim families.

When you reach Lahore, daytime temperatures will average well over 100 degrees Fahrenheit. Our houses are not air-conditioned but we do use electric fans. Eventually you will become accustomed to our tropical seasons but you must be prepared to bear the first onslaught of this extreme climate.

I am writing a separate letter to your parents. I advise you to introduce me to them yourself and show them some of my letters so they may be able to grasp fully the background of my present letter to them.

Your brother in Islam,
ABUL ALA

Larchmont Acres Apartments, Apt 223-C
Mamaroneck, NY
USA

May 2, 1962

Dear Mr. Mawdoodi,

I am grateful for your kind letter of April 18th, extending to my daughter, Margaret, an invitation to live in your home. My wife and I are deeply moved by your gracious offer of hospitality.

Since embracing Islam, particularly as an ardent convert, it seems that living in our society presents practical difficulties. Margaret is anxious to accept your invitation, and as her parents, we are amenable, although it means going to live in a distant land. Particularly in view of the enthusiasm she has evinced, we are hopeful it would give her the opportunity for a happy and meaningful existence.

[Going to] a country with a very different culture will surely require a degree of forbearance during a period of adjustment. With the sympathy and understanding indicated in your letters, combined with Margaret's ardor, I am confident that her entrance into your family life will be successful.

I was pleased to note in your letter to Margaret the advice regarding change of citizenship and marriage. It is my paternal wish that she take irrevocable steps only after a reasonable period of residence.

She goes to your country with our full consent and especially as [she is] a person of fine character we shall maintain a continuous

5

interest in her welfare. Therefore, please feel at liberty to write me at any time.

Mrs. Marcus joins me in conveying to you, your wife and children our heartfelt gratitude.

Very sincerely,
Herbert S. Marcus

The Hellenic Torch
Alexandria
EGYPT

May 1962

After all our good-byes, after you, Mother, Betty, and Walter walked down the gangplank and drove off, I was overcome by a profound sense of dread. I stood at the deck rail for a long time completely stricken, the excitement of the weeks leading up to my departure gone. When the ship finally pulled away from the Brooklyn pier, the lights of the city began to dim and the engines seemed to echo the pounding of my heart. A black and fathomless ocean was slowly swallowing everything I had ever known. It took some time and many prayers before my fears began to subside.

The crossing thus far has not been without incident. At first, my fellow shipmates distracted me from my panic. There is an Indian boy on board named Jehangir Govind. He is returning home to Bombay after his studies in America. He snootily insists on being called Jack because he says I mispronounce his name. There was also a young man named Sherman accompanied by an older, alcoholic wife named Thelma. The Greek captain and his crew, along with several Greek deportees, completed the passenger list. After ten days at sea in close quarters with all of them, I ended up taking a number of meals alone in my room to spare myself their comments about my clothes.

Mother, you imagined that I was going to need my nice silk dress for dining and dancing on board, as if my passage had been booked on a cruise ship instead of a cheap Greek freighter! I was happy to leave that dress behind with Betty (along with my girdle and corset). And my high heels I gave to the colored lady who lived in the room next to mine at the Martha Washington Women's Residence. Dressed now in my hand-sewn, ankle-length dirndl skirt and high-necked long-sleeve blouse, I certainly can see that I cut an unlikely figure. Anyone might well ask: why would an otherwise attractive Western woman insist on dressing in such a manner? Honestly? I don't blame them.

The captain tells me that he has just returned from Turkey. Despite Mustapha Kemal Ataturk's best efforts to persecute Muslims by outlawing polygamy, the hajj, and the Arabic script, it seems that the captain found no dearth of religious fanatics. I asked him what he meant by religious fanatic.

Muslims who refuse to eat pork for fear of hell, he informed me. Muslims who avoid non-Muslims like the plague. He would be perfectly happy to see the Muslim religion eradicated, he said, because everyone knows Western civilization is superior. While Istanbul and Ankara are fairly Westernized and home to many Europeans, he assured us that the rest of Turkey is as backward and reactionary as ever. A young Greek sailor chimed in: You will see for yourself the filth and poverty of the Arabs when you get there.

This is the tenor of the nightly commentary on board.

My first thought was that I was sorry Turkey was not on the *Hellenic Torch*'s itinerary. I am frankly surprised to learn that there are that many Turks who have resisted Ataturk's effort to turn them into modern Europeans. The secular and nationalist leaders of Egypt, Pakistan, Turkey, Tunisia, and Morocco have all been desperately eager to put development before everything else, to Westernize and modernize away every last evidence of their traditional Islamic cultures in frantic pursuit of Western standards of urban living and dress. It's been a constant worry that the world I am looking for will be gone by the time I arrive. Would I arrive at my destination forty years, seventy years, a century too late?

Jehangir tells me that if I want to pray five times a day that is my own business, but he just doesn't see what possible difference it makes. He can't tell one religion from another. And it is a complete fairy tale, he insists, that God is everywhere watching to see whether I behave. Once he became a man he found he could dispense with such fantasies; he is now in the habit of being good. Jehangir reminded me of those young men at the Columbia University Muslim Students Association whose mission in life is to modernize Islam to death, gutting it of its essentials.

Thelma and Sherman disembarked at Crete with the Greeks. By the time they left, their conversation had become increasingly unpleasant. Thelma persisted in her drunken insistence that the Arabs live in filth and squalor. I wasn't surprised to find that when she invited me to her room to help her pack there was a surfeit of empty liquor bottles under the bed, cigarette stubs stuck in every dish and glass, and a carpet covered with stains. I held my tongue.

Five days later the sun rose on Alexandria. Watching from the captain's deck after my early-morning salat, I saw the coast come into focus. Dozens of feluccas manned by men in skullcaps and flowing white jellabiya skirted across the harbor out of the morning mist. It was a most incredible sight. Clearly recognizing me as a fellow Muslim, they called out "asalaam aleikum" and my heart practically lifted me off my feet. I was no longer traveling in the West. I had finally crossed over.

Soon after we docked, a dragoman arrived and offered to show me the sights of the city, pulling an official permit out of his pocket to alleviate my concern that I might be taken advantage of. Once I made it clear that I was a convert and only wanted to attend a prayer service, his distant manner gave way to warmth and he immediately hailed a taxi to take us both to the Old City.

All my life I have heard about the backwardness of the Arabs. I have read the accounts of Christian missionaries, Orientalists, and Zionists. You, Mother, and the Greek sailor gave me the same refrain, though after the war the polite word became *under-developed*. Indeed, in Egypt I saw poverty everywhere I looked. Horse-drawn carts plied cratered roads and the buildings looked on the verge of collapse. Some of the men I saw were indeed indescribably filthy. Children in rags played in the street with toys engineered from bits of wire and rubbish; hawkers sang out their wares in a sweet singsong fashion. The vast majority of men, women, and children wore traditional native dress, including one woman fully clad in a burqa carrying a crate of live chickens on her head.

In your eyes, this scene would look like something out of the Middle Ages. You would withdraw in disgust at the unsanitary conditions, cluck at the crude dwellings in which they live, quote me child mortality statistics. You couldn't get out of here fast enough. But I see something else. I see their dignity and gentleness, their exquisite manners and open-arm hospitality, their unquestioning faith. I envy them their lives, beyond the reach of "technical assistance" and the poisoned fruit of modernization. Pure sentiment, you would insist.

Before taking me to the mosque, the dragoman invited me to his home to meet his family. We found his wife preparing the noon meal in a soot-covered kitchen over a kerosene stove, chickens and roosters quick-stepping around her, as if impatient to be fed. His older daughter held a severely malnourished baby. His fourteen-year-old son looked more like a ten-year-old, but read from the Qur'an fluently. After lunch my guide took me on a tour of saints' tombs in his neighborhood. We entered a schoolroom filled with boys studying the Qur'an. When I was introduced, they were all astonished to meet an American woman who chose to be a Muslim and live in a Muslim country. Under their reverent gaze, I felt something like a saint myself.

Our last stop was for the midday prayer. At the mosque, I was the only woman among fifteen men, kneeling on reed mats under

9

rafters filled with sparrows. The prayer service was exactly the same in Alexandria as it had been in my little storefront mosque in Brooklyn. Afterward the imam invited me back to his office and offered to answer any questions I had about Islam. I told him I was traveling to Pakistan at the invitation of Mawlana Abul Ala Mawdudi. I was going to live with his family as his adopted daughter. He said that Mawlana Mawdudi was the holiest man in Pakistan.

One of the men from the mosque asked me how it was I came to embrace Islam. Daddy, whenever your friends asked me this, I always knew they were secretly looking for a complicated psychological explanation. While there is no use crying over spilt milk, I deeply regret all my lost years in America, struggling to find my way. Like your friends, you believed there *had* to be something wrong with a person who chose to live according to her most deeply held beliefs. Such a thought would never occur to the men who had prayed with me.

"Allah guides to the Truth whomsoever He pleases," I answered, and every man in the room nodded in understanding. Wandering the streets of Alexandria, my first experience of a real Muslim country outside of books and *National Geographic,* I never once felt I was in a foreign place. Though I have yet another month at sea before I reach Pakistan, I will post this letter here. I wanted to reassure you that for the first time in my life I feel I have finally arrived at a place I can call home.

Anonymity is my vocation. I inhabit the lives of my subjects until I think like them. Behind the doors of my study, I wear them like a suit of out-of-date clothes, telling their stories, interpreting their dreams, mimicking their voices as I type. I find myself most susceptible to those tuned to an impossible pitch, poets and wild-eyed visionaries who live their lives close to the bone. Haunting archives, reading letters composed in agony and journals thick with unspeakable thoughts, I sound the innermost chambers of unquiet souls; unearth dramas no one would ever think to make up.

The reading room of the Manuscripts and Archives Division is located in the very heart of the marble library, which is itself sited in the heart of the city where I live. There are long tables with elegant brass lamps that take a few minutes to warm up, shining their brightening eyes on the rare volumes and papers of our illustrious forebears. Scholars hunch over them, bathed in their reflected glow, like medieval scribes. You need special permission to enter the reading room where all the manuscript collections are held, but the catalog itself is available online from anywhere, even in the reading room itself.

One morning in the library I was idly clicking through the listing of the papers on deposit. I wasn't looking for anything in particular. I was on the prowl. The Henry Kittredge Norton Papers (b. 1884; 4 boxes) first snagged my attention. From the archivist's cover note, I learned that Norton had spent his entire life dedicated to the proposition that the future of urban mass transportation lay in aerial transit. This man, I imagined, was haunted by dreams of flying. I once wrote a book about a woman who spent fifty years trying to provide a single meaning for every word in the dictionary. She dreamed of words as numbers. Once her book was completed, she expected that it would make lying impossible and humankind would finally learn to speak the truth. Another subject of mine dreamed of heaven. He traveled to Mexican jungles and the farthest reaches of the Himalayas, convinced he would eventually find a teacher who would show him the way there.

In a vast, exquisitely maintained law library in a former colonial outpost, I once stumbled upon a casebook. Inside this casebook, like a small pulsing heart, lay a warm knot of baby mice nesting in a hollow of shredded legal citations. The fragility of the lives represented by the rarely opened boxes in special collections and archives held for me a similarly subversive and hidden promise. In these boxes I searched for secret or alternate histories, an overlooked rebel whose life work might overturn commonplace understandings.

Many of the less familiar names in the library's archives are bygone titans of the social register, well-heeled library patrons whose achievements in finance, real estate, and charitable works are entombed in thousands of anonymous gray boxes like the bones of obscure saints. But that morning it was the dissonance of a lone Muslim name, among the commonplace Jewish and Christian ones, that waylaid me. That name, wedged between a nineteenth-century nun and a twenty-first-century animal rights activist, was Maryam Jameelah. From the finding aid's descriptive overview of her life and work, it was evident Maryam Jameelah was a well-known figure in the Islamic world.

The boxes arrived just before lunch, retrieved from the locked cages of the library's deepest recesses. According to the index, the first two boxes of the Jameelah archive contained correspondence, newspaper interviews, and a few of her many books. There were also reviews, a bibliography, and a detailed timeline of her life. The next four boxes contained the handwritten manuscript of a novel and a selection of artwork. There were childhood crayon drawings on yellowing paper by "Peggy" and vivid pastel works depicting the daily lives of Arab peasants—juvenilia from Maryam Jameelah's beginnings as Margaret Marcus. Predominantly, however, the archive represented Maryam Jameelah's life and work after she had left America for Pakistan. The last of the boxes included innumerable family photographs of heavily made up Pakistani bridal parties.

Maryam Jameelah's bibliography listed a number of books and pamphlets all first published out of Lahore, the state capital of Pakistan's Punjab province, near the Indian border. They bore bristling and grandiose titles: *Modern Technology and the Dehumanization of Man, Islam Face to Face with the Current Crisis, Western Materialism Menaces Muslims, The Resurgence of*

Islam and Our Liberation from the Colonial Yoke. For her portrayal of Western culture and social mores Jameelah drew on an array of magazines and books sent to her by her mother back in New York. There are citations of popular social critics like Oscar Lewis and Lance Packard as well as racier fare like "I Was an Alcoholic Housewife" from *Reader's Digest.* In her two-volume work *Western Civilization Condemned by Itself,* a pirated chapter from *Catcher in the Rye* is used to illustrate the misery of the typical American adolescent. Selections from T. S. Eliot's poem "The Waste Land" evoke the psychic toll of godless living. Each excerpted work was pitched as a cautionary tale intended to stiffen the spine of those who might be tempted to stray from Islam and be drawn into the clutches of the West.

But the true source of Maryam Jameelah's authority arose not from her readings and argument, but from the circumstances of her life, haphazardly documented by her nine boxes. By any measure, hers was an unusual story. Every book she wrote is framed by an account of how as a young girl growing up in Mamaroneck, New York, the daughter of secular Jewish parents, she came to reject America and embrace Islam. Self-taught, untraveled, and unlearned in any foreign language, Margaret Marcus had sacrificed the supposed freedoms and privileges of a Western lifestyle to live in upright exile in Pakistan. The choice she lays out for her readers is stark and familiar: a life lived by the sacred laws laid out in the Holy Qur'an or one blackened by hell-bent secular materialism.

Jameelah's output trailed off in the mid-1980s. But her books, translated and distributed through Islamic centers, reading libraries, and bookshops all over the world, continue to influence the way the Islamic world thinks of the West—America in particular. "Maryam Jameelah's significance [lies] in the manner with which she articulates an internally consistent paradigm for [Islamic] revivalism's rejection of the West," her entry in *The Oxford Encyclopedia of the Modern Islamic World* reads. "In this regard, her influence far exceeds [that of] the Jamaat [e-Islami] and has been important in the development of revivalist thought across the Muslim world."

The Jamaat-e-Islami was the brainchild of the man who had first invited Margaret Marcus to live in Pakistan as his adopted daughter. His name was Abul Ala Mawdudi and he was known throughout the Islamic world both for his writings on Islam and for his tireless advocacy of an Islamic political order. In 1941 Mawdudi founded the Jamaat-e-Islami in pre-Partition India. Like the Islamic Brotherhood of Egypt (founded in 1928 by Hassan al-Banna), the Jamaat was initially a movement dedicated to advancing the cause of an Islamic rebirth and the establishment of a pan-Islamic state. Margaret Marcus's earliest writings entailed a similar vision.

Vali Nasr, Mawdudi's biographer and an authority on political Islam (also referred to as Islamic revivalism), describes Maryam Jameelah as broadly responsible for cementing the global cultural divide between Islam and the West. His father, Seyyed Hossein Nasr, one of the preeminent scholars of traditional Islam living in the West, is more precise: "Maryam Jameelah began to write at a time when few in the Islamic world were criticizing western culture in any depth. While there were mullahs who made superficial critiques, say of western women's scandalous clothing, for someone from within the West to criticize modernism, in an articulate and logical way, was revolutionary."

But I knew none of this that first morning. I had never heard of Maryam Jameelah or Abul Ala Mawdudi. I only thought to wonder how such an archive ended up at the Manuscripts and Archives Division of the New York Public Library. That day I merely glanced at her books and letters before turning to a series of photographs I found in one of her books. A family portrait taken in 1938 showed the future revolutionary as a four-year-old in a smocked dress, gazing at a distant point with large brown eyes while her older sister, Betty, mugged coyly for the camera.

I noticed that as Margaret Marcus grew older, the photographs became less forgiving. Awkwardness radiated from her. Trussed in fancy dresses, she stood apart from her respectable-looking parents and lipsticked sister, gamely smiling and looking as if she wanted to disappear. By her midtwenties, she began wearing a scarf to cover her hair. Finally, a news photo taken soon after her arrival in Pakistan showed her in a burqa posed standing in front of a sunlit door, only her hands and feet visible. By then she was living in the home of Mawlana Mawdudi and her first book, *Islam versus the West,* was a best-seller, soon to be translated into a dozen languages. This image of her would appear in nearly every book that followed.

I looked at that photograph for a long time.

It was a photograph of a woman who, after a lifetime of hiding, now wanted to be seen. It was a photograph of someone who could only be herself beneath a pitch-black burqa. Twenty-eight years into her life, Margaret Marcus had been transformed. Through this veil Maryam Jameelah saw the world and her place in it with absolute clarity.

"These shall be the clothes I shall wear from now on," she wrote her parents happily. "I wish you could see me now! I wonder if you would recognize me as the same old Peggy!"

So Margaret, too, had managed to slip out of one life and into the clothes of another. Only for her it was a real life, not an imagined one. For her there was no going back. However unknown to me, in this unlikely firmament and under this impenetrable habit, Maryam Jameelah was a star. I put the photograph aside and returned to the first thick folder of letters.

By the time the closing bell rang I was surprised to find I was not on the prow of a Greek freighter gliding through the Suez Canal, but in the cool marble hold of the manuscript reading room. Putting the boxes on reserve, I packed up my notes and made plans to return and read further.

5-A Zaildar Park
Icchra
Lahore
PAKISTAN

Early July 1962

Now that I have settled myself here, I would like to explain how I came to be a part of the Mawlana Mawdudi's family. It seems I have spent my entire life trying to get to this moment, to explain myself in terms that make sense to you. I'm not sure I ever will. But if I don't try then we will never be able to put the difficulties of the last ten years behind us.

According to the Mawlana, among every people in every period of history there have been the good and the righteous and, whatever creed they professed, they are the true Muslims.* He saw these qualities in me. There were even true Muslims before the time of the Prophet (peace be upon him), a period traditionally held to be a time of total pagan ignorance, or *jahiliyya*. The Mawlana believes that Western values exported to the Muslim world by colonialism created only the most recent manifestation of this sorry state, and, like me, he went through a period of ignorance and upheaval before alighting on the Right Path. In Arabic they call this path the Sunnah, meaning the Way of the Prophet.

On the advice of the jailed Islamic leader Sayyid Qutb of the Muslim Brotherhood in Cairo, over a year ago I sent the Mawlana Mawdudi some of my writings on Islam as a way of introducing myself.** He responded with an invitation to share the coming

---

* Translated from the Arabic word for "master," on the subcontinent *mawlana* is used as a title to refer to learned religious men.

** Sayyid (or Seyyed in Persian, Syed in Urdu) is an honorific indicating a person who is a descendant of the Prophet Muhammad. In the case of Qutb, however, Sayyid is also his first name.

Ramadan holiday with his family in Pakistan. "When I was reading your articles," Mawdudi wrote me, "I felt as if I were reading my own mind." He was certain I'd feel the same when I read his work and of course I did. He was impressed but only mildly surprised that a girl born and brought up in America could come to hold the *exact same* views he had been preaching for the past thirty years of his life. Naturally, Mawlana Mawdudi wanted to know how a young American girl, from a Jewish family, no less, could arrive at a clear and genuine conception of Islam all by herself. He asked if I might find the time to write a brief story of my mental evolution and send it to him.

So I wrote him of my typical American girlhood, my secular education, and my abortive religious one. Though my interest in Arab culture predated the founding of the state of Israel, you will remember that 1948 was also the year I began reading deeply in Arab history, poetry, and writings. It was a book by a Jewish convert to Islam who eventually showed me my path, I told him. That was the book you and Mother would not let me check out of the Larchmont Public Library, *The Road to Mecca* by Muhammad Asad. I read it dozens of times.

With the Mawlana's encouragement I marked the end of Ramadan in the spring of 1961 by taking my vows at the Islamic Mission of America in Brooklyn. It was the day after my twenty-seventh birthday. Whenever you tried to talk me out of converting, Daddy, it never had anything to do with giving up Judaism, it had to do with my finding a place in American society. You warned me that I would become a stranger in the family and the community. As you well knew, by then I already was a stranger. I had been for a long time. Yet I found converting to Islam was not the end of my difficulties.

In late March, after you left for Trinidad and Tobago, I made up my mind. As soon as you returned from your holiday, I handed you Mawlana Mawdudi's letter. There was no time to argue; I had six weeks to prepare for my journey. I emptied my bank account, bought a portable Smith Corona, shipped ahead my library of Islamic books, applied for a passport, and secured the recommended immunizations.

As I went about these tasks, I discovered in myself a sense of purpose. I was resourceful, efficient. For the first time, I realized how long I had been stuck in this netherworld between childhood and adulthood, alone in my room with my books, practically friendless, unhappy and frustrated. And then Mawlana Mawdudi opened a door. He showed me how I might escape the awful destiny that awaited me if I remained in America. Approaching my twenty-eighth year, I had the sense that his invitation had arrived not a moment too soon. I was grateful. I am still grateful.

That is how I now find myself, finishing this letter to you while sitting on a narrow bed across from a wall of thousands of books, just outside the study of Mawlana Abul Ala Mawdudi.

Like many children, I had once been haunted by big questions. Who created us? What is it to be good? Is there life after death? I took on the question of how to live my life and what to believe in dutifully, like a somber homework assignment. In church, I knelt at the communion rail to contemplate the man hanging immobile before me, forlorn and defeated yet also impossibly beautiful.

As I grew older the big questions receded; my mind would wander off before I could get anywhere near them. In my work I tended to stick with smaller questions and look for larger meanings in the answers I found. Of Margaret Marcus's life I might have asked: How did she come to reject America and all it stood for? Did she ever regret her decision to leave? Of the man who invited her to live in Pakistan as his daughter, I might have wondered: Who was he and where did he come from? What did he believe and what did he see in Margaret Marcus? Contemplating Marcus's letters and writings, I wondered if littler questions were the wrong ones, or equally unanswerable. Whether only the big metaphysical questions were worth asking. Margaret Marcus struck me as the sort of person who wouldn't settle for less. I found something to admire in that and wondered how well the answers she found served her.

Margaret's life, too, went straight to the heart of the heated debate over the notion of a divide between Islam and the West. Many Western scholars and diplomats, thoughtful editorial writers, and old-fashioned Orientalists, even a few secular-minded Muslim writers, are convinced this divide is real and irreconcilable. "Islam's borders are bloody and so are its innards," one influential scholar insists. "The fundamental problem for the West is not Islamic fundamentalism. It is Islam, a different civilization whose people are convinced of the superiority of their culture." Maryam Jameelah echoed these convictions from the opposite shore. For Margaret and Maryam, it was always the West that persisted in considering itself the superior civilization, with inevitably tragic results. Far from seeing her own life as a bridge between America and the Muslim world, Maryam believed that Western civilization and Islamic civilization were implacably opposed: "any compromise with the former," she writes, "equaled defeat of the latter."

In works spanning three decades Maryam deconstructed and denounced the work of those Orientalists and theologians trying to find common ground between the values of the God-centered Muslim universe and those of the secular and scientific West. She encouraged readers of her books to have nothing to do with them: "This kind of sophistry fails to strike the slightest response in me," she writes primly. "After Copernicus, the western astronomer saw man as a puny speck on a tiny planet revolving around a tenth-rate star, drifting aimlessly in a cosmic ocean . . . his creation perhaps only an accident or a mistake." There was something slightly enviable in Maryam Jameelah's clarity of purpose, in her insistence on meaning over meaninglessness, on a divinely directed life over aimless drifting, on big questions over small ones.

However, it still struck me that, in the effort to claim the superior culture or civilization, both sides traded in caricatures and insights of varying subtlety. Both seemed to use or abuse history, particularly histories of violence and cruelty, to further their agendas. Both sides wrote from Olympian heights of authority and scholarly erudition. And, inevitably, both shed tears over the treatment of women. Crocodile tears, Maryam Jameelah sniffed. Confronted by the clashing assumptions of the morning newspaper and the message of Maryam's books I often felt that the impasse between "Islam" and "the West" was truly unbridgeable. Confused by the warring abstractions, seduced by one view at one moment only to betray it in favor of its opposite the next, I was wary of stepping between them.

My attitude toward Maryam Jameelah was, initially at least, curious but distant.

5-A Zaildar Park
Icchra
Lahore
PAKISTAN

Mid-July 1962

After a few anxious days, I am now completely at home in the Mawdudi household. Language is my principal difficulty. Everyone seems more interested in practicing English than in teaching me Urdu. I feel that Humaira and Asma, not to mention the numerous neighborhood ladies who drop by to meet me, are crushed to see me dressed in the shalwar kameez provided me by the Karachi ladies I met upon my arrival in Pakistan. They were doubtless expecting a bobbed and blond memsahib with white skin and blue eyes, dressed in a short skirt. Instead, with my black hair and Semitic coloring, I really don't look that much different from them. Used to hearing precise and British-inflected English, they all find my American accent impossible to follow. As for Lahore, unlike the bit of Karachi I saw in my few days there, it has lovely tree-lined streets. Beyond that, I thought very little of it, as I went immediately from the airport to purdah.

The house itself is somewhat dingy and primitive, at least by the materialist standards of Americans, but is well built of stone and cement. A Westinghouse fridge sits in the dining room but the two bathrooms consist of nothing more than chamber pots and a cold-water shower with an unreliable pump. As there are no closets, no one knew what to do with my hangers. There aren't even chests of drawers. Everyone merely folds clothes and puts them away on shelves. It is far too hot for my cotton stockings and the bulky black sweaters I got at Gimbels bargain basement but they will be useful in winter as there is no such thing as central heating. For the midday nap everyone, with the exception of the Mawlana, takes to the largest room in the house, settling down on Indian bedspreads and pillows. At night we sleep in rope beds and on the hottest nights the servants carry these beds to the roof. To escape the mosquitoes, we all pull our covers over our heads, giving the roof the appearance of being littered with corpses.

At first I shared a room with Humaira but given the strain of my journey, the Mawlana decided I could have a room to myself. Not a bedroom, because there wasn't one to spare, but the corridor adjoining his study. Here floor-to-ceiling bookshelves contain Mawdudi's vast library of English, Arabic, Persian, and Urdu titles. There is also a lower shelf filled with magazines from all over the world. With a space cleared for my own books and a little wooden table for my typewriter, I have my own office.

I would never have guessed that Humaira and Asma were only two of the Mawlana's children since he hadn't mentioned the other *seven* in his letters. Umar Farooq is his oldest son and a student of Arabic. Next is twenty-five-year-old Ahmad Farooq, who is on summer leave from a medical college in Karachi. Both are so deeply immersed in their studies that neither pays me the least attention. Indeed, they behave as if I didn't exist. Begum Mawdudi tells me that this is because Islam forbids young men to talk to strange women.* The entire household treats them, as the eldest sons, with great respect.

Twenty-three-year-old Humaira is hard at work studying for her finals. We are all obliged to be deadly quiet. Though the exam is eight months away, she reads *Richard III* and *The Canterbury Tales* in Old English for at least fifteen hours a day. She is shocked at my indifference to English literature. When she isn't reading the classics, she rereads *Gone with the Wind*. She is so besotted with that novel that the other night she dreamed she was Scarlett O'Hara! When I asked her about her appreciation of the great Urdu poets Iqbal and Ghalib, she did not disguise her scorn. She said their work was "sentimental." Asma, barely nineteen, is already embarked upon a master's degree in economics. Though both girls are perfectly polite and obedient, with exceptionally refined manners, I was astonished that the Mawlana had agreed to such Western courses of study. He explained to me that in Pakistan, until one mastered Western subjects, a person wasn't considered truly educated.

After Asma and Humaira comes Muhammad Farooq, in his last year of high school, and then my favorite, fifteen-year-old Haider Farooq. I think of all the children, the sweetness of this boy sets him apart. Haider, like many boys his age, has a soft spot for animals and promises to take me to the Lahore zoo. For more than a week, he nursed a baby pigeon in his room. His mother told me he had once brought a stray dog into the house, to his father's absolute fury. Muslims consider dogs unclean. On my arrival, Haider presented me with a silly ring with imitation diamonds, which I wore until all the stones fell out. Even though he speaks

---

* *Begum* is an honorific title given to high-ranking Muslim women of South Asia.

little English he still manages to make me laugh, relieving me of some of my loneliness.

Finally, there is ten-year-old Khalid and the family favorite, six-year-old Ayesha. As the "baby," she is spoiled, bright, and mischievous. When she refuses to eat, the Mawlana takes her on his lap and feeds her like a baby bird. I am nothing to her but the butt of her jokes; she loves nothing better than to mimic my English. The household staff includes a cook and a twelve-year-old servant boy from rural Punjab named Hidris. No one seems to think it strange he isn't in school. To round it off, friends and relations of the Mawlana and the Begum arrive in a steady stream, sometimes for tea and sometimes for months at a time.

Begum Mawdudi is forty years old but looks nearly fifty. She also gives lectures on the Qur'an and the Hadith at the homes of various women in the neighborhood. I always accompany her and sit on the floor with the rest of the women and their babies. I'm only sorry I can't understand what she is saying, so I content myself with observing all very closely. Naturally, everyone in Begum Mawdudi's social circle and immediate family has been eager to meet me. My early weeks in Lahore have been filled with tea parties. It won't surprise you to hear that even in Pakistan where there is not a cocktail to be seen, I have no patience for such occasions.

All but one of the Begum's younger brothers and sisters (she is the eldest of ten) live in Lahore and they are all far wealthier than we are. I couldn't help but contrast these teas with the attitude of my hosts during my brief stopover in Karachi. They wanted nothing to do with the Peace Corps. They knew that if they accepted "technical assistance" from the Americans, vulgar Hollywood films and books were sure to follow, with the aim of turning Muslim youths away from Islam. My arrival in Lahore coincided with Jackie Kennedy's visit with her foolish sister Princess Radziwill. Their exploits and shameless clothes were an inevitable topic of teatime conversation. Until I learn Urdu I am, alas, at the mercy of the English-speaking and Westernized upper crust of Pakistani society.

I did visit one household where I found the true Islamic atmosphere I had feared was lost forever (apart from our own, of course). This was the home of a man named Mohammad Yusuf Khan, a longtime worker for the Mawlana's Jamaat-e-Islami party. The household includes his wife and children, his married and unmarried brothers and sisters and their small children, his mother, and various elderly aunts. While the young women looked quite vibrant and beautiful, the babies seemed malnourished. They were unnaturally still, with large unblinking black eyes, just like my paintings of poor starving Arabs you so disliked.

There must have been more than thirty people living there and though the family was obviously poor, the women of the household put out a most showy tea with fine china and white tablecloths in honor of my visit. I couldn't help but calculate what such a spread must have cost them and how hungry they would be in the days to come. Nonetheless, they persisted in offering me cake after cake, biscuit after biscuit, sweet after sweet. All I could do was smile and say "asalaam aleikum" while they repeated over and over "a hundred times welcome." I noticed a lone youth on a charpoy in the corner; he was nothing but skin and bones. Begum Mawdudi told me he was not right in the head and had been that way since he was a baby. His sisters looked after him lovingly, talking to him softly as we said our good-byes. That image stayed with me.

At dinner that night the Mawlana told me that Mohammad Yusuf Khan was an upright man. In India his family had been wealthy landowners but in 1947, when the Indian subcontinent was divided, they were forced to flee Hindu India. When they arrived here in Pakistan, honest people like him found nothing, while the crafty and the cunning made off with everything.

In her first book Maryam Jameelah argued that Western civilization had been on the wrong track pretty much from its beginnings in Greek philosophy but sealed its fate with the French Enlightenment. Subsequent books focused their critique on contemporary Western values and culture: "The destruction of the natural environment by modern technology for the short-sighted profit of the affluent countries of the West, threatens to destroy mankind, if not all life on earth." For so-called "primitive" peoples, "the impact of modernization is inseparable from their degradation and often their extinction." Nor had the more developed cultures of the formerly colonized been spared. She was a fierce critic of American foreign policy, its unfettered support of Israel, its meddling in the affairs of Muslim countries, and its headlong and blind belief in the notion of "progress." American oil companies had insinuated themselves into the very heartland of Islam, she held, breeding greed and corruption where there once had been a proud desert culture. For Muslim nations governed by a secular Westernized elite, "our political sovereignty is more nominal than real and the Western powers . . . are determined to keep it that way."

With assurance and finesse she captured, too, the more subtle ways in which the West had sought to undermine far older cultures and societies. In a line of argument that would later become familiar to the readers of Edward Said's *Orientalism* (1978), in the sixties and seventies she described the implicit racism of this project precisely and instructively: "Orientalism is not a dispassionate, objective study of Islam and its culture by the erudite, faithful to the best traditions of scholarship . . . but an organized conspiracy [. . .]." Where Said simply saw a secular and imperialist agenda, Maryam also felt these works were motivated by the desire "to incite our youth to revolt against their faith, and scorn the entire legacy of Islamic history and culture as obsolete." She tasked the *New York Times* and *Time* magazine on their constant inveighing against the medieval mind-set and backwardness of the Arabs. Quoting Malcolm X, she wrote of the shame that compelled young Muslims to affect Western manners and dress, the ways in which they were coached to question the validity and relevance of their traditions and faith. Finally, she offered an iron-clad vision of Islam that promised a way to make Muslims whole again, undivided against themselves.

Maryam Jameelah's works are unsettling as much for the tone in which they are written as for their content. There is, first of all, their hectoring know-it-all voice. Wasn't it just like an American to go marching off to a foreign country and tell them what was what. Who was Margaret Marcus to tell anyone what being a Muslim was all about, as if it were just one thing? And yet whenever I tried to turn away, something in her letters to her parents from Pakistan kept bringing me back.

For over thirty years, Margaret Marcus corresponded with her parents, Herbert and Myra Marcus, back home. These letters begin in May 1962 with her departure for Pakistan and end in 1996 with her father's death at age 101 in a Boca Raton nursing home. Her parents' replies are not among her papers; I presumed they had remained in Lahore while her own letters somehow made their way to the archive of the marble library. Of the letters from "Peggy," however, there are hundreds of pages, both typed and handwritten in a painstaking grade school hand. The letters describe in great detail the circumstances of her life in Pakistan.

But it was the first twenty-four letters, loose in a folder and filed apart from the two bound volumes of the later years, that riveted me. Beginning with the letters Maryam Jameelah wrote aboard the Greek freighter that took her to Pakistan, this series ends abruptly eighteen months later with her marriage. This denouement was as surprising and impenetrable as nearly every twist and turn of her fate that preceded it.

At a time when the handwritten word on a piece of paper is becoming more and more fleeting, postmarked letters and private journals have acquired the quaintly self-conscious air of relics. Reading rooms have become shrines with rules and esoteric rituals to observe. These letters and journals, as well as first drafts and photographs, remain the raw materials of any work of history or biography. Puzzling out a story from fragmented records, interrogating and adjudicating conflicting accounts, establishing precise chronologies, and teasing the color of emotion from taciturn documents still constitute the daily practice of scholarship. Yet in the archive of Maryam Jameelah such skills felt almost entirely wasted. Here was a helpful list of every article, review, and book she had ever written, as well as a month-by-month accounting of her every school, summer camp, hospital stay, and illness. The date of her first period is included, as is the date of her last one. Furthermore, her early letters to her parents read nothing like her polemical writing. Her voice is fresh and ingenuous, and even at times unintentionally comical. While Margaret never hesitates to express an opinion, in her letters she is also a careful observer, with an anthropologist's cool eye. Her lectures on Islam and secular materialism largely make way for the story of plucky Peggy Marcus in Pakistan, complete with dramatic dialogue and vivid description. Each letter reads like a serial installment on the progress of an improbable adventure but with details too real to have been invented. Mailed at nearly weekly intervals, they run pages and pages long with scarcely an interrupting typo. They are wildly chatty. Perusing them, puzzling over them day after day, I soon began to think of Margaret Marcus, with both fondness and slight condescension, as Peggy.

In these letters there was an implicit rebuke of her parents' lifestyle whenever Margaret describes her encounters with poor and humble Arabs or the heartwarming sight of "fuzzy wuzzies" at midday prayer. Herbert and Myra Marcus were at best indifferent to questions about the meaning of it all; they seemed to live for their Caribbean vacations in Trinidad and Tobago. Yet Margaret is never simply the scold. She is a deeply affectionate daughter. Her bouts of soul searching, her expressions of joy and clear-eyed thinking, blunt her sharp and humorless edges.

But dark notes remain. In a letter written at Jeddah, Saudi Arabia, en route to Karachi, Margaret found that no matter how insistently she dropped the Mawlana Mawdudi's name, she was not allowed off the boat. "The border officials have seen far too many pilgrims take up permanent residence in the Holy Land," she explained to Herbert and Myra. Yet she airily pronounced on the entire country, having gleaned what she could from a shipping agent and close observation of the activity on the pier. "The visitor to Saudi Arabia is never for a single instant allowed to forget that he or she is in a Muslim country," she wrote from her high perch on the captain's deck, the whiff of her approval unmistakable. "In Saudi Arabia, they don't stand for any nonsense; the thief gets his right hand chopped off and the stump dipped in boiling oil." Even such sentiments failed to convey just how far from home her tale would take her. Still, from the very beginning, it seemed certain that Peggy's grand adventure would not end well.

Margaret's critique of America's tawdry social mores, its blatant civil and racial injustices, was scarcely original; it marked her as part of the troublesome generation that came of age during the postwar period. Many of her generation questioned the 1950s cold war consensus in similarly spectacular ways. But Margaret's contrariness was unusually precocious. In 1945, on her first and only trip to the Deep South for a cousin's wedding, Peggy found an empty seat at the back of a Savannah bus. The imposing black woman she sat next to burst into laughter while the white passengers all looked back at her, their faces contorted in silent fury.

Margaret was ten years old. The memory haunted her for years and found its way into her writings. She blamed her parents; they had neglected to explain the rules of the Jim Crow South. The encounter would provide Margaret with yet another example of the inadequacy of her parents' view of the world. In their anxious bid to assimilate, they had failed to notice and question the evils and hypocrisies that surrounded them.

Yet at the heart of all her letters and books lay another question; how and why did Islam become the remedy? Not long after I started combing the archive, I began to suspect that Peggy's correspondence had all along been directed not simply at Herbert and Myra, but past them, to posterity. In a cover note written some years after those first twenty-four letters had been sent, Maryam promised future readers that, considered on their own, these letters would provide "ample response" to the following question: why would a modern American girl seek her happiness and fulfillment in a "poverty-stricken, so-called backward, Third World country"?

Yet for every question the letters promised to answer, many more arose to take their place. Some of these questions were small and niggling; others seemed so vast I could only dimly fathom their scale. Was the enmity between Islam and the West metaphysical or historical? Was it ironic or inevitable that the age of liberal democracy had also been the age of imperialism? What was the relationship between the principles enshrined in a constitution and a country's culture and politics? How, exactly, had the American Cold War found its sequel in the war against Islamic terror?

There were days when, on leaving the library, I could barely account for what I had been doing. Standing on the street waiting for the light to change after another day in the archive, I was gripped by the effort to grasp the precise logic of these events. Inevitably my questions drew me further and further into the archive and into the writings and life of Maryam Jameelah and Margaret Marcus. Whenever I felt I was getting in over my head, I returned to Peggy's story as it unfolded in these twenty-four letters to her parents.

And it was here that I began to catch glimpses of another,

more intractable and human tale. Unlike the triumphant account of Margaret Marcus's journey to Islam, which prefaced every single one of her books, between the lines of her letters to Herbert and Myra Marcus the war of ideas between Islam and the West seemed neither so stark nor so immutable. In these two dozen letters the answers to small questions promised to unlock larger ones. By tracing the thread of how a woman like Margaret Marcus became Maryam Jameelah and following it to Pakistan, I felt sure that I could find a way out of the trap history had set.

Or so I thought at the time.

5-A Zaildar Park
Icchra
Lahore
PAKISTAN

Late July 1962

Your exhaustive description of Mother's birthday dinner at that fancy Westchester restaurant was well nigh unbearable to read. I am still unaccustomed to the Pakistani diet and to hear of the rich menu of foods you are enjoying is a torment. When I am most hungry I have visions of steak and pot roast and meat loaf and mashed potatoes, finished off with a thick slice of Sara Lee cheesecake and ice cream. The Mawlana confided to me that he experienced similar visions of Begum Mawdudi's dishes when he was being feted as an honored guest of King Saud in the tents of Saudi Arabia. On his yearly visit he is expected to relish the sight of an entire roast camel. The hump is served as appetizer. As the honored guest, he is presented the platter of testicles and eyeballs. I expect I will soon grow used to the chilies and will find food tasteless without them. Until then I dream of Sara Lee.

Mian Tufail Muhammad is both the secretary general of the

Jamaat-e-Islami and the Mawlana's publisher. In his flowing, immaculately white shalwar kameez, he was the picture of elegance when he arrived to collect me at the airport. He has a gray beard and, like the Mawlana, wears a lambskin cap. In one of the Mawlana's last letters to me he wrote that Mian Tufail Muhammad had not had an opportunity to read my novel for possible publication. The reason was that he had been arrested and thrown in jail without trial for having written a pamphlet against the anti-Islamic Family Laws Ordinance recently passed by the government. Thinking he was still in prison, I was astonished when he introduced himself. And before I knew it I heard myself asking him if he had been tortured.

It is good to suffer for the cause of Allah, he said in a most solemn voice.

The Mawlana Mawdudi is not long out of prison himself. On first meeting him, I could scarcely believe that he was only sixty-one years old. His white beard, lined face, and stiff movements made him seem ancient. Jail took such a toll on his health that he has enough medicines to stock an entire dispensary! I was told by one of his associates that in an effort to make him "confess," he was beaten and tortured. Even the threat of execution did not budge him from his principles.

I was disconcerted to learn, however, that he chews betel nut throughout the day so that his mouth is an unnatural shade of red. It is a very expensive habit. Begum Mawdudi restricts herself to a mouthful after every meal but the Mawlana is never far from the family's heirloom silver spittoon. I've noticed that one betel leaf, prepared with tobacco and red betel sap, lasts about three hours.

Yet despite his ill health, the Mawlana is a tireless political leader. He is a bitter enemy of President Ayub Khan and the Western "intelligentsia," precisely because he is one of the most important Muslim thinkers in the entire world and the message of his teachings is the exact opposite of what they represent. I don't believe I've ever met anyone more widely read in so many languages. I'd be surprised if there was anything he didn't know about Islam. And like me he acquired his knowledge largely by his own efforts, with little formal education. On a recent visit to Saudi Arabia he conferred with King Saud about his plan for a new Islamic university at Medina. As a gesture of solicitude and respect, King Saud sent him a large piece of the black covering of the Holy Kaaba at Mecca, with verses of the Qur'an embroidered on it. The entire household was awestruck when it was spread out on the bed.*

From five o'clock in the morning until nearly midnight about two dozen bearded brown men in white pyjamas visit the Mawlana's study. There they carry on grave conversations about the work of his political party, the Jamaat-e-Islami, which has been banned by the government. Just like the Society of the Muslim Brotherhood in Egypt, they are seeking to make Pakistan a fully-fledged Islamic state with the Qur'an as the law of the land. In fact, Sayyid Qutb has been greatly influenced by Mawlana Mawdudi's writings on this. During the day the Jamaati leaders sit in the back garden enrapt in the Mawlana's discourses, Mian Tufail Muhammad among them. When the muezzin calls they form their own congregation with the Mawlana as imam leading them in prayer. "My father's family!" as my dear Haider Farooq once joked.

It is only now, after I've been at the Mawdudi household for several weeks, that I have met the last of the nine Mawdudi children. Seventeen-year-old Hussain Farooq had been spending part of his summer holiday with his uncle in Karachi. He returned home with suitcases bursting with up-to-the-minute Western fashions, including pointy shoes, cartons of American cigarettes,

---

* Holy Kaaba—the black granite cube marking the most sacred site of Islam and around which pilgrims to Mecca circumambulate. The covering cloth is called a *kiswah*. This cloth is embroidered with Islamic inscription of the *shahada*, the profession of faith. The cloth is replaced every year.

and girlie magazines. Apparently this uncle, one more of Begum Mawdudi's numerous brothers, was a Muslim in name only. In America Hussain would be immediately recognized as a juvenile delinquent. In Pakistan such youths are known by the British terms: teddy boys and teddy girls. Naturally, I am concerned about the poor example he is setting for the younger boys, Muhammad, Khalid, and, most particularly, Haider.

Though there are aspects of my life in Mawdudi's household that give me pause, my one real complaint is that the Mawlana has no time to spare for me. Even when he does make the time, his English isn't nearly as fluent as his letters had led me to believe. He had written them in Urdu and his secretary translated them. Left on my own, I have no choice but to return to my writing and study of Urdu. I am also writing a weekly column for the Friday Islamic supplement of the *Pakistan Daily Times.* One new book I am planning is to be titled *Islam and Modernism,* and another *Islam in Theory and Practice.* I also have ideas for a revised edition of my first book, *Islam versus the West.* Naturally, I wish to discuss all my thoughts with the Mawlana and when his duties do not permit this, it is frustrating.

In the meantime, I decided to introduce myself to my new country by writing an autobiographical essay for the *Pakistan Times,* revisiting my journey from America to Pakistan. No sooner was this published than I began receiving an avalanche of letters proposing marriage. The Mawlana had predicted this in one of his letters to me. He wrote that all those qualities that would make me a good Muslim wife would be considered faults in America, and that if I stayed in New York I couldn't possibly hope to find a husband to be my true life-companion. He said he knew a great number of virtuous young Muslims and imagined a match that would prove to be of great help in his movement. Once I arrived in Pakistan, he promised, I would have no cause to worry about my future.

By far most of these marriage proposals were addressed to the

Mawlana, as he is my guardian, but once in a while there would be a letter addressed to me. "I am a lonely tree parched in the wilderness of the desert!" one suitor proclaimed. "A fire for you is burning in the furnace of my chest!" He went on to reassure me that he had nearly eight thousand rupees in his savings account. I read these letters aloud to Asma and Humaira, and we fell over laughing. After we received fifty such proposals, the Mawlana informed me that I was now the most sought after spinster in all of Pakistan. It was hard for me to take any of these letters as seriously as the Mawlana Mawdudi did.

One night over dinner the Mawlana returned from taking a call in his study to inform me that I had been offered a full-time job teaching English at a local madrasa. I had neither interest in nor qualifications for such work, having long ago decided that I would be incapable of disciplining a class of ill-behaved children, much less inspire in them a love of learning. This was not what he wanted to hear. "You must think of what kind of work you would like to do so that you can earn enough to live decently," he admonished me. "I am old now and in poor health and I am very much worried about your future."

When I pointed out that this was exactly the dilemma you both had been faced with, he interrupted me to say that my welfare was now his concern. I would not be able to make a living from my writing because Pakistan was a poor and illiterate country. Nor can I make a living as a typist or a secretary as Betty once did because here only men fill these jobs.

"If you do not want to work," he concluded, "then the only alternative is marriage. I am convinced that marriage is the best thing for you, no matter how much you insist that you do not want it. Believe me, Maryam, the woman in you is not absent, she is only sleeping."

CHAPTER 2

The Mawlana

Remind them, for you are but an admonisher,
You are not at all a warden over them.
But who is averse and disbelieves,
Allah will punish him with direst punishment.

Qur'an, 88:21–24

This was the family story.

When Abul Ala Mawdudi's grandfather heard that his son, in his first year at the brand-new university at Aligarh, had been seen playing cricket in infidel clothing, he immediately withdrew him. The great modernizer and reformer Sir Syed Ahmad Khan, a relation of his wife's family, had founded the experimental "Anglo-Oriental" college. Like many former members of Mughal court society, he had felt obliged to send Ahmad Hasan there. But the spectacle of his son kitted out in white trousers and jacket was too much for a man who had witnessed the Mutiny of 1857 and the subsequent brutal dismemberment of the Mughal Empire by the British. He transferred Ahmad Hasan to Allahabad to study law, abruptly suspending the experiment with English education. Yet the legacy of Ahmad Hasan's engagement with the West, however glancing, would be passed along to his youngest son. Abul Ala Mawdudi was born twenty-five years later, on September 25, 1903, in Aurangabad, India, the last of Ahmad Hasan's children.

At the turn of the twentieth century, Lord Curzon was viceroy of India and the British Empire was at the zenith of its rule over the Indian subcontinent. By then the disgraced cricketer was a practicing solicitor, husband, and father. Soon after Abul Ala's birth, however, Ahmad Hasan abandoned the law to devote himself, like his own saintly forefathers, to Sufi thought. Yet when he left the messy world of human strife for the realm of prayer and ascetic practices, he took along his family. He raised his youngest son in similar seclusion, shielding him from foreign influence and the rough manners of less lettered schoolboys. Until Abul Ala turned eight, he was his sole teacher. Thereupon he consigned the boy to the local madrasa, intent on securing his son's future among the learned and devout.

Only when the family found itself on the brink of destitution was Mawdudi's father persuaded to resume his legal practice. Ahmad Hasan did so on one condition: he would only represent the innocent. The rest of his life was spent living out this seeming paradox: a Sufi ascetic immersed in the affairs of men. He died after a long illness when Mawdudi was seventeen, a learned man, gently devout, but stubbornly at odds with the world as it was.

I was reminded of Ahmad Hasan after reading two speeches Mawdudi gave at Lahore Law College soon after the founding of Pakistan on August 14, 1947. Muhammad Ali Jinnah, the "Father of the Nation," had labored to forge a national creed out of another seeming paradox: even as its borders were drawn along the lines of faith, Jinnah insisted that Pakistan would be a secular democracy. Mawdudi's speeches in January and February 1948 were a last-ditch effort to forestall this outcome and the beginnings of his long struggle to write Islam into both the constitution and the consciousness of the new nation.

For Mawdudi, secularism, nationalism, and multiparty democracy were emblematic of the false philosophies of the West to which Muslims had for too long been enslaved. They had nothing to do with Islam. Jinnah and the Westernized political elite poised to consolidate their power represented neither the voice of the masses nor the future of Pakistan; Mawdudi did. In 1948 he warned the students of Lahore Law College that these men would hijack Pakistan for their own ends.

Long before the idea of Pakistan had taken hold, in editorials and books published in the 1920s and 1930s in India, the Mawlana Mawdudi had argued that there was no need to partition the subcontinent once the English had left. Mawdudi never wanted a separate homeland for Muslims. He did not foresee a democratic state that would give voice to a formerly abused minority. Instead he wanted to pick up where the Mughal Empire had left off, resume a moment in history when Islam was glorious and powerful and sure of itself, impervious to Hindu influence. Islam alone could replace British rule.

There would of course be critical improvements, none designed to appease the Hindu majority of the subcontinent. In the Qur'an and the Hadith, the record of the Prophet's sayings and doings, Mawdudi had discovered the makings of a blueprint for an entirely new social contract: "a revolutionary ideology and program which seeks to alter the social order of the whole world and rebuild it in conformity with its own tenets and ideals." He accused Jawaharlal Nehru and the Indian National Congress of plotting to impose a Hindu raj in India, yet in these early years his proposed Islamic state often sounded like a Muslim one. The longer he thought about it, the more perfect and inevitable such a state became.

But who would lead it? The British had sent the last Mughal emperor into exile in 1858, ending three centuries of Muslim rule over the subcontinent. The Turkish Caliphate disappeared with the Ottoman Empire in 1924. As the outlines of his dream took shape in the years before the 1947 Partition, Mawdudi found allies in the Muslim Brotherhood of Egypt, also locked in opposition to British rule. But even after the British Empire was dismantled, the Brotherhood found itself under siege, its leaders arrested or executed, its members exiled. Perhaps Mawdudi entertained the hope that Lahore—once the sixteenth century seat of the Mughal emperors Akbar the Great and his son Jahangir—might replace Cairo as the center of an Islamic renaissance. Lahore would once again become a great capital city, the throne of an Islamic empire overseen by a reconstituted caliph.

In classical and medieval Islam, the caliph represented the Prophet's successor, the supreme political leader of the world Muslim community. A caliph's life was a grimly titanic labor, Mawdudi held, a life that sacrificed wealth, pleasure, and carnal desires in service to Islam. Such a leader could not live in a palace or indulge in the pomp of a powerful head of state as he would be constrained by fears of judgment day. Should this caliph take a single rupee, a single patch of land, betray even a hint of arrogance or indulge a careless moment of lust, he would know that Allah would be unsparing in the hereafter. There seemed to be something inescapably innocent in Mawdudi's belief that the threat of hell was the only check required on a man's pursuit of power. Not surprisingly, Maryam Jameelah's description of the unsmiling leader of the Jamaat-e-Islami bore some resemblance to Mawdudi's model caliph.

After Pakistan became a reality, Mawdudi set out to define more precisely what he envisioned. In the Islamic Republic of Pakistan, he promised, men would be enslaved only to God and God's laws, not to infidels and their man-made ones. That meant the reestablishment of Sharia law. Drawn from the Qur'an and the Hadith as well as a host of traditional works on Islamic jurisprudence, the imposition of Sharia would ensure that Islamic moral values replaced Western ones. The Muslims of India had been the first to abandon Sharia, Mawdudi told the students at Lahore Law College. Then Egypt embraced the Napoleonic code. Turkey and

Albania appropriated various European constitutions. Though Sharia was still in force in Saudi Arabia and Afghanistan, the spirit of it was gone, and enforcement was erratic. Among the many challenges Pakistan now faced, he said, was the need to extract a clear set of criminal and civil laws from the complex and contradictory custom-based traditions of Sharia. He bemoaned how his peers among the ulema were unequal to the task of translating the rich heritage of Islamic law into contemporary constitutional frameworks.*

Mawdudi called his envisioned state a theo-democracy, suggesting that the people of Pakistan would have some undefined role to play in the new body politic. At the same time Mawdudi tried to allay the misgivings of those who were wary of introducing Islamic law into the legal code of the new nation. Some feared that Sharia, however one codified it, would hobble Pakistan's effort to find its feet in the modern secular world. What about the non-Muslim minorities within the borders? Wouldn't they resist the imposition of Muslim religious law? Would Islamic rule actually mean chopping off the hands of thieves and stoning adulterers? For the Oxbridge-educated political elite, like Mawdudi's hated rival Jinnah (who would be dead before the end of the year), Sharia was tantamount to institutionalized barbarism.

All these questions, Mawdudi held, were prompted by ignorance. The humiliations we have suffered, the battles we have waged, he said, would be redeemed only if Islamic law was enshrined. If British civil and criminal codes were instituted instead, what sense was there in the fight for independence? Sayyid Qutb of the Muslim Brotherhood echoed Mawdudi's argument in Egypt. For those who held that establishing a state on the basis of religion and religious law was backward and reactionary, he raised the inexorable question: was not Israel founded on this basis?

Mawdudi addressed the first concern with sweeping promises.

---

* *Ulema* or *ulama* refers to a religious scholar of Islam.

Once the fundamental principles of Sharia were grasped, he said, and a study was done of the ways in which it had evolved over time, there would be no doubt that Sharia would be as responsive to the demands of contemporary society as it once had been in the past. Naturally, religious minorities would be entitled to demand safeguards for their rights and interests and beliefs, he exclaimed. Historically, the magnanimity of Islam was unparalleled. They would absolutely be allowed their rituals and customs, even their practice of eating pork and drinking wine. Such safeguards are written in the laws of Sharia, and would be diligently enforced during times of peace and prosperity. There was a note of imperial officiousness in the way Mawdudi flipped through these points.

However, non-Muslims, like women, would not be allowed to hold public office or weigh in on matters of policy. And gambling parlors and houses of prostitution would be closed. And cinemas. And women of minority communities would have to cover themselves. The Islamic state could not be expected to accept evil practices that violate Islamic principles simply for the sake of appeasing minorities. Indeed it would be the duty of the state to enforce observance of these laws. But there would be no need for opposition parties because the Islamic state, by definition, would be just.

If the Mawdudi imagined he had quieted everyone's concerns with these broad assurances, he was mistaken. Subsequent speeches and editorials would gradually refine his argument and address "liberal" objections. But it was when he came to address the more savage aspects of the penal code that his cavalier manner seemed most jarring. The classic Orientalist argument against the imposition of the Sharia, he pointed out, involved ignoring an entire body of law to focus on "minor" points of *hudud,* the most merciless of the four categories of punishment in the Islamic penal code.

Mawdudi didn't hesitate. The Sharia dictates a hundred lashes for the unmarried fornicator and the stoning to death of the married adulterer. Such punishments could only seem outrageous in a society where risqué pictures and vulgar music were commonplace, he argued; where men and women mingled promiscuously. Similarly, it is only unjust to cut off the hand of a thief in a society where many go without. Once a truly Islamic state was achieved, such sins would become inconceivable. Virtue, piety, and the unrelenting awareness of God and the hereafter would keep all citizens chaste and honest. This would be in stark contrast to the depraved and thieving state of affairs one found in the West. The political mechanism for achieving such an upright state remained mysterious, but Mawdudi conceded that it would involve a gradual spiritual evolution of the populace. Such a transformation could not be achieved by fiat.

Anyone who has ever been subject to fierce catechisms might easily imagine the heavy hand of such a penal code. Under these laws, the inner hagglings of conscience might worry and blacken even the most blameless of hearts. And what of those Muslim youth already divided by the powerful pull of the freewheeling West? Their moral confusion might easily become handmaiden to cruelty. And who would stone the adulterer, whip the unmarried fornicator, who would brandish the swords? What minority would want to be subject to such punishments? What kind of authority would want to inflict them? Would Mawdudi be willing to lift the lash against his sons and daughters?

But these were my questions, not Mawdudi's. The machinery of governance and jurisprudence, the institutions that would be required to exert the will of the state, did not interest him quite so much as his arguments against adopting Western values in adjudicating these issues. He also glossed over the question of how the state's political leadership would be chosen. Candidates for office had to be put forward by others; they could not volunteer themselves. Mawdudi seemed to think that the choice of leader would be obvious to all. Qualifications included political and military sagacity, worldliness, statesmanship, and "unusually deep insight into all the current branches of knowledge and all the major problems of life." Should the fear of hell prove insufficient to curb the carnal desires of the individual selected, by what mechanism might he be removed? Mawdudi didn't say. But if the Mawlana was short on the specifics of a workable Islamic state, he was long on ambition.

In 1956, after eight years of impassioned speeches, pamphlets, and protests, as well as several changes of administration, the constitution of Pakistan was eventually complete. The final draft included a toothless provision proclaiming that all laws would be written in accordance with the teachings of the Qur'an. The Jamaat declared itself victorious, but Mawdudi was noticeably restrained. Was this evidence of his essential lack of interest in complex questions of jurisprudence and governance? Or did it signal ambivalence about his ends? Or perhaps the Mawlana Mawdudi was simply willing to settle, temporarily at least, for a symbolic acknowledgment of his power.

However loosely phrased, the provision that all laws must be "Islamic" would nonetheless cast a fatal shadow over the legitimacy of Pakistan's leaders and the legal code that supported them. Two years later, in 1958, General Ayub Khan seized power in Pakistan, declared a state of emergency, and suspended the newly completed constitution. He banned all opposition parties, among them the Jamaat-e-Islami.

Though his speeches, writings, and travel were now closely monitored, Mawdudi redoubled his efforts. Though its treasury was confiscated, the Jamaat organization remained intact not only in Lahore but also in the countryside. There it was active, distributing Mawdudi's writings to thousands of reading rooms. The party administered medical clinics and flood relief centers and agitated both for the cause of an Islamic state and for a return to the democratic process. The effort to sustain his party under the ban, combined with his stints in jail on charges of sedition, eventually led Mawdudi to appreciate the necessity of due process and an independent judiciary.

Of course this was the conclusion many Westerners might hope he would draw. "They need to become like us," purveyors of Western cultural commentary were constantly saying, as if room would be made for them. As if the world would be a richer place if they did. As if the secular West had everything figured. Had the checks and balances woven into our most sacred laws proven any more effective than the threat of damnation in curbing our darkest impulses? If so, the twentieth century bore scant evidence of it.

Yet however many obstacles Ayub Khan placed in Mawdudi's path, his conviction that an Islamic state was inevitable only grew stronger. "If the expectation that Islam will eventually dominate the world of thought, culture, and politics is genuine," he wrote in 1963, "then the coming of a Great Leader under whose comprehensive and forceful leadership such Revolution is to come about is also certain. . . . When leaders of iniquity like Lenin and Hitler can appear on the stage of this world, why should the appearance of a Leader of Goodness be regarded as remote and uncertain?" Should the man who wrote this ever grasp the reins of power, it seemed unlikely he would ever relinquish them.

The Jamaat-e-Islami was originally conceived not simply as a political party but also as the nucleus of a holy community, much like the one that collected around the Prophet during his early years in Mecca. Or that was the conceit. It was actually formed in August 1941 in reaction to the Jinnah-led Muslim League's call for a division of the subcontinent along religious lines. Once the Jamaat lost the fight against partition and became focused on the struggle over Pakistan's constitution, Mawdudi's party began to act more like a shadow government. Hierarchical, tightly knit, and ideologically vetted, his followers were groomed to step into positions of moral leadership in Pakistan and elsewhere. After 1947, branches of the Jamaat-e-Islami sprang up in India, Jammu and Kashmir, East Pakistan, and Afghanistan.

Mawdudi's writings had even wider reach than his political party.

In them he expressed his hope that Islam would replace Marxism and capitalism as the new global paradigm. His vision of an Islamic world order that would spread the benefits of Islam to all of mankind was no less high minded and no less sincere, I supposed, than the promises of freedom and democracy hawked by the West. The profession of faith, the daily prayers, fasting, charity, and pilgrimage—the five pillars of Islam—were the means both to train party cadres for their mission and to sustain a sense of holy community across the Muslim world. Mawdudi compared this mandate to the training other nations gave their military and police.

Correspondence was another means Mawdudi used to reach out to the world's Muslim leadership from the confines of his Lahore home. In December 1960 Margaret Marcus initiated their correspondence with a letter expressing admiration for an essay Mawdudi wrote on the certainty of an afterlife. The essay had appeared in the *Muslim Digest,* an English-language magazine out of South Africa, which had published her own essays. Reading one of them, enclosed with her letter, Mawdudi immediately recognized a kindred spirit. He responded at length to her observations about Muslim students she had come across in New York and on the shameless fashions of Western women's clothing. As her letters became more personal, he responded with a litany of his illnesses. Though she had yet to convert, he expressed concern for her plight in the land of infidels. "I fully realize the ordeals which a person must endure when he or she embraces Islam in a land of Kufr," he wrote her. "A woman faces a thousand-fold more trials than a man. Through bitter personal experience, you have come to know how tolerant and broadminded these modern Westerners are!" Despite his long days as the leader of the Jamaat-e-Islami, it seemed as though Mawdudi had all the time in the world for Margaret Marcus.

Margaret's remedies for the political challenges facing the Muslim world were uncannily similar to those proposed in Mawdudi's writings and speeches of the thirties and forties, and often equally vague. In her very first letter to him, Margaret described her mission "to devote my life to the struggle against materialistic philosophic-secularism and nationalism which are still so rampant in the world today and threaten not only the survival of Islam but the whole human race."

Like Mawdudi, Margaret focused her energies more on disputing the work of others than on presenting concrete proposals for what was now required to embed specific Islamic values in newly sovereign Muslim countries. In the essays that would make up her first book, she refuted "point by point" the work of Wilfred Cantwell Smith, the director of the Islamic Institute at McGill University; Asaf A. Fyzee, the vice chancellor of Kashmir University; the Turkish sociologist Ziya Gokalp; Sir Syed Ahmad Khan, "who took for his god, nineteenth century European science and philosophy"; and Taha Hussain, the blind Egyptian intellectual writer and eventual minister of education. "All these so-called Muslim intellectuals," Margaret explained to Mawdudi, "are far more dangerous than any external enemies for they are attacking the very foundations of Islam from within. In writing my articles, my goal is to open the eyes of my Muslim readers to this fact."

For Margaret, too, Sharia was somehow central and Sharia largely equaled *hudud.* Her argument in support of the punishments for adultery or drinking or theft involved no interpretation, no higher legal principle than "the law is the law." As for the idea that the punishments were medieval, cruel, or inhuman, she asked, "Does not an evil remain an evil regardless of time or place? Is the merit of a law to be judged according to its leniency? Does the criminal deserve more sympathy than society?" Suppose the American government, she wrote, threatened by the Soviet Union, decided to abandon its Constitution and the Bill of Rights and put in their place a police state so as to better defend itself and its sovereignty: "Would this [sovereignty] not be meaningless after losing its very *raison d'etre*?" Maryam assumed America's founding documents were as transparent, simplistic, and non-negotiable as her notions of Sharia.

By the time Mawdudi described his threefold political strategy to Margaret in December 1961, however, the plan to extract an array of criminal and civil laws from the complex traditions of Sharia was no longer a priority. Instead, he seemed more focused on explaining the continuing grip of the West on his compatriots. His first priority, he now wrote, was to undermine the ideological foundations of Western culture. Second, he would elucidate as clearly as possible the Islamic way of life and mark the ways in which it is superior to that of the West. Finally, he would provide practical Islamic solutions to all of "life's main problems," so as to show those who might feel they have no choice but to follow the West that there is another way. This read more like the outline for a long sermon than the template for a lawbound, constitutionally inscribed state embodying the highest ideals of Islam.

The Mawlana allowed himself a moment of satisfaction at all he had achieved. It was no exaggeration to say, he told his young American admirer, that as a result of his efforts millions of Muslims in Pakistan and India had come to share his yearning for an Islamic order. Further, they nurtured a strong wave of resentment against the Westernized and educated political elites who stood in their way. Once the ban on the Jamaat-e-Islami was lifted, Mawdudi suggested, the voice of the masses would be heard.

Margaret was not Mawdudi's only correspondent abroad. He also exchanged letters with Ayatollah Ruhollah Khomeini, whom he would meet for the first time in 1963. Khomeini would later become Mawdudi's Farsi translator. Sayyid Qutb, in his Cairo prison, was also among his correspondents. That an American Jew, an Iranian Shiite cleric, and an Egyptian man of letters could find common ground with a man who traced his ancestry to a twelfth-century Sufi master from Afghanistan suggests that at the heart of their shared worldview there was something more than a traditional religious sensibility in play.

Like a figure from ancient history, the Mawlana was a difficult man to see clearly.

In her letters home Margaret reported the Mawlana's teachings to her parents without gloss, as if his authority had supplanted her own. Like the subcontinent he came from, the Mawlana's world was divided into two camps: observant Muslims and everyone else. The former represents the epitome of good, Peggy wrote gravely from her rope bed in Icchra, and the latter the apogee of evil, Herbert and Myra Marcus presumably included. She seemed to relish the prospect of being at the center of the Mawlana's struggle, confident that her own role in the looming contest would be significant. Indeed, within a month of her arrival in Lahore, the fortunes of the Jamaat-e-Islami seemed to shift.

In the late afternoon of July 16, 1962, the Mawdudi household was startled to learn that General Ayub Khan had signed legislation that lifted the ban on political parties. Mawdudi immediately drew up a list of charges and demands addressed to Ayub Khan's government. In between her accounts of Haider Farooq's new family of kittens, the doings of the Sufi neighbors she'd seen from the upstairs bathroom window, and the servant boy's attack of malaria, Margaret wrote her parents of the air of anticipation in the back of the house, where Mawdudi was holding an emergency meeting with his party workers.

What part would Maryam Jameelah be given to play in the political drama the Mawlana mapped out that afternoon? Mawdudi had already made space for her in his party as he had in his family. Before she arrived, he had published translated extracts of her letters in his party publication, introducing them as an "eye-opener for Muslim youth." Clearly her arrival had been greatly anticipated and, given the success of her first book and the visibility of her writings in the popular press, she had proven something of a sensation. But beyond her serving as an example to his daughters, had Mawdudi envisioned her as his helpmeet, a translator to

47

help his writings reach a broader audience? Or something else? Perhaps he calculated that an American might not suffer the same kind of surveillance and political restraints that he was subject to. Perhaps he hoped Maryam Jameelah might act as his proxy. What exactly were his thoughts when he heard the constant tapping of the Smith Corona just beyond his study door? Did he read Margaret's letters before he posted them? If the Mawlana's entourage considered her at all, were they inclined to view Maryam Jameelah not as a propaganda tool but as an interloper, even an American spy? Pakistan had long been a willing U.S. partner in the new Great Game of the cold war. There was no shortage of CIA agents about. The Mawlana had already spent several years in jail. He was not a well man. They needed to look out for him.

Despite her volubility, Margaret's letters from the Mawlana's house conveyed little on these matters. She seemed oblivious to the anomalousness of her position: an innocent abroad. Margaret may have assumed the Mawlana had invited her to Pakistan and taken up guardianship of her simply because he was as invested in her writings on Islam as she was. She often betrayed a sense of entitlement, styling herself as Mawdudi did, as the last word on what it meant to be a faithful Muslim and what a proper Islamic state required of its citizens.

And the Begum? What were her thoughts regarding the arrival of a young woman in her already crowded household? As part of the requirements of purdah, the women of the Mawdudi household were allowed to use only the front lawn and front portion of the house. The back garden and the Mawlana's study, with the pile of books and papers spilling over his desk, constituted the inviolate men's realm. Begum Mawdudi never acknowledged her husband's associates or ventured into his study, Peggy boasted to her parents; she didn't even know Mian Tufail Muhammad. Margaret did. She was proud of her space in the narrow corridor opposite the Mawlana's library, intimating to Herbert and Myra that she was privy to the men's world as well as that world of beautifully appointed teas and suckling babies. Herbert Marcus had always held that women in Muslim societies were treated no better than slaves, but here she was, their dear Peggy, not simply respected but lionized.

Meanwhile, purdah meant that the Mawlana made phone calls on her behalf. Her watch, broken on the journey over, required repair. He or some underling filled her prescriptions for vitamins and acne cream. The American consulate needed a photograph of her face; she required a chaperone if she was to be unveiled in front of a strange man. On any particular day there might be a letter to her editor at the *Voice of Islam* to be posted or a thank-you note to Dr. Said Ramadan. Ramadan was the son-in-law of Hassan al-Banna, living in exile in Switzerland to escape an Egyptian death sentence. She also corresponded with Sayyid Qutb's sister Amina in Cairo and Muhammad al-Bahy, the director of cultural affairs at al-Azhar University, not to mention her parents, Betty, cousins, and aunts. Furthermore, upon the publication of "How I Became Interested in Islam," magazine editors, newspaper interviewers, and prospective suitors deluged Mawlana Mawdudi with requests for interviews with Maryam Jameelah just as the prospects for the Jamaat-e-Islami were looking up.

Whatever Margaret's role was to be, whatever merit her proximity to the Mawlana afforded her, it seemed purdah proved less of an obstacle than Urdu. Margaret could hear the low voices of the Mawlana's "family" on the other side of the door, but she could not yet understand them. The typing continued.

Yet before I could begin to fathom the political and familial dynamics of the Mawdudi household, Margaret Marcus's letters to her parents were suddenly all about a man named Hakim Rai Naimat Ali Khan and his wife, Khurshid Bibi. The return address was no longer the Mawlana's house in Lahore but a place called Pattoki. A month into her stay, Peggy explained, she had received a kind letter from these friends of Mawdudi. Khan and his wife had invited her for a visit. After three days her childless hosts, whom she soon referred to familiarly as Baijan and Appa, asked her to stay on permanently as their daughter. Margaret gladly accepted, returning only briefly to Lahore to collect her clothes and books.

The lifting of the ban on the Jamaat had occasioned her move, she explained in her second letter from Pattoki, responding to her parents' concerns and questions about these developments. The Mawlana had been overwhelmed by work, leaving him no time for his wife and family, much less for her. This had created a certain amount of tension in the house, which had its effect on everybody. In fact, it was the Mawlana who initiated the new arrangement.

So, with barely a backward glance, Peggy introduced a whole new cast of characters. Liberated from those Westernized and urbane Lahoris, and the close quarters of the Mawdudi household, she was in the thick of this new life in no time at all. Though Mawdudi remained her guardian and she continued to correspond with him, her letters to her parents now filled up with the minutiae of life in a small town an hour south of Lahore. For eight months the letters from Pattoki poured out in a bubbling current.

I let myself be carried along by these new developments, losing myself in Margaret's slipstream account of a busy household in a small town in the Punjab half a century before. Then, in the second to last of those twenty-four letters, I was furiously trying to back away from the precipice in front of me. After an unexplained five-month lapse in correspondence, Peggy wrote from yet another address. The building on Jail Road in Lahore was known locally as Paagal Khanaah. Just under a year after her arrival in Pakistan, Maryam Jameelah had been committed to the madhouse.

July 1963

The more I considered it, the more convinced I became that the Mawlana and his political cadres had taken against me. Baijan, I now saw, was in league with him, however reluctantly. He and Appa had been nothing but kind to me. But not one week before I received the Mawlana's letter, I had noticed that Baijan had grown quiet and withdrawn. He and Appa had recently returned from Lahore, where they had gone to see a doctor about Appa's migraines. Or so I had been led to believe.

Except for that single trip, whenever he wasn't at the medical dispensary or at meals, Baijan spent hours on the roof, pacing, repeating his Dhikr and running his fingers through his prayer beads over and over again. Long after the electric and kerosene lights went out, I could hear Baijan pace above my head, alone with Allah. When I commented on Baijan's distraction and absorption in his prayers, Appa suggested that perhaps Baijan was planning to become a Sufi. Now I could only conclude that after wrestling at length with his conscience, Baijan felt that he had no choice but to agree to Mawdudi's plan. That was when I first became frightened.

I immediately took refuge with a village neighbor so I could collect my thoughts. I tried my best to keep a rein on my fears. This was very difficult. Not since my departure from New York had I known such unceasing torment. Of my many correspondents, however, there was one man I trusted implicitly. He was a journalist in Karachi named Shaheer Niazi. He alone had expressed a frank skepticism as to the saintliness of Mawlana Mawdudi.

I wrote to him of my deepest fears concerning Mawdudi's intentions. As it seemed impossible for me to stay on in Pattoki under Mawdudi's guardianship, I needed his advice. Could he come to Pattoki? I needed help figuring out what I had to do to extract myself from Mawdudi's control. I would require new lodgings. I wanted nothing more than to remain in Pakistan and live simply and independently. He wrote back immediately. He would come as soon as he could get away.

But before Shaheer Niazi had time to arrange his journey, Mian Tufail Muhammad, the secretary general of Jamaat-e-Islami Party, arrived in his sparkling white shalwar kameez. He was accompanied by a pretty young Peace Corps volunteer named Janet Hanneman and a nondescript man from the U.S. consulate. Hanging back was yet another man, handsome and heavyset, whom Mian Tufail Muhammad introduced mysteriously as Dr. Rashid, a personal friend.

After an awkward round of tea, I was told to pack and get ready to go. Filled with foreboding, I nonetheless acquiesced. I was entirely at their mercy. Of course, the entire village turned out to get a glimpse of the uncovered, slim, and attractive "Memsahib" Janet and that only added to the spectacle. After an hour or so, the car stopped. Even before I looked out the window, I had somehow known where I was being taken. I turned to Janet.

It's the mental hospital, isn't it? She nodded sadly.

We thought it was the best place, she said.

Once I had been admitted, I snuck a look at my case file. There I discovered a copy of the Mawlana's March 12 letter to me and all my suspicions were confirmed. Dr. Rashid turned out to be the hospital director and answerable to the Jamaat-e-Islami.

I wondered if Shaheer Niazi would ever find me.

According to Margaret, the crisis had been set in motion when she received a letter from Mawlana Mawdudi. Dated March 12, 1963, nearly eight months after she had left his home, his letter was quite different from earlier ones, she told her parents, so distinct as to make her think Mawdudi had not written it. She studied it with a wary eye, each time testing it for a false note. Leaving aside an account of its content, she was suddenly struck by its tone. Mawdudi had never addressed her with such detachment before! He did not mince words, Peggy reported; it was a cold and ruthless letter. She couldn't help but conclude that it was not addressed to her, but written so that the Mawlana might justify his subsequent actions to himself. The thought terrified her. After this preamble, Peggy then provided a bare summary of the letter's contents.

Mawdudi began by saying that it had always been his intention to find her a suitable young man to marry. He had first thought her misbehavior was due to the frustration of her unmarried state. Given the most recent report from Pattoki, he now felt he didn't want to risk the ruin of a good man's life. The Mawlana then proceeded not only to outline her transgressions in Pattoki but to list those she had committed in Lahore as well.

Earlier, Peggy had assured her parents that it had been entirely her own decision to leave Mawdudi's home. She now admitted this wasn't the case. The Mawlana had sent her to Pattoki to be "rehabilitated," and on the evidence of Baijan's testimony he had evidently determined that her rehabilitation had failed.

If Herbert and Myra expected to learn the substance of the Mawlana's complaints from their daughter, they would have been disappointed. Whatever Margaret stood accused of doing, her crimes appeared to be either so inconsequential or so damning that she couldn't bear to repeat them when she came to account for how she happened to be writing from an insane asylum.

I assumed evidence in the archive or the library would settle such questions and determine the direction of the story. But the March 12 letter was not among the letters in the Maryam Jameelah Papers. All I had was Margaret's account of events: an account that, she now admitted, hadn't been entirely truthful. I was thus obliged to consider, too, whether Margaret Marcus's panic over

Mawdudi's intentions was, like her ardent religious zeal, a symptom of some deeper and more private pathos.

Or was it that beneath the story that Margaret's letters told, there had all along been another story, a shadow story in which Herbert and Myra's deepest fears about their daughter and the man into whose care they sent her were realized? Was she truly in danger? Had she been dispatched to Pattoki because she had displeased Mawdudi in refusing to marry? Had party elders or a jealous wife turned him against her? Was the lifting of the ban on his party somehow related to this development?

Perhaps Maryam had tried to argue some point about Islam with him. Mawdudi had written that for those "self-deceived" people who imagined they could get him to change his views, the "rightful place to accommodate them and their like is in an 'asylum.'" Mawdudi also believed that women, by their very nature, posed a clear danger to the Islamic state; he traced the collapse and destruction of every great civilization to the moral decay and weakening of the social fabric that occurred when women were granted "undue freedoms." In his view women needed to be restrained and sequestered; men needed to be vigilant "lest [they] should, like Adam himself, be lured into a life of pleasure."

Every narrative possibility turns on a question of character. In this case, the characters of the Mawlana Mawdudi and Maryam Jameelah. I could imagine any of these as possible scenarios, but before I could advance any further, there was one more question I was obliged to consider.

Which one did I secretly want to be true?

I had been in the city that morning.

In the days that followed I waited with a friend for the phone to ring. Our children were in and out of each other's houses more than usual. We shared meals when we could and I smoked cigarettes for the first time in years. Though we recognized the irrevocability of what had happened, I echoed her quiet certainty that there would be a phone call. But little by little the outlines of the event became sharper, and the day finally came when we could sum it all up in a sentence. The husband this woman had left behind on the 88th floor had not followed her out and would never. I listened to the explanation she provided her children. They had asked: Why hadn't their father left with her? How had she been spared? Why was he dead?

He never imagined the towers would collapse, she replied. He stayed behind to help others find a way down.

It never occurred to me that the explanation could be that simple.

But after the children were put to bed and she was lying alone in her room trying to sleep, how did she begin to account for what had happened? Did she ever think to ask herself the larger questions? Why this? Who were these men? In all the time we spent together I could never bring myself to raise these questions. I was in awe of her quiet composure, perhaps, or fearful of unsettling it. So when I turned, alone, to thinking about the hatred that occasioned the attacks, I didn't doubt it was real and it was frightening but it was hard, at first, to catch hold of. The act itself was so far outside what I knew that, like many others in the city, I couldn't bear to contemplate it for long. That was not a mark of how much we were suffering, I felt certain, but of how much suffering history had spared us.

The city's heart was left open in a way that left everyone dazed. In the early weeks I was swept up in an atmosphere that mixed dread and exaltation. It was months before I could bring myself to leave the city limits. How much longer would it take to circumnavigate the question of what had happened and why, to take its complete measure? Ten years? Twenty? The meanings already being worked out of the event from Washington were incomprehensible and, I foolishly imagined, beside the point.

But the details kept coming. Once I began to hear about the men in the planes, I couldn't stop imagining them waiting their turn at the ticket counter, fingering their box cutters and their awful purpose. The unfolding accounts of the horror on the planes and inside the buildings, the calm expressions of love that poured into phones and message machines, were unbearable to fathom. At a certain point there was no disguising my revulsion.

The hatred when it came seemed as if it had always been there. I turned it over and over, rattled but also subtly empowered by the clarity of it. Yet, like the dread that preceded the hatred, this also subsided. Only after I stumbled across the Jameelah archive did the questions that haunted me during those days begin to flare up once again. At a certain point I realized that this was something I could do. I would find better answers than the hasty ones we managed to put together in those days. I would find answers more lasting than the easy ones provided for us.

By then, of course, years had passed. By then the American proxy wars on the Muslim world Maryam Jameelah had written about had become cataclysmic and genuine, no more so than in the aftermath of the attacks. My country now became directly and irretrievably responsible for the deaths of thousands upon thousands of Muslims. That is how, I learned, our new enemies imagined we thought of them. Not by their ethnicities or nationalities or family names, but by their religious beliefs. And this, a war on Muslims, had been our plan all along, they insisted, conveniently refusing to credit those behind the attacks. And yet were they entirely wrong? There was now reason to wonder. Had Maryam grasped something about America that I had missed? Had Mawdudi? As the years wore on, their war dead made up in numbers what they lacked in novelty, immediate impact, and intimate proximity. Yet these escalating figures—20,000, 50,000, 100,000, and more—rendered in simple, disposable newsprint, never seemed to register in quite the same way as the Technicolor ones we had suffered.

As with the attacks on the city, however, questions touching on the guilt or innocence of the dead were largely beside the point.

Either they were all innocent and we were all guilty or *we* were all innocent and *they* were all guilty. We shared our enemies' faith in the power of violent spectacle, in shock and awe. In kidnappings and secret prisons. Did we take after them, or did they take after us? A few voices entertained lingering doubts over our leaders' rationale for the war; most seemed readily appeased by the bland promises of liberation from tyranny. I imagined my growing sense of shame and alarm equaled that felt by those families who, in the wake of the attacks, had sat quiet and thunderstruck in their homes, hoping against hope that their coreligionists had not been behind them.

I saw, too, how long-standing legal protections ordinary Americans considered their due might simply disappear. Surveillance could become a free-for-all. Language, too, had become a game; just how far could the leaders we heard from in those days take words from their meanings? The Patriot Act? Homeland Security? Total Information Awareness? In this new season every mention of the word *terror* had the power to make cowards or dupes or bigots of reasonable people. The word *freedom* summoned righteous legions at home while elsewhere cynicism and rage proliferated. Maryam's question echoed in my head: Suppose the American government decided to abandon its Constitution and Bill of Rights and put in their place a police state so as to better defend itself. Would not sovereignty be meaningless after we lost our very *raison d'être*? I began to think that something essential in the entire project of my country had come undone.

I couldn't help but ask, how much had my trust in America been a cipher for a deeper and more lasting set of beliefs? How much of what I considered right and wrong was predicated on being a citizen of a well-armed country? I was exiled to a state of devastation and doubt. This was my new nationality.

The discovery of the archive had become the crooked key to understanding how all this had come about. Here there would be an explanation. Who were these nineteen men? Who were we?

Who was their God? Who was ours? It hadn't escaped my notice that Maryam's letters also gave me the chance to peer in the window of the house of the aging leader who first issued the call for global jihad. Did Margaret live to see the attacks? What did she make of them? Did she watch the city she had once known so well fall to pieces? Had she changed her mind about the evils of the West or did she remain resolute? Would she defend the indefensible? What could she tell me?

"There are certain eras which are too complex, too deafened by contradictory historical and intellectual experiences, to hear the voice of sanity," Susan Sontag once wrote. "The truths we respect are those born of affliction." It wasn't that I hadn't questioned Maryam's reason. Rather, I looked to her for the outsider's crucial insight, a blind seer's clarifying truth. I found in her story a secret history that would challenge those we had been telling ourselves. The wars we were selling.

I couldn't shake the sense, too, that the new wars were being waged by the same flinty-eyed men whose aggressive intentions, a scant generation before, were focused elsewhere. "America is allegedly determined to bestow upon Viet Nam a truly free democratic society," Maryam Jameelah wrote in 1969. "But while buckets of crocodile tears are shed by officials in Washington over Viet Nam's backwardness and miserable living standards, four million are slain." These same men had watched that war unfold from lowly government desks and decades later thought they could do better. They wanted a different ending and would stop at nothing to get it. Where others were inclined to give them the benefit of the doubt, the shock of this fact kept me nailed squarely in place. That war, too, was painted as a war between freedom and tyranny. "They hate our freedom," the speechwriters now wrote, picking up where the earlier litanies had left off.

Like the young Margaret, I began to feel maladjusted, to harbor grudges. I kept a blacklist of those who had written in measured, manly tones about the unpleasant necessity, the sober duty, of choosing this war. Not the war against those who had attacked us, but a fatter, easier, and far more profitable target: conveniently Muslim, as if that were a bonus. In those long years I veered toward shrillness, oppressed by people talking about children and real estate. Friends became strangers. And when conversation turned to the war (and only then, it seemed, because it was going so badly), the general tone was either complacent or meekly despairing. Every day I raked the news for a story that would open everyone's eyes. But even the most outrageous accounts of torture and mendacity were fleeting distractions. Something more final was required. An unnamed thought lodged inside me like a swallowed curse, a thought heretical and traitorous. By then my widowed friend had left for a new neighborhood; her children grew older in different schools. I lost track of her.

Once in a while I would stop spinning and remember I wasn't always like this. But still I wanted to know: By what mechanism did America and the world's Muslims suddenly become each other's evil caricature? Metaphor? Narrative? Racist propaganda? In moments of clarity, it seemed to me that whichever side of this war one was on had nothing to do with who believed in divine revelation or who had the most righteous cause. Nor did it have to do with who was Muslim and who was Jewish or Christian. Rather, it seemed simply that neither side really wanted this train to stop, with the possible exception of those families who were actually on board. And no one knew in what direction it was headed. This was the drill on both sides: let the drama play out, then commemorate the heroes and the martyrs.

It was really a very simple story, I thought bitterly, as I returned with relief to the letters in the marble library. By then I knew that the answers to my questions weren't all to be found there. By then I knew I would go to Lahore.

CHAPTER 3

Doubt

Accounts of the Prophet Muhammad began to be recorded during his lifetime, but the first printed collection of his words and deeds (the Sunnah) did not appear until well after his death. Each of the biographical scraps in these collections was known as a hadith (ahadith, plural). Where God's emissary, the angel Gabriel, was believed to have dictated the Qur'an to the Prophet, ahadith were culled from the Prophet's family and early followers. Only those who shared his day-to-day existence, who were privy to his most intimate reflections, were sanctified. Khadijah, the Prophet's first wife and first convert, their daughter Fatimah, and his third wife, Aishah, were all considered Companions. They were all trusted sources for compilations of the Hadith.

But unlike the Qur'an, with its unchanging 114 suras, ahadith proliferated wildly after the death of Muhammad. As the Prophet's life receded into the distance, the circle of those who claimed to have known him widened. Many embroidered a slight acquaintance or a chance meeting to claim the status of Companion. Others fantasized a nonexistent friendship into an intimate one, plying stories of the Prophet to feed the hunger of his followers for guidance in the long years without him. The decision to commit the ahadith to print was an effort to curtail these inventions and establish a canon. Yet from the start doubts trailed ahadith like the tail of a kite.

In Sunni Islam, there are six major compilations of the Prophet's sayings and doings. Each reflects the temperament of the compiler and the methodology used to judge which sayings out of hundreds of thousands were authentic and trustworthy, and which were weak or entirely made up. To settle competing versions, the science of Hadith study—*ulam al-hadith*—arose. To evaluate a specific hadith, each compiler focused not only on the human links in the chain of transmission, called *sanad,* but also on the precise wordings of their texts, or *matn.*

The finest, most sensitive minds applied themselves to the arduous task of authentication. Which Companion first recounted this hadith and to which Successor? Apocryphal anecdotes needed to be identified. Biographical methods were employed to weigh the character of the witness who first proffered testimony. In Arabic this was called *ilm al-rijal.* Where a teacher in the line of transmission passed along the Prophet's words to various pupils, his credibility was enhanced. Some of the less punctilious compilers invented entirely new Companions for the Prophet; one trespasser was snuck in as a servant in the Prophet's household. Yet even the early ahadith that were flagged as fiction remained part of the canon, providing insight into how judgments of authenticity were determined.

The process of ahadith winnowing by these early scholars seemed an effort to find a way back to the clarity and compassion Muhammad had first bequeathed to them. Through this exacting discipline they would recapture the sense of certainty about how Allah expected them to conduct their lives. Whatever the truth or falsehood of any particular anecdote, each wisp of testimony gave evidence of their community's strenuous effort to inhabit the Prophet's thinking and, by extension, the mind of God. From this effort would arise the beginnings of Islamic jurisprudence, wherein civil laws were either extrapolated from the judgments implied by the Prophet's actions or arose directly from his statements. One of the earliest compilations of ahadith came out of Medina, the city where the Prophet and his early followers took shelter from persecution. This was a work called *al-Muwatta*. Compiled over four decades by Imam Malik, its authenticity was universally agreed upon as second only to that of the Qur'an. One of his ahadith read: "You people bring disputes to me," the Prophet said, "but it may be that some of you are able to put your case better than others. I have to decide on evidence that is before me. If I happen to expropriate the right of anyone in favor of his brother let the latter not take it, for in that case I have given him a piece of hell-fire."

This suggested that while direct testimony and material evidence can tell part of the story, it is still possible for a miscarriage of justice to take place. The law is applied according to the information at hand, the Prophet intimated, but damnation awaits those who have been unfairly rewarded at the expense of the innocent. Reading this, an early scholar concluded that the Prophet was telling his followers that those who possessed only the law were not infallible, not even the Prophet himself. Equally, this scholar went on to say, those who relied purely on inner conviction while remaining ignorant of the law were not true Muslims. From the earliest days of Islam, it seems, there was a running conversation between the mandates of Sharia and the lawgivers' search of their own faithful hearts and consciences.

As with the hadith, there were competing methodologies for arriving at legal judgments. One school of law might arrive at a ruling through the rigorous application of legal principle and inductive reasoning. Another might take its lead from long-established legal precedents. And yet another might find guidance in the more fluid realm of community consensus. Whatever the school or tradition, the spirit of critical inquiry was evident from the very beginning.

These early jurists seemed to be assembling the pieces of a vast puzzle, certain only that when they were finished, when they had cast their judgment, the spirit of Islam would once again be passed on, whole and complete. Naturally, this sense of completion would last only until it was time for the next generation to further finesse the struggle of interpretation, of *ijtihad*. Mastering the cautious logic of generations of lawgivers would provide not only subtle training in the unreliability of texts, but also a lesson in humility. However theoretical and inconclusive, however antique and esoteric the skills required, the care with which these fragile wares were parsed stands as testament to the sincerity and doggedness of faith.

The Mawlana, however, was impatient with medieval hermeneutics. Perhaps justifiably, he wanted Islam to move on, to engage with the world outside these learned tomes. Having made his own study of the Qur'an and the various permutations of Hadith, he was ready to pronounce upon the true intentions of the Prophet and draw from them an entire schema of legal opinion, indeed an entire constitution for the state of Pakistan, if he but had the time. And just as he had insisted that the pure and essential laws of Islam were practically self-evident, he made hadith study sound quite simple. He claimed he could tell at a glance whether the hadith in question was truly an authentic account of something the Prophet had actually said, or a later corruption. In short, he had no single critical method, no precisely unfolding argument, just his own intuitive grasp of the Prophet's intentions.

There was something of this improvised attitude in his handling of Maryam Jameelah. Within days of her commitment, Mawdudi and his family had embarked on a long-planned pilgrimage to Mecca. While he was in the Holy Land, Mawdudi met with King Saud bin Abdul Aziz and received honors from many Saudi dignitaries and ulema. He had had the pleasure of participating in a special sacred ceremony in which an exquisite black *kiswah*, handwoven and embroidered with gold thread in Lahore, was placed over the Holy Kaaba of Mecca. Two special trains manned by Jamaati workers had ferried this *kiswah* across the length of Pakistan, stopping at rail depots to meet ecstatic crowds waiting to kiss and weep over the precious cloth. This was considered a great diplomatic coup for Pakistan and served to burnish Mawdudi's spiritual credentials among the traditional ulema. When he called a press conference on his return six weeks later, the Mawlana was prepared to answer questions about the many honors bestowed upon him by the Saudis. He was not expecting questions about the fate of his wayward American charge.

In carrying the Mawlana's remarks, the editors of Pakistan's major Urdu-language daily, the *Nawai Waqt*, were doubtless answerable to the Mawlana's avowed enemy, President Ayub Khan. Their account of Mawdudi's press conference gave them an opportunity to ingratiate themselves with the president and embarrass and undermine an increasingly powerful adversary at the same time. It was they who first publicly revealed that the Mawlana Mawdudi's celebrated protégée, Maryam Jameelah, had been committed to the madhouse.

"She is simply suffering from hysteria," Mawdudi began, trying to play down the significance of Maryam's plight. He had left everything to Mian Tufail Muhammad and had yet even to visit her at the Paagal Khanaah. He had only just begun to sort through the stack of mail that awaited him on his desk in Icchra.

"I received a letter from her a few days ago written from the hospital," he continued. "The manner and style of this letter is so logical and rational that it is inconceivable to me it could have been written by a madwoman."

Of course, the Mawlana could not admit publicly that he might have been mistaken in his previous appraisal of Maryam Jameelah; his judgment might be questioned. Furthermore, Maryam wasn't a cynical political adversary; to the general public she was for all intents and purposes his daughter. Nonetheless, it seemed a feeble defense for the Mawlana to cite the logical manner in which Maryam's letters were written as proof of her sanity.

Perhaps he felt more comfortable drawing conclusions from textual study than from going to see her in the hospital. If so, this was of a piece with his overly bookish take on the world, not to mention a definite skittishness when it came to unmarried women. It was as if he now regarded Maryam not as his daughter, but as yet another difficult text, written in a language he didn't entirely understand, which, like German or English, he would master once he found the time.

Perhaps this is unfair. I might have asked the same question of myself. Was the Peggy Marcus of the letters an altogether different person from the woman the Mawlana encountered at the dinner table or the one Appa taught to make rotis in Pattoki? Could one be crazy and the other sane? If Maryam's letters to the Mawlana seemed entirely rational, perhaps that was the point in writing them: to convince Mawdudi that she remained the true and earnest Muslim daughter he had first taken her for. Peggy's letters to her parents would have a similar intent. These letters were filled with endless details engineered to allay her parents' concern about her welfare and perhaps, like a person whistling in the dark, her own. Whatever conflicts had arisen out of the difficulties of her life in Pakistan, in her letters at least, Peggy held tight to the Right Path.

The Mawlana expressed his complete confidence that Maryam would recover her senses in a matter of days, two weeks at most. Then, rather than returning her to live with his family, he planned to arrange a separate residence for her.

"This lady is a true Muslim who came to Pakistan to join a true Islamic society," the Mawlana concluded, deftly working his way round to his final pitch: "We are also interested in arranging her marriage to a like-minded Muslim gentleman."

Though news of Maryam Jameelah's commitment six weeks before had doubtless already reached him, Mawlana Mawdudi's published remarks caught the eye of Ghulam Ahmad Parwez. Born the same year as Mawdudi and the author of a competing commentary on the Qur'an, Parwez was the Mawlana's archnemesis. A self-styled Islamic thinker not unlike Mawdudi, Parwez exhibited a similar impatience with the subtleties of Hadith study. Only he went even further. He thought nearly everything about it spurious. Instead, he brought his focus to bear entirely on the Qur'an. This evidently granted him far greater latitude when it came to his vision of what Islam entailed.

Rejecting Hadith as a source of Islamic law and practice also proved amenable to the secular leadership of Pakistan. Parwez was one of the authors of the recently implemented Family Laws Ordinance, the new civil code of Pakistan. He and Mawlana Mawdudi had fought a pitched battle over the legislation. In a failed effort to derail its passage, the Mawlana had joined forces with the more traditional ulema to pronounce the ordinance un-Islamic. Among other innovations, the Family Laws Ordinance made taking a second wife subject to the first wife's consent, required that divorce be processed and mediated in civil as opposed to religious courts, and outlawed child marriage.

Thus the fate of Maryam Jameelah at the hands of Mawlana Mawdudi and his party was of more than passing interest to Ghulam Ahmad Parwez. An unsigned editorial published in his organization's official magazine that July made clear that he intended to extract his pound of flesh by parsing Mawdudi's comments on her fate. This amounted to his own biographical study, an *ilm al-rijal* in Urdu on the character of both Mawlana Mawdudi and that of his ward, Maryam Jameelah.

Mawlana Mawdudi has said that Maryam has not become insane while at the same time he says she is hospitalized due to hysteria. We would be grateful if someone could explain how hysteria is not madness. To cite her coherent prose as evidence of her sanity is to overlook the fact that many crazy people sound perfectly sane, showing no evidence of mental imbalance until that moment when sanity deserts them. And we have heard that she is in the notorious Paagal Khanaah. No one is hospitalized in the Paagal Khanaah unless they are unlikely ever to recover, much less in a matter of weeks. And we now understand that Maryam Jameelah has already been in residence for over a month.

We know from her own writings and from newspaper interviews that Maryam has come from America and has long searched for spiritual peace in a community of like-minded souls. Such a community was not to be found in her native country. Nor did she find spiritual peace in her native religion of Judaism. This search brought her to Islam. In theory, no doubt Islam seemed to her an eminently practical religion. Unlike Judaism, for example, a faith limited to Jews, Islam is one that she might share with the whole of humanity. From her books she doubtless learned that the ummah embraces all human beings, whatever their race or nationality or station in life; it is a faith, too, that holds women in the highest esteem.

In Pakistan Maryam Jameelah expected to find this true Islamic society she had read of in her books. This was why she left her home and family, her childhood memories, her entire American identity. She left behind everything for Allah. All these wonderful thoughts were in her heart and mind when she reached our shores.

Yet as soon as she arrived here she was offered a burqa.

In America her natural modesty was deeply offended by the clothes worn by the typical Western woman. And so she embraced the burqa with relief and joy, equating it with her natural chasteness. She did not immediately grasp that a woman can be modest without a burqa and immodest beneath one. I imagine it did not take her long to realize the hypocrisy of those sisters for whom the burqa is an empty affectation. I have no doubt that this was a deeply unsettling discovery.

Any psychiatrist or psychologist will agree that those who become insane are oversensitive. For a person like Maryam Jameelah, the discrepancy between her dream of an Islamic society and the reality of what she found here would be shattering.

What else did she learn about the Jamaat-e-Islami version of Islam? What were the rights they sought to uphold in the face of the recently imposed Muslim Family Laws Ordinance?

A man can marry off his four-year-old daughter.

A man can take four wives whenever he wants.

A man, whenever he wants and without providing any reason, can divorce his wife, but if a woman wants a divorce she faces enormous obstacles.

If a woman does not agree with her husband he may beat her.

The purpose of marriage is to satisfy man's sexual cravings or to have children, so he can have sex with four different women and impregnate all of them. A woman may have relations with only one man.

Our sister Maryam came from a society where humans are completely controlled by the capitalist machine, where human beings are treated like slaves. She had no idea that she would be joining a community where not only is the human body enslaved, but the soul is as well. In this world, there is no prospect of freedom. She might have been unhappy in American society, she might have been unhappy as a Jew, but at least she had the choice to question her society and renounce her family's beliefs.

Now I will again return to the Mawlana Mawdudi's comments about the fate of Maryam Jameelah. When this lady recovers, he tells us, he plans to find separate accommodation for her. I find this a subtle way of distancing himself. She is obviously being pushed out of his house. Then he will arrange a marriage with a man not of her choosing, a like-minded Muslim gentleman, he suggests.

The word arrange used here is typical. For in the Islam of the Jamaat-e-Islami, Maryam Jameelah cannot select her husband by herself. Here the right to select a husband is the prerogative of her guardian. The Mawlana Mawdudi will decide whom she is to marry.

I've discussed this case in detail because I feel strongly that whoever is involved in treating Maryam Jameelah should be aware of the conditions under which her breakdown occurred. And this is not only her tragedy. It is the tragedy of hundreds of thousands of Maryams who are crucified on the cross of religion. These girls are neither living nor dead. Before marriage their life is criminalized; they are made to wear burqas as if to bare their God-given face was a sin. They are never certain whether the man who comes to the door to marry them brings with him their freedom from this bondage or a knife across the throat.

There used to be a time when suffering people would come to find refuge within Muslim homes. There they were assured of being taken care of until they were healed. Now the situation has deteriorated to the point where people arrive completely sane and are turned out when they go crazy.

Unfortunate daughters of Islam! I implore you to wait for the day when a man will come with the light of the Qur'an in his heart. Only then will husbands understand that in nurturing you and all your gifts, we as a nation can change our destiny.

The New York Public Library has dozens of books in various languages on Mawdudi. There is a two-volume work that tracks his life practically month by month. There are books that herald him as the founding father of political Islam and a pioneer of Islam's twentieth-century revival. There are even hints throughout the party literature that he might have been the prophesied Redeemer, whose arrival heralds the day of Resurrection. The Mawlana did little to discourage this particular view. Finally, there are works that trace the influence of his writings (and that of others) on the teachers of Osama bin Laden and his proliferating jihadi stepchildren. Just as a librarian named Mr. Parr in the Oriental Division had once helped Maryam find the books she needed in her study of Islam, the librarians of the (renamed) Asian and Middle East Division were unfailingly helpful in my study of Mawdudi. I was even allowed to enter the closed stacks in search of particular titles and obscure journals. The books on Mawdudi rarely stray into intimate territory. Abul Ala Mawdudi as a husband or brother, son or father, is almost entirely absent. His motivation for inviting Maryam Jameelah to Lahore remains a mystery. The crisis over her commitment is passed over in similar silence, as if what happens in real life isn't nearly as important as what is pronounced upon in speeches or written down in books. However partial or impartial, all these books portray Mawdudi as he portrays himself: as a commanding voice of political and religious authority. He is a Mujaddid: a Renewer of the Faith.

Many of the works that Mawdudi wrote are also available in the library stacks. In one hundred and fifty books and countless issues of his journal *Tarjuman al-Qur'an*, Mawdudi holds forth tirelessly on purdah, education, birth control, law, morality, war, marriage, governance, and the treatment of religious minorities. His unpublished memoirs (quoted by a few writers) tell the story of his intellectual evolution, beginning with his schooling in his saintly father's library, followed by a period in the wilderness after his father's death, and climaxing with his triumphant embrace of the Qur'an as his "beacon," "master-key," and "true benefactor."

Even in translation, Mawdudi's voice is lucid and muscular, a seductive symphony of learning and worldliness. He broadcasts the authority of a man who traffics in realities, not the trivia of scholarship, mystic vagueness, or defensive apologetics. He refuses to let centuries of debate over questions of interpretation mediate his response to the holy texts. Even the great Urdu poet and philosopher Muhammad Iqbal found himself fortified by Mawdudi's brush-clearing, hortatory tone. Both his English translator and his Urdu biographer are compelled to remark admiringly on Mawdudi's scientific and logical approach to Islam. Mawdudi himself characterized his approach to Islam as "scientific."

Yet though Mawdudi often uses the language of science, engineering, and logic to make his points, his rhetorical feints would exasperate the most cool-headed scientist or logician. A 1947 address given at his father's alma mater, Aligarh University, is typical. In this speech Mawdudi takes pains to establish that the arrival of an Islamic state was an entirely natural and inexorable eventuality, historically determined: "Just as in logic, deduction always follows the arrangement of premises; in chemistry a chemical compound is formed by the combination, in a particular way, of certain ingredients . . . likewise it is an undeniable fact that in sociology a state is merely the natural consequence of the circumstances which pre-exist in a particular society." In Mawdudi's thinking, science and "Nature's plan" are interchangeable: the "laws of Nature" are a cover for the hand of Allah (the "Engineer" and "Designer") at work in human events. And Allah, he believed, was intent on delivering to the subcontinent an Islamic state. There was clearly more alchemist than scientist in Mawdudi.

Mawdudi's occasional gestures of humility, like his tone of rationality, can also seem like a rhetorical trick. From the evidence of his written work, he does not allow much in the way of personal reflection or doubt to temper his cast-iron judgments. "Now that I have access to the roots of knowledge and the world of reality," he writes casually, "Kant, Nietzsche, Hegel, Marx and other secular thinkers began to look like pygmies. In fact, I began to pity them, for they could not resolve issues, despite grappling with them throughout their life and producing thereon huge volumes." No one else need bother with these men and their tedious inconclusive books, he seems to say; I've read them for you.

Mawdudi's most widely read book is undoubtedly the brief introductory primer *Towards Understanding Islam,* a required text in nearly every madrasa curriculum in Pakistan and elsewhere. But it was the multivolume *Tafhim al-Qur'an,* a work of translation and Qur'anic commentary, that established the foundation of Mawdudi's intellectual authority and provides the key to the leader he struggled to become. The revelations contained in the Qur'an, Mawdudi writes in the introduction, "drove a quiet, kind-hearted man from his isolation and seclusion, and placed him upon the battlefield of life to challenge a world gone astray." This was a reference to Muhammad's transformation, but perhaps there was something of Mawlana Mawdudi, too, to be found here.

Begun in February 1942, *Tafhim al-Qur'an* occupied Mawdudi during his years of incarceration at the New Central Jail in Multan. By the time he finished thirty years later, Mawdudi had at last retired from his leadership of the Jamaat-e-Islami. After his death in 1979, Zafar Ishaq Ansari translated this work into English as *Towards Understanding the Qur'an*. Unlike his primer, which invited shortcuts, these volumes of "interpretative exposition," Mawdudi felt, would help orient a student on the Right Path of understanding Allah's message.

He begins his masterwork by stating that the Qur'an is neither a narrative nor a closely reasoned argument. It is made up of seemingly random verses, exhortations, and divine fiats, arranged in no particular order. It is not sufficient to simply read it from beginning to end. To find the Right Path, Mawdudi counsels, the reader of the Qur'an must do exactly as he did. In the introduction he outlines the steps of the path he took.

First, as the Qur'an is a book like no other, the earnest seeker must abandon all preconceived notions of what will be found between its covers. Then, he must grasp the Qur'an's fundamental claims. First among these claims is that God has conveyed upon every rational man and woman the gift of understanding. This understanding includes the ability to choose between good and evil, and the power to exercise one's full potential. With these gifts alone, every human being will have what is needed to reach a sincere faith and an explicit grasp of God's commands. There is no question for which the Qur'an and the various books of Hadith do not contain the answer. "Nothing is missing," he writes elsewhere; "no part is vague or wanting."

According to Mawdudi, what the Qur'an asked of its readers was clearly no different from any other disciplined course of study; there was something comforting and encouraging in that. But as he continued with his instruction on how to read it, the path seemed to get more and more treacherous. Each of the Qur'an's 114 suras requires careful examination, the Mawlana cautions. The seeker must take notes, organize verses with similar themes together, and compare and contrast the Qur'an's teachings with those found in other books, ancient and modern, sacred and secular, that have addressed the same large questions.

There will also be linguistic difficulties, he warns, even for those fluent in classical Arabic. The problem with literal translations, he explains, is that even though the Qur'an was written in "clear Arabic," its terminology "may give rise to ambiguities." One word may have several meanings or be used to denote different states of mind. There will be words whose meanings will have to be rethought and retooled, since they have been so long in disuse.

Despite all the subtlety and finesse required to thread these needles, Mawdudi didn't believe that his representation of the Right Path signified new or idiosyncratic interpretation of the Qur'an. He was simply preserving the "primordial" and "pristine" Islam that was in danger of being lost forever in a thicket of scholarly obscurantism. This conviction might account for Mawdudi's excitement over his discovery of a young American woman who had arrived at exactly the same understanding of Islam as he had, without any knowledge of classical Arabic or familiarity with all those antique debates. From vastly different starting points, their shared methodology of rationality, diligence, and sincerity had led them to the exact same Right Path. Of course, that was until Maryam veered off and ended up in the madhouse.

There is room, Mawdudi goes on to insist, for healthy debate. Such differences are the soul of a free society and a sign of intellectual vigor. In sorting out God's intentions, even the Prophet is no greater authority on the text than his companions. To suggest that the meaning of individual suras is unchanging is the conclusion of a society of unthinking "blocks of wood."

What then of his invocation of a primordial Islam? What of his insistence that no part of the Qur'an is vague or wanting? But Mawdudi continues on blithely, the tone of reasoned discourse obscuring the contradiction, as if it were possible to have it both ways. Only those who read the work to quibble over split hairs are unwelcome, he writes. The Qur'an absolutely condemns to perdition those who create mischief by sowing endless picky controversies. Those who induce schisms by misunderstanding the fundamental truths of Islam are similarly damned.

But who is to decide what constitutes a quibble and what a subject for healthy debate? Who is to decide what the fundamental truths of Islam are or aren't? Is questioning Mawdudi's authority, in itself, divisive? But Mawdudi did not stop to consider such questions. For those who bring an earnest and open mind, he maintains, all that remains is the choice to adopt the way of life outlined in the Qur'an, or not. In the Mawlana's mind, the right choice is perfectly clear. Only the most perverse or ungrateful person will spurn it.

So there is, in effect, no choice at all. Mawdudi skillfully peddled the illusion of independent choice, the illusion of debate, the illusion that everyone has been given the gift of understanding. But what he is really saying is that he doesn't actually trust anyone's reading but his own, thus the need for an "interpretative exposition" of the Qur'an. In *Towards Understanding Islam*, he is nearly venomous toward those "kufr" who persist in questioning. The person who, after reading the Qur'an, nonetheless rejects Islam will inevitably "spread confusion and disorder. He will, without the least compunction, shed blood, violate other men's rights and generally act destructively. His perverted thoughts and ambitions, his blurred vision and distorted scale of values, and his evil activities will make life bitter for him and for all around him."

The animus here, the departure from his signature lofty tone, suggests that Mawdudi was writing from personal experience. Did he have scheming and two-faced British officials in mind? Or was he thinking of those puppets of his enemies, the slavish ulema? They were the ones who presumed to correct his understanding of classical Arabic and tried to hustle him out of the political arena. Or perhaps he was thinking of those cynical and secular adversaries who, year after year, decade after decade, refused to recognize his moral authority? Was Maryam now considered perverse and ungrateful, her vision blurred and distorted? Perhaps the Mawlana had, on closer inspection, discovered that Maryam Jameelah didn't see the rightful path exactly as he saw it. Was this why he had committed her?

For Mawdudi, it was "a principle of creation" that women be docile and acquiescent. Yet whatever respect Maryam may have had for the Mawlana's learning, she could be intractable, as her parents well knew. Even before she arrived in his household, Margaret had disobeyed an explicit command from the Mawlana. In one of her letters to him she had mentioned her love of painting and, as she contemplated her departure, raised the question of what she should do with her artwork. Countering her suggestion that perhaps the Islamic prohibition against figurative art was directed solely at portrayals of false gods and idols, the Mawlana was firm. This was no quibble. The Holy Prophet categorically prohibited Muslims from drawing pictures of living beings.

Picture making was the first step toward idolatry, he wrote back to her, striking an uncharacteristically harsh note. Idolatry is not simply worshipping an idol. The proliferation of pictures of leaders and celebrities inevitably led to reverence for them instead of for Allah. This too was a form of idol worship, he said. From earliest times, even in the Arab world, pictures served as the greatest vehicle for spreading immorality and lewdness. Now more than ever, he insisted, indecent literature, music, pictures, and statues are the most potent instigators of adultery and fornication. He insisted that Margaret destroy all her artwork before coming to Pakistan.

In the interviews she gave upon her arrival in Lahore, Margaret spoke about how dutifully she had abandoned painting once she realized it was forbidden. In his editorial excoriating Mawdudi, Ghulam Ahmad Parwez had insisted that this constituted yet another deep psychological blow. Through painting, he said, Maryam expressed her emotions and feelings. "How could it be considered haram when one of the avatars of Allah was a painter? God has said in the *Qur'an* that one of his great prophets, Suleiman, used to ask artists to make paintings." Even if Mawdudi had believed it wrong, Parwez suggested, he might have brought Maryam to the stage where her creative powers could find some other outlet. For Parwez, this was more evidence of the Jamaat's inhumanity and their tendency to impose Islam by force.

But though Margaret had renounced her art, she couldn't bring herself to destroy her youthful paintings and drawings. Instead she donated them to the Oriental Division of the New York Public Library. After consulting with the art department, Mr. Parr had agreed to take possession of them. In her mournful cover note to a bound portfolio of early artwork, was there a measure of ambivalence in Maryam's decision to give up her art? "Now that I am a Muslim, I hereby stop making pictures and embark instead on a literary career in service of the Faith," she vowed. Had there been backsliding? Had Maryam disobeyed another of Mawdudi's strictures while she was a member of his household?

There was reason to be skeptical of Ghulam Ahmad Parwez's account of Maryam's state of mind. Mawdudi hadn't tried to force Maryam into marriage with a groom of his choosing. Similarly, Parwez's description of Maryam's romance with Islam coming up against a brutal reality was not in the least borne out by her letters home, though admittedly it was now clear that she had not been altogether forthcoming. And Margaret rarely let ten days go by between letters, yet there was that inexplicable gap of five months between the last letter from Pattoki and the one from the madhouse. If letters were missing, what else was?

Maryam was well aware of the symbolic weight of her decision to leave America. Her journey to Lahore was self-consciously styled to echo the journey of those early Muslims who followed the Prophet from Mecca to Medina to escape persecution. In Arabic this was known as the *al-hijrah*. In leaving Mecca, they abandoned the only home they had ever known, sacrificed family ties, and suffered terrible hardships. Yet it was also an action that bestowed upon them great merit. So it stood to reason that the details of Maryam Jameelah's fate were destined to become political fodder, for both Mawdudi and Parwez.

But Parwez levels a more serious accusation. Reading between the lines of Mawdudi's newspaper interview, and perhaps listening to the gossip in political quarters, he concludes that Maryam Jameelah had suffered a crisis of faith. According to the Islam of the Jamaat-e-Islami, should an avowed Muslim renounce his faith, such a person would be accused of apostasy, otherwise known as *murtad*. The sentence for apostasy is death. Mawdudi had pronounced the entire community of Ahmadiyya Muslims, a reform movement launched toward the end of the nineteenth century and dedicated to the peaceful propagation and revival of Islam, non-Muslims. To identify them as apostates would require a death sentence. Parwez trotted out his final diagnosis: fear for her life as an apostate had precipitated Maryam's mental collapse.

But how could this be? Maryam Jameelah organized her entire existence around the fact that she had embraced Islam and Islamic society in a way that precluded her return to the life she had known as Margaret Marcus. No matter what she had suffered in Lahore or Pattoki, no matter how homesick or hungry or lonely or difficult her existence had become, such sufferings were more likely to have strengthened than weakened her beliefs. Also,

I knew that Maryam had never returned to America; all her books were published out of Lahore. Whatever his argument with her, Mawdudi still considered Maryam a Muslim, however misguided. Yet even if Parwez was wrong as to the reason, even if his concerned and paternal tone was a cover for scoring political points, Maryam was indeed in fear for her life.

The Paagal Khanaah on Jail Road is a huge asylum located in central Lahore. In 1962 it encompassed two main hospital buildings housing fifteen hundred inmates, among them five hundred women. One building was off-limits to all but the hospital staff. This housed the chronically and criminally insane. There, patients with shaved heads were kept in locked cells. They were served food that consisted of little more than stale rotis and watery dal, slopped on the bare floor outside their doors. Most weighed no more than ninety pounds and many weighed less than that, their bodies wasted by dysentery. If they wore any clothes at all, it was often no better than a burlap sack. They were rarely bathed. Sanitary conditions were unspeakable.

Though she found the chronic ward frightening, Margaret couldn't seem to keep away, sneaking in from her accommodations in the private ward to take stock of the patients and their living conditions. She compared their appearance to that of Jewish concentration camp victims whose photographs she'd pored over as a young girl. Few ever made it out of this building alive, she reported to Herbert and Myra.

Patients with better prognoses slept in dormitories in the public wards of the second building, a multistory brick edifice organized around a large central courtyard lined with walkways and trees. There disturbed and mentally deficient children, small skeletons covered in filth, ran wild. The patients of the public wards paid little or nothing for their beds and treatment. This part of the hospital also housed the private women's ward to which Margaret was assigned. The cost of a bed in the private ward was such that only the very rich could afford one, but even by the standards of the private ward Margaret's accommodation was lavish. Because she was an American citizen, she was assigned a large sunny room to herself with three ayahs to attend to her needs.

Treatment at the Paagal Khanaah included electric shock, sedatives, and any other medication required to stave off malaria, tuberculosis, typhoid, dysentery, and malaria. During the hottest summer season, patients bathed only once or twice weekly. Still, on the first of the month, every single patient was given a physical and mental examination. Two weeks later a committee of doctors would meet with Dr. Rashid to determine who was ready to be released. Only private inmates could be released on Dr. Rashid's say-so alone.

As there was no wall between the private quarters and the public wards, the public patients were constantly stealing. As a result, most of the private rooms were sparsely furnished with perhaps a transistor radio kept under lock and key. Even though Margaret had ayahs to watch her things, she soon lost a blue silk shalwar kameez trimmed with Appa's handworked lace. She suspected one of the ayahs but there was nothing to be done. Margaret told her parents she tried to cultivate a philosophical attitude toward those things she didn't feel she could change. Yet this hadn't stopped her from trying to smuggle letters out.

Where other patients lolled about on their beds all day, or spent their time praying, Margaret continued to write articles for various Islamic periodicals using—with his permission—the Mawlana's address on the return envelope. She also spent a great deal of time socializing with her fellow patients, the handful of nurses, and Dr. Rashid. Among the high society of the private ward, there was a very pretty young girl of seventeen who had been committed by her parents when they found her collection of beautiful little bottles filled with poison. She couldn't resist tasting them.

In the room next door was a drug addict. Not yet twenty, she

was the daughter of one of the richest zamindars in the Punjab.*
Married off at twelve and already the mother of three, she described the battalions of servants at her command. Her father
had ten thousand buffalo, she boasted, an equal number of sheep,
and enough orchards and fields on her family's vast estate to feed
everyone in their district. She crowed that one of her uncles had
been educated in America and now kept thirty wives.

This Maryam found hard to credit, a story out of *A Thousand
and One Nights*. How was that possible? she asked. The Holy
Qur'an allows only *four*.

My uncle is a king, the girl replied with a toss of her bony head,
covered with sores. Who will stop him?

And finally there was the exquisitely beautiful woman with
whom Maryam spent most of her time. This woman, a Pakistani
Christian, had become obsessed with the thought that a man
named Ali Rizi was attempting to blackmail her. So vivid was her
description of this man and his wicked clan that Maryam began
to believe her. Dr. Rashid, however, assured her that the allegations had been thoroughly investigated. Despite this one delusion,
Peggy wrote her parents, she considered her friend quite sensible
on other subjects.

Did Maryam, sounding so sensible on other subjects, also suffer from paranoia? Was she at the mercy of a similar idée fixe? It
didn't seem so. In her letter from the madhouse Margaret mentioned that before she left for Pattoki, Begum Mawdudi had promised her she would accompany the family on their pilgrimage to
Mecca. Within days of her commitment, however, she learned
that Mawlana Mawdudi and his family had left without her.

Hearing this news from Dr. Rashid, Maryam was filled with
a sense of desolation so all-encompassing that she had to remind
herself to breathe. "If circumstances had only been different!"
she wrote. Rather than holding firm to the conviction that she

---

* A zamindar is a feudal landowner.

was being unjustly persecuted or that her life was in danger, she wrote as if she secretly agreed that she had been committed for her own good. Nonetheless, she tried to smuggle out a second letter to the journalist Shaheer Niazi, her possible savior. Once again Dr. Rashid intercepted it.

The line that divides sickness from sanity, real danger from imaginary persecution, is not always clearly drawn. I decided to reread Peggy's voluminous eight months of correspondence from Pattoki more carefully. Perhaps I had overlooked something. Pattoki was no more than a tiny provincial town, one step up from a village. There were no telephones and few cars. The narrow lanes between houses were largely reserved for donkeys, water buffalo, and the odd pony cart. Residents walked from one end to the other via rooftops. Maryam herself rarely set foot outside the house. Despite these conditions, Margaret's letters from Pattoki were not entirely uneventful.

The house had two bedrooms on either side of a central courtyard, each with whitewashed walls and decorated with calligraphic inscriptions from the Qur'an. One of these was set aside for Maryam, with two stuffed chairs, a sofa, and a dressing table for a desk where she worked on her Urdu. At the back of the courtyard was a hole in the wall where the neighborhood women could be summoned, saving them from the effort of putting on burqas.

Maryam's respectful affection for Baijan and Appa is a constant theme of the letters (though neither spoke any English). There was also the colorful but inconsequential village gossip; the brother of her Urdu teacher dressed as a woman to dance at wedding parties. Their water buffalo gave birth to the most beautiful calf. The calf died despite Baijan's best efforts to save it. The weather is an inevitable topic; they slept on the roof when it was hot, and plagues of insects invaded her room once the monsoon rains arrived. And food is a staple: Margaret announced to her parents that she had acquired a taste for a dish of goat's brains and eggs. There are the occasional visitors: the water seller's wives, two backpacking Western college girls wearing obscenely tight sweaters, the ubiquitous neighborhood ladies. And inevitably, there is illness: Appa suffered from headaches and sciatica, one neighbor dropped dead from malaria, another of typhoid. A child fell off a roof. Each letter is pages and pages long. Reading them is like trying to scry a pattern in the arrangement of rabbit entrails.

Then, sometime in the fall, before the nights became too cool to sleep outside, Peggy told her parents she had abandoned any hope of becoming a wife and mother. On reflection, she had decided that she was temperamentally, emotionally, and mentally unsuited. Unlike in America, where single women languished when their friends abandoned them for marriage, she reasoned, purdah provided even single women the companionship of other women and an endless number of children to care for and look after. Margaret had an appealing habit of finding the bright side of whatever it was that troubled her.

Margaret had always lacked social graces; she was clumsy and bereft of those feminine charms that are the currency of an open marriage market. "Nobody who knows me or has seen me has ever or can truthfully ever describe me as 'charming,'" she once commented. In this she couldn't help but compare herself to her older sister. Where Betty Marcus had once worshipped Shirley Temple and fretted about her weight, Margaret spent her childhood play-acting adventures in the Syrian Desert. After graduating from the University of Michigan, Betty had found a great match in Walter Herz, a Harvard graduate and soon-to-be-successful businessman. She was living quite happily as a housewife and mother to two little girls in Plainfield, New Jersey. If, as Mawdudi claimed, the woman in Maryam was asleep, in Pattoki she had resigned herself to letting that sleeping woman lie.

Margaret's desire to get married never seemed entirely serious. She had suggested to Mawdudi that her difficulty in finding a spiritual partner played a role in her decision to emigrate, but perhaps she said that because she thought Mawdudi might find it odd if she expressed no desire whatsoever for a husband. Margaret now announced her plan to serve the cause of Islam through her writings instead of marriage. To her parents, she betrayed no trace of regret in the trade-off. But if this was the end result, it would have been far easier to stay in New York, where books and research materials were more easily obtained. In Pattoki even English-language newspapers were hard to come by. Perhaps Maryam's failure to take any of her suitors seriously was a greater source of regret than I had supposed.

Despite the difficulty of obtaining books, by the end of her third month in Pattoki, Maryam Jameelah had written four new articles. There was one condemning Western efforts to influence the Muslim world; another criticized the ill-begotten efforts of the modernizing reformers of Islam. Her work began to appear in translation in the Arab daily *An Nadwah,* out of Mecca; in the *Daily Kohistan,* a Karachi monthly; in a newspaper out of Kerala, in India; as well as in a few Urdu publications out of Lahore. A collection of essays was released in Istanbul.

Her progress in Urdu was slow, Peggy confessed, but she planned to tackle Arabic and Persian once she had mastered it. In the meantime, she began work on another book project. *Western Civilization Condemned by Itself* would be an anthology in which she would take on the greatest thinkers of Western civilization (beginning with Plato) to demonstrate how their ideas had brought the world to the brink of extinction. Her ambitions certainly hadn't deserted her.

But for this work, Margaret's life seemed a lonely and parched existence, and except for the occasional rat in her room, an exceptionally dull one. Yet for the most part, however, her letters expressed near perfect contentment. If she had any complaint it was that that the neighborhood ladies tended to sit and stare at her as if she were some kind of exotic animal. Pattoki retained aspects of the traditional peasant society she had always longed for, at least as it had been prettily photographed by *National Geographic.*

There was no more joyful way to start the day, she insisted, than with the sound of the muezzin's call at dawn—"Prayer is better than sleep! Prayer is better than sleep!"—followed by dogs barking, buffalo lowing, and babies crying. Here, Peggy wrote her parents, she was truly happy. She had always felt that to live the life she had always wanted, she would have to leave America. She now insisted that she couldn't imagine what circumstances might compel her to return, even for a brief visit. She promised never to forget all her parents had done for her, but she knew now they were on different paths.

On their journey through life, she had once told Herbert and Myra, they had always focused on the scenery and accommodations, anticipating with pleasure their next cocktail hour or hand of bridge. They had never considered where life might be taking them. But she was different. She needed to get to the absolute heart of things. To do this, she constantly reminded herself that she might die at *any* moment and would have to answer for the life she had lived. To achieve something noteworthy and enduring with the few gifts God had provided her was her keenest desire. Only then would God realize that she had not squandered her life, dishonored her limited time on earth by meaningless pursuits or sinful behavior. She planned to give a good account of herself.

By the time Margaret left for Pakistan, Herbert and Myra had become members of the Unitarian Church, forsaking their Jewish heritage much as their daughter had, yet remaining within the American pale. What were they thinking? Were they simply leaving behind burdensome beliefs like a closetful of clothes that no longer fit? Were they trying to elude what Margaret called "the tragic history of the Jews" in favor of one that was sunnier, more sensible, and quintessentially American? Whatever their reasons, I didn't fault them. Faith can be a slippery thing.

As a young man in love, my father had converted to Catholicism. He schooled himself in every facet of Catholic doctrine and every chapter of church history. Yet by the time we came along he went his own way on Sunday mornings, never accompanying the rest of us to Mass. Over dinner he would hold forth on corrupt and hypocritical popes, lecturing us on their self-serving encyclicals on birth control and infallibility—his own version of a Sunday sermon. In this way he took the thin cloth of my belief and poked it with holes.

When I asked him what then had led him to convert, he said simply, "I was young," as if having once believed in something inaccessible to reason was a romance he had long since outgrown. Family arguments over religion continued until the last of us grew up and moved away. My siblings found the answers they needed (pagan, yogi, evangelical Christian), but I never had. Instead I looked to poetry and the lives of poets to get me to that ineffable and absolute "heart of things." Like Margaret, I aspired to give a good account of myself.

Suddenly, in Margaret's letters from Pattoki, I came to this: "I have completely stopped taking the Compazine pills. I don't think I need them anymore. This is fortunate since they can not be obtained here."

PART II

JAHILIYYA
THE AGE OF BARBARISM AND IGNORANCE

Uthman b. Haif told that a blind man came to the Prophet and asked him to pray to God to cure him. He replied, "If you wish, I shall make supplication to God, but if you endure, that is better for you."

Mishkat al-Masabih

CHAPTER 4

The Misfit

Maryam's letter from the madhouse was written on the eve of her release. In it she proposed to answer all her parents' questions. To do this properly she would have to start at the beginning and tell Herbert and Myra what had really happened upon her arrival in Pakistan. In the light of these subsequent revelations, she would then revisit her stay in the Mawlana's house and the circumstances of her move to Pattoki. She would tell the whole story of how she ended up at the madhouse and what was now in store for her. Everything would be explained.

I found something amiss in the fact that Margaret felt free to write frankly about her life in Pakistan only once she was certain of leaving the Paagal Khanaah, as if she had first to wait and see how her fate would be decided. What had happened during those five months when there were no letters from Pattoki? Was she loath to concede that her parents might have been right about the treatment of women in Muslim countries? Perhaps she had simply been bullied into writing this new letter in exchange for freedom. Perhaps the letter was a closely supervised exercise in self-criticism.

But of course Maryam's arrival in Lahore is not actually where her story begins. In file 5 of Box 2 of the Jameelah collection there is an odd little book published in July 1989 by Mohammad Yusuf

Khan and Sons, and printed off Ferozepur Road in Lahore. The front cover reads *Quest for the Truth: Memoirs of Childhood and Youth in America (1945–1962): The Story of One Western Convert* by Maryam Jameelah (formerly Margaret Marcus).

Larchmont Acres Apartments, Apt 223-C
Mamaroneck, NY

November 1959

Until I was four years old I was completely silent. My mother even took me to the Neurological Institute in White Plains so the doctors could tell her what was wrong with me. When I finally began speaking, my mother said, it wasn't baby talk but complete sentences. After worrying so much about the fact that I wasn't talking, suddenly she was driven to distraction by my unending questions. Why was this and why was that. Questions she never gave much thought to. That first year my father bought me a gramophone so that I might give her a moment's peace.

There were some things I didn't question. I believed in the Easter Bunny until I was six. I didn't stop believing in Santa Claus until I was in the third grade. Even after Betty convinced me otherwise, the Easter baskets filled with chocolate eggs kept coming and I received just as many Christmas presents as before. I never really made the connection between these holidays and being Christian until Julia Bustin, the smartest girl in my class, refused to sing Christmas carols in school and told me she celebrated Hanukah, not Christmas. I loved to sing carols and act in pageants and decorate our Christmas tree; I'd even go to the candlelight service at Saint Thomas Episcopal Church. Julia Bustin didn't get nearly as many presents at Hanukah as I got at Christmas. I didn't entirely understand why anyone, if they had a choice, would want to miss out on Christmas.

It was Ellen Barrett and Joan Armstrong who let me know I

wasn't a Christian but a Jew. I met them in the fall of 1939, soon after we moved into the two-bedroom in the Larchmont Acres apartment complex and just after I started kindergarten. The following spring, I was on the swing set behind Saint Augustine's Church when a procession of fourth-grade Catholic girls and boys waving palm fronds came after me throwing rocks. Ellen and Joan led their taunts of "Christ killer, Christ killer." The same thing happened at Central Elementary playground with the older boys. I complained to the teacher and my mother spoke with the principal. I asked a boy in my class why he and his friends tormented me and he said the priest told them to. For the next three years Ellen and Joan made my life completely miserable, but it was that first year at Larchmont Acres that I learned I was a Jew. Every Easter after that it was the same story.

Unlike those poor Jews who came from ghettos in Russia and Poland, my mother's great grandparents weren't driven out of Germany by pogroms. They came to America in search of greater economic opportunities. Their ancestors had been followers of Moses Mendelssohn. His movement to get Jews to assimilate and embrace Western culture and secular education, I learned, was called "the Haskalah," or the Enlightenment. Later I would compare the reforms of Moses Mendelssohn to those pushed by Shaikh Muhammad Abduh in Egypt and Sir Syed Ahmad Khan in India on behalf of the Muslims. They, too, wanted the Muslims to assimilate Western values. By the time my mother's great grandmother came to America she was in the habit of celebrating Christmas and didn't know the first thing about Judaism. Her son, my grandfather, was always scornful of religion, but he nonetheless married a woman who never failed to attend Friday services and observe the Sabbath. I called her Nana. When Nana came to visit us, she wouldn't even allow me to draw pictures or sew clothes for my dolls on the Sabbath. I adored Nana.

In contrast to Mother's side of the family, my father's grandfather came to America from East Prussia and was an Orthodox rabbi and not nearly so assimilated. My father once told me that his only memory of his grandfather was the day he boxed his ears when he caught him reading Horatio Alger stories instead of studying his catechism. Perhaps it wasn't surprising, then, that my father's father had nothing but contempt for Judaism. As soon as he could he moved to New York, where he started his own business manufacturing and selling men's neckties. After graduating from Brooklyn Boys High, my father briefly considered rabbinical school but his father forced him to go straight into the family business. By the time he was twenty he had traveled all over America selling neckties. I often wonder if things would have turned out differently if my father had become a rabbi. The Depression killed the market for ties.

We celebrated the Jewish holidays in the same spirit in which we celebrated Easter and Christmas. On the High Holy Days Betty and I would be kept home from school, and if Grandfather and Nana were visiting from Savannah we would go for a drive in the country and have dinner at a nice restaurant. One year a man saw me on the playground and asked me why I wasn't in school. It was Yom Kippur, I said innocently. He must have been a Jew because he gave me a dark look and asked me why I wasn't in synagogue. Suddenly ashamed, I realized I had been stuffing myself with food and playing when real Jews like Julia Bustin were fasting and sitting in temple.

After that I never went outside on a Jewish holiday and I became intent on learning what it meant to be a good Jew. This led my mother to enroll Betty and me in two years of classes in the Reformed Liberal Sunday School at Temple Israel in October 1943. I was nine years old before I learned anything about Judaism but once I began reading about the tragic history of the Jews, I was unable to stop. But in the very years when the Jews of Europe were suffering untold horrors at the hands of the Nazis, my classmates at Temple Israel were horsing around or reading Superman comics hidden in their prayer books. I found this disgraceful.

In my Bible study textbooks I learned that both Arabs and Jews claimed Abraham as their patriarch and that the Arabs had offered the Jews sanctuary from Christian persecution in medieval Spain. There, under Arab rule and protection, the Jews experienced a golden age of literature. The Oriental Jews of Cairo and Palestine, and the Sephardic Jews of Granada, interested me far more than the hypocritical Reformed Jews of Westchester. When my English teacher asked which poets I liked to read, I mentioned the turn-of-the-century Hebrew poet Chaim Nachman Bialik. Bialik wrote gloomy poems about the Russian pogroms and exhorted the Jews to rise up in self-defense. From the way my teacher looked at me, I'm sure she had never heard of him. Obviously, her idea of a poet was Keats or Shelley. My parents always tried to pretend we were no different from the Christians, but the Christians didn't see it that way. For a time, I decided I'd rather have been born an Orthodox Jew. They, at least, never apologized for being Jews.

At home I pored over the *Saturday Evening Post, Holiday,* and *Look* magazines, ignoring the spreads of Hollywood starlets in swimsuits to follow the progress of the war in Europe. When the German army invaded Russia in 1941, my mother hid the *Life* magazine issue that showed the horrible pictures of frozen Russian and German soldiers, bloodied and distorted, lying in the snow. After the war, she hid the dreadful photographs of the concentration camps. But I always found them. I read all the newspaper accounts of how the Nazis tortured and gassed the Jews. I had nightmares for years afterward but I studied the photographs and never forgot a thing.

Quest for the Truth appeared to be a collection of Peggy Marcus's thank-you notes to her grandparents and homesick letters from summer camp. There are lengthy missives addressed to her sister, Betty, at the University of Michigan, and letters to her parents away on Caribbean holidays and business trips. She also included copies of her expansive letters to prominent Islamic leaders, like the one above describing her ancestry, upbringing, and intellectual evolution, mapping each turn on the path to Islam. Taken together, the collection offers a self-portrait of her childhood and coming-of-age up to the moment Margaret Marcus sets off for Pakistan to become, more fully, Maryam Jameelah.

The letters portray a fairly typical suburban childhood. Herbert and Myra Marcus had provided their daughters a home that, like America itself, appeared to be a fundamentally benevolent and sunny place. As a little girl Peggy had fully embraced her parents' view of the world, just as readily as she believed in Santa Claus and the Easter Bunny. Yet soon enough Peggy realized, as every child must, that this wasn't nearly the whole story. Indeed, there were certain ugly truths for which this outlook was wholly insufficient. The inevitability of death was one. When their daughter came to their bed in the middle of the night to ask, tearfully, why she had to die and what would happen when she did, what could they say? There was nothing to do but accept that death was inevitable. By the time Peggy grew up, Herbert and Myra promised her, medical science would enable her to live one hundred years or more. That was the sum of their consolation. How could Peggy not have felt betrayed?

The schoolyard bullies were mere nuisances. If Peggy faced any unpleasantness, a visit to the principal's office, Myra assured her daughter, was all it took to set things right. Both Myra and Herbert were of the mind that American Jews needed to think, live, look, and behave exactly like other Americans. That was the kind of country America was. Until the liberation of the camps began in the fall of 1944, this viewpoint sufficed.

Accounts of what had been happening in the eastern parts of Europe had been largely dismissed as somebody's propaganda or downplayed as isolated incidents. Those stories that did make the newspapers reflected this general disbelief, taking the form of brief mentions relegated to the back pages. It was not as if the rest of the war was going so well, such a placement seemed to suggest, that there was anything anyone could actually do about what was happening. Providing the stories were even true. The *New York Times* remained unconvinced. The photographs from the spring of 1945 changed that. Margaret would have just turned eleven.

Herbert and Myra Marcus were not the only ones to turn away from the utter ghastliness of the photographs. The war was over; better times lay ahead; never in America. Of course Myra might have known that her Peggy would refuse to leave well enough alone. And Myra knew she would never be able to answer all her daughter's questions. There were always so many questions. It was upsetting. So she hid the newspapers and magazines. Finally, after discussing it with Herbert, Myra took her daughter to see a child psychologist.

Unimpressed with the principal's handling of her tormentors, Peggy might have begun to suspect that once again her parents didn't really grasp the larger implications of the crime. Perhaps they just preferred to close their eyes, refusing to admit what was perfectly clear. Even the journalists reported what they saw in the camps in a tone of bewilderment, awestruck at the scale of the extermination. They might have been covering a manufacturing industry dedicated to the marvels of mass production and cost-saving efficiencies. The photo captions of the newspaper and magazine coverage of the camps identified the bodies on display as concentration camp prisoners or concentration camp survivors. While there was always an obligatory reference to Nazi atrocities, there were few allusions to Jews.

That Halloween, Margaret went to a party dressed up as a ghost, with skulls and skeletons dangling around her neck and won an award for Most Original Costume and a write-up in the *Mamaroneck Daily Times*. Eventually she would see that the story behind the photographs wasn't simply one of Nazi atrocity and concentration camps. It was about the Jews and it was about evil, and the question of what happened after one died could not be simply brushed off. There had to be an accounting. Otherwise . . . well, the prospect of that kept her awake at night. This is what I imagined Margaret Marcus would not forget.

Larchmont Acres Apartments, Apt 223-C
Mamaroneck, NY

February 1945

At school I always limit myself to drawing pictures of typical American children, though seldom blondes: portraits, largely, rarely landscapes. I am something of an expert when it comes to portraits of Chinese people and Negroes. At home, however, I draw only Arabs. Not from life, Nana, because I have never ever seen an actual Arab, but from the *National Geographic* photographs I've seen in the Central Elementary library.

Mother and Daddy hate my drawings of Arabs. They imagine I draw them the way I do so everybody will feel sorry for them. I once spent an entire afternoon painting a huge mural of Arab village life, using poster paints and crayons. When Daddy came home from work that day, he came into my bedroom and sat on the edge of my bed. He told me that the Arabs were a low people. They were backward, dirty, and evil. They had supported the Nazis during the war and were constantly rioting and massacring the Jews of Palestine. They treat their women like slaves, he added.

As soon as he left, I got out of bed and destroyed all my sketches. I promised God that I would be a good Jew and wouldn't write the novel I'd been planning about Palestine. Three days later, I broke my vow by going to the Larchmont Public Library to read everything I could find about the Arabs so that I could prove to Mother and Daddy that they were just prejudiced. I felt certain I could change their minds. Of course most of the books in the public library were by Christian missionaries and Zionists. They had exactly the same prejudices against the Arabs as my parents had. Mother said perhaps I was just trying to prove that I was right. Why couldn't I accept any evidence that challenged my own views?

Was I simply being stubborn, Nana? It seems perfectly clear to me. When Grandfather tells his stories about Negroes, referring to them as darkies or niggers, he always laughs at Mother's discomfort. At Smith College, Mother learned to abhor race prejudice. Not only does she believe that Negroes deserve complete equality of opportunity, she also feels that social intermingling is acceptable and to be encouraged. Even racial intermarriage is not a mortal sin in her eyes.

So why are the Arabs any different from Negroes? Grandfather's life revolved around the secret meetings of the Ancient Arabic Order of the Nobles of the Mystic Shrine. Daddy, too, keeps a red felt fez with a silk tassel on his dresser. When I asked him what they did at Shriner meetings, he said they wore Arab robes and bowed in the direction of Mecca before sitting down to crack jokes over dinner. They could play at praying to Allah, play at being Arabs, but the real Arabs mean less than nothing to them. God means nothing.

Jews like us have become just like the Christians. We really don't know what we believe. When I grow up, I plan to live in Palestine or Egypt as a painter and a missionary to the Arabs. Not to convert them, but to make sure they stay just as they are.

It seems very odd that such an idea would occur to an eleven-year-old. It was striking, too, how Peggy seemed to treat the events and characters of the storybooks she was reading with as much seriousness as she did the events and people in her own life. It was as if she had been born in the wrong place and time and was looking for another that would suit her better. She surrendered herself to her books in an unusually intense way, providing elaborate plot summaries in her childhood letters. A set of cloth books, each set in a different country and featuring a child with whom Peggy invariably identified, was described in great detail.

Her favorite was the story of a little American Indian girl living in the time "before the white men came and ruined everything." There was *Boy of the Desert* by Eunice Tietjens, *Camel Bells: A Boy of Baghdad* by Anna Ratzesberger, *The Forgotten Village* by John Steinbeck, and *Theras and His Town* by Caroline Dale Snedeker. Even before she could read, she told one correspondent, she made her mother read the *Just So* stories so many times that she memorized every word. Thereafter she would lie in bed, turning the pages of Kipling's book as if she could read the stories to herself, reliving every twist and turn. The book eventually fell to pieces.

After a series of uncharacteristically joyful letters to her parents from the Noyes Camp for Modern Dance, Peggy recounted a grim exchange with the camp director. When Peggy told her how happy she'd been and that she looked forward to returning the following summer, the director looked at her coldly and said that was impossible. Admitting her had been a terrible mistake. You have no talent, absolutely no promise at all, she said. Certainly you are the queerest child I have ever met. The next time they come here to visit you, Margaret, I will advise your parents to send you to a psychiatrist. While the camp director was describing Peggy's lack of physical grace, she seemed to be offering a devastating appraisal of her femininity as well. It was the last camp she ever attended. Peggy told her parents that they were wasting their money.

Her letters gave the impression that Margaret could make sense of something that had happened to her only by writing it down in every detail. It didn't matter if she was rehashing incidents of family history her parents or sister or grandparents were no doubt well aware of; the important thing seemed to be getting in every particular, as if she were a storyteller not entirely in control of her material. Perhaps the letters were just another manifestation of her tone-deaf and autistic sort of talkativeness. Or perhaps they were the only means she had of making herself heard in the face of a suburban milieu intent on pretending that this awkward, socially inept little girl didn't exist.

Larchmont Acres Apartments, Apt 223-C
Mamaroneck, NY

September 1948

Until my periods started, I dressed like a boy. It was perfectly clear to me that boys' lives are vastly more interesting than the dull routine of my mother's life as a housewife. I wanted to be good at sports, particularly football, but I wasn't any better at them than I was at ballroom dancing. Outside school, I was a different person. Karen Wanberg and I would organize hunting expeditions to the forests and perilous cliffs of Westchester County, risking bloody knees and bruised shins in heedless pursuit of game and adventure. As an Arab raider, swathed in bedsheets, I added Barbara Kenny to my collection of wives. As a Japanese samurai, I would commit hara-kiri rather than allow myself to be taken prisoner by an American soldier. As a noble Indian chief, I would raid settlers' cabins, scalping left and right; I save only a little girl who, after a time with my tribe, will refuse to return to her people.

Once I started to develop, I had to give up all these games. I now wear saddle shoes and skirts and sweaters and cotton blouses with ruffles just like every other high school or college girl. I also abandoned my fantasy of living life as a boy. In sixth grade Karen Wanberg insisted upon throwing a Valentine's Day party, complete with Bing Crosby and Frank Sinatra records, which I was obliged to borrow from Betty. This was never music I took any pleasure in. Music should be transporting, not nerve shattering. I spent the entire party sitting outside on the steps in my party dress and winter coat, counting the hours until I could go home. Karen accused me of ruining everything and thereafter refused to speak to me.

The whole project of being a teenager, with its incessant talk of boys, dates, dances, parties, clothes, and film stars is too silly for words. I think Julia Bustin and Barbara Kenny feel the same way, but they go along with it all because they don't want to stand out. I refuse to and pay the price for that. My whole life has moved indoors with books. This is just as well, because from day one of seventh grade none of my friends from elementary school wanted to have anything to do with me.

The summer before eighth grade my counselor at the Noyes Camp for Modern Dance found *The Lance of Kanana: A Story of Arabia* by Harry W. French at the public library in Provincetown for me. Though I like just about any story about children in different countries, I asked her to look out for anything with an Arab theme. By then I'd begun my drawings and paintings of Palestinian Arabs for the novel I am planning to write. In the story, Kanana is a Bedouin tribal boy of thirteen, scorned by everyone as a perfect coward and misfit, all because he will not participate in mindless tribal warfare. I know all about tribal warfare.

Only when the Byzantines descend on Arabia and capture his beloved father does Kanana join the army of General Khalid ibn al-Walid, pledging to fight on behalf of Allah and Arabia. When Kanana is captured as a spy and brought before a Greek general to negotiate for his elderly father's release, he is told that the price of his father's freedom will be the life of an Arab soldier. Plunging a lance into his own breast, Kanana shouts, "Here is your Arab!" and swiftly expires, the savior of Arabia and a martyr in the jihad. It is a most thrilling story. The Arabs really seem to know what they are about. This is in perfect contrast to the Jews of Mamaroneck and Larchmont.

Eventually, my mother withdrew us from Bible school because Betty hated it and refused to leave her bed without a screaming match. Nineteen forty-five was pretty much the end of Judaism for the entire family, and the beginning of my adolescence. After Betty went off to college, my parents and I started attending the Ethical Culture Society of Westchester, where I was put in the most advanced class with a bunch of other ex-Jews. The founder of the Society for Ethical Culture, Dr. Felix Adler, rejected organized religion altogether. He wrote that ethics had nothing to do with God and that you could be perfectly good without the fear of damnation hanging over your head. Most everybody in Ethical Culture has embraced agnostic humanism, but our teacher that first year was an out-and-out atheist. His name was Dr. Shoop.

Dr. Shoop was convinced that soon the very idea of God would be regarded as superstitious nonsense arising from a simple fear of death. Eventually, he promised, science would do away with death altogether. His ideas were terrifying to me, but even the most badly behaved classmates were mesmerized by the gleam in his eyes. There was no fidgeting or comic book reading in this class. The following year we had a different teacher and it was only much later that I discovered Dr. Shoop had been hounded out of his job in the public schools for teaching the theory of evolution. No one would hire him after that. He became convinced that everyone was out to get him and had to be committed. There was little hope for his recovery.

After three years at Ethical Culture, I am now scornful of all religion and don't believe in God at all. Judaism is still, in essence, tribal and has retained its tribal nationalistic character. Even if there is a God, what sense did it make for Him to restrict His truth to a single people? Truth by definition has to be universal.

However, like nearly every other Jew and ex-Jew I know, I am excited by the prospect of the new state of Israel. Living in New York seems almost like living in Israel. There are Israeli flags flying from nearly every window on Fifth Avenue, and everywhere radios blare advertisements urging everyone to contribute to the United Jewish Appeal for Refugees and Overseas Needs. We can't even eat dinner without being interrupted by the doorbell and some lady asking for donations. At the Larchmont railway station there are UJA advertisements on the platform billboards featuring photographs of starving Jewish children from Europe waiting to immigrate to Israel. Even the Larchmont Public Library now has a special exhibition of Israeli books depicting all the blessings the Jews are bringing to Palestine.

I am convinced that the Jews and Arabs will cooperate and together create a new golden age such as occurred in medieval Spain. Under Arab protection from Christian persecution, Jews will become real Jews and their lives will once again be filled with meaning.

One afternoon I drove up to the town where Margaret grew up. Larchmont is a wealthy suburb of mock-Tudor homes with wrap-around porches and carefully landscaped yards. But the streets were empty. No one seemed to be home. I drove by landed estates, country clubs, golf courses, and two different yacht clubs on Long Island Sound. None of these are mentioned in Peggy's letters. Margaret's world consisted entirely of Central Elementary, Mamaroneck High School, the playgrounds, and the Larchmont Public Library. At the center of this world was the Larchmont Acres apartment complex where Herbert and Myra Marcus lived for thirty years, raising their two daughters, in a modest two-bedroom.

The move had been a comedown from the little house in White Plains where Margaret was born. Herbert Marcus regretted the social slippage, though Margaret wouldn't become aware of it until middle school. The six-story apartment complex, with its concrete pathways and sloping lawns edged in bushes, was actually in Mamaroneck, its nomenclature a transparent sleight of hand by a property developer. Its proximity to Larchmont, however, gave the address some necessary social stature, straddling the divide between Larchmont's detached homes and the Italian working-class enclave of "the Flats" in Mamaroneck.

I got out of the car only once. The Larchmont Public Library was packed with mothers and strollers and children, bereft of the silence and old book smell it once must have had. Its shelves were a fruity cornucopia of Disney DVDs and movie videos; computer terminals lined a wall in the back room. Margaret's treasured book, Muhammad Asad's *The Road to Mecca,* had been deaccessioned. The shelves of *National Geographic* magazines that had given her a window on the world outside Larchmont were gone. Immediately behind the library was Saint Augustine's Church. The parochial school had long been closed, its playground also gone.

Larchmont Acres Apartments, Apt 223-C
Mamaroneck, NY

November 1949

After I heard Umm Kulthum on one of those tiny radio stations for immigrants, Betty, I wouldn't let Mother be until Daddy took me to the Syrian section of Brooklyn. At Rashid's record shop on Atlantic Avenue I spent all my allowance on a stack of her recordings. I immediately lost all interest in the Wagner and Verdi operas and Beethoven symphonies I'd been listening to since I was four. Mother detests Umm Kulthum so I wait for her to leave the apartment before I take out the records. Then I play them at top volume with all our windows open. The ancient sound of her voice transports me. I so like to watch the response of the people walking on the streets below.

After art, music has always been my second-best subject in school. I could read music in the second grade. But it wasn't long before my choir director began complaining that listening to Umm Kulthum had ruined my singing. He had often praised my strong clear voice to Mother, but he always chose Sally McArthur for all the solos. Every year she completely monopolizes the school program of the annual Christmas pageant. I have now outgrown all of this. I only have ears for Middle Eastern music.

I had once imagined that with the founding of the state of Israel the Jews would rediscover their faith and reconnect with their Semitic roots in the land of Abraham. I even attended a meeting of the Zionist youth group Mizrachi Hatzair. Yet as soon as they discovered that I was raised in a liberal nonkosher household, they wanted nothing to do with me. The coup de grâce was the screening of a pro-Israeli propaganda film in which the Arabs were once again grossly misrepresented. I got into a terrible argument and soon realized that Israel would not mean a return to the golden age of the tenth-century caliphate of al-Andalus. It would be something else entirely. Still, when the hostilities broke out between Jews and Arabs in Palestine, I was devastated.

New York has now become the center of Zionist propaganda, to which Mother and Daddy all too readily subscribe. Not one of the Zionist leaders who pass through New York to address the Security Council or the General Assembly of the United Nations seems to feel the least twinge of conscience for the terrible wrong being done. As soon as I get home from school I race to listen to their speeches on WNYC.

What possible justification can there be to deprive an entire people of their homeland and rights as human beings? Hadn't the Jews just suffered such a crime based on equally specious propaganda? And what was Palestine to them? Moses received his revelation in Egypt. The most important part of the Talmud was codified in what is now Iraq. But for the Zionists and their sympathizers, the "backward" fellaheen of Palestine now constitute a grave obstacle to the march of progress. The more I read of the

Zionist project in the *New York Times*, Betty, the more I realize that the rubric of "progress" has blinded everyone, even our parents, to the bleak fate of the fellaheen. Are they not human, too?

Last night Eleanor Roosevelt, a member of the Commission on Human Rights and chief delegate of the United States to the United Nations, came to Mamaroneck High School to give an address to commemorate the first anniversary of Human Rights Day. I went with Mother and was shocked when Mrs. Roosevelt spent nearly all her time extolling all that was going on in Israel. The Jews had every right to the whole of Palestine on both sides of the Jordan River, she said. Where there once were only sand dunes and swamps, there are now farms and thriving industry. Should Palestine be returned to the Arabs, she warned, the country would relapse into medieval poverty. She contrasted the corruption of the Arabs with the idealism and vigor of the Jews.

I couldn't help but wonder what any of this had to do with human rights. During the question and answer period I was tempted to ask her about the massacre at Deir Yassin in April 1948 and the expulsion of Arabs from their villages all over Palestine, but Mother stopped me. She said I'd be lynched. We argued all the way home and continued the argument in the apartment until midnight. Why don't the Arabs just make peace and be willing to live and let live? Mother asked me.

What if a robber came into our house and forced us out into the streets, penniless and starving? I replied. And then to ease his conscience, the robber asked us to sign a peace treaty that would essentially legalize his seizure of everything that was once ours. Would you do it?

But Israel had been recognized by the entire world. The Arab world should accept it as a fait accompli.

I said that this was injustice, plain and simple.

It was the way of the world, she countered, where the strong triumph over the weak. If one demands that Palestine be returned to the Arabs, then one must also demand that America be returned to the Indians. America could not have been created without the seizure of their land and the killings of large numbers of them. Now we are the most powerful country in the world! Compare modern Tel Aviv with medieval Jaffa and that alone justifies the Zionist cause.

I no longer consider myself a Jew.

CHAPTER 5

Paagal Khanaah

There was a vogue in those years to blame the undemonstrative mother for whatever difficulties beset the child. Myra Marcus had often wondered how much she was responsible for her daughter's difficulties. In the years Maryam lived in Pakistan, it was Myra who devotedly filled her stream of requests for American books and magazines, as if to compensate her daughter for whatever she had failed to give her as a child.

A month before Maryam received the threatening letter from Mawdudi, she asked her mother to write what she remembered of her early years in White Plains and Larchmont Acres. It was as if Maryam suddenly needed to look elsewhere for answers to her troubles and had again turned to her mother for help. Perhaps she had already sensed a storm was brewing. In her reply, Myra answered her daughter as best she could. She did not shy from reliving the struggles they'd faced. Maryam included her letter in the opening pages of *Quest for the Truth.*

Betty was the first to fall sick, Myra began. The strep infection spread to her ears, accompanied by a desperately high fever. With Peggy on the way and only a modest savings account, suddenly they found there was an expensive mastoid operation to pay for. Eventually, they all were stricken. Myra couldn't help but compare the fever to the Depression that had gripped the country, bringing down her father-in-law's tie factory, throwing her husband and his brothers out of work. The whole country seemed to be caught in its terrible grip. Yet though economic conditions were worse than ever, there was nothing in the world she and Herbert wanted more than another child. Peggy was born in the spring of 1934 out of their shared faith that the future would be better.

The string of illnesses, like the Depression, eventually subsided, but from the beginning Myra worried. As a baby Peggy was easily startled by loud noises and laughter. The sound of crumpling paper made her cry. Standing in her crib, she would chew up the wood railings like a trapped animal. And long after she learned to walk, she was intensely fearful of falling. Facing a slight incline, Peggy would get down on her hands and knees rather than risk losing her balance. The hisses and knocks of the radiator alarmed her, and the sight of a machine spewing insulation into the roof of the house next door was a vision of such terror that she awoke screaming in nightmares for weeks afterward.

Perhaps because Peggy had such a difficult time of it, she was especially loved. But her parents' love was never enough. As Peggy grew older, Myra noticed how her daughter found it increasingly difficult to make and keep friends her own age. She often ended up playing with younger children. She was thin skinned and high strung and stubbornly resisted advice and criticism. "Were we too overprotective, too permissive," Myra asked, "or too anxious and concerned?" Yet it seemed that there was nothing Peggy wanted more than to be liked. "Perhaps because you found that impossible, you would rebel."

If she were given another chance to raise her daughter, Myra wrote in February 1963, she couldn't say what she would do differently. Were the doctors they sent her to at fault? Clearly something in the Bible stories Peggy had read at Temple Israel had struck a chord that no one else in the family seemed to hear. Betty had never felt the lack of spirituality in their home that Peggy complained of. On the bright side, she told her daughter, her teachers, relatives, and close friends all considered her an exceptionally gifted young girl. Her paintings were always praised in school and she had a beautiful singing voice. These were tremendous assets.

Myra had always marveled, too, at Peggy's capacity for joy—in music, in family outings, picnics, walks in the countryside, holiday meals. Beyond these thoughts, however, Myra felt too close to her to analyze the reasons for the difficulty of her adolescence. "We loved you dearly," Myra wrote.

Larchmont Acres Apartments, Apt 223-C
Mamaroneck, NY

December 1956

My life is at a complete standstill. Did Mother tell you about Dr. Harper? After my nervous breakdown, I began seeing a psychiatrist. I never even made it to the classroom before the college authorities at the University of Rochester sent me packing. Dr. Harper was the third psychiatrist I tried, and the least upsetting. He is soft-spoken and has only recently begun a private practice. Psychoanalysis involves lying down on a couch and launching into an hour-long monologue while your doctor sits in a chair behind you taking notes and asking irrelevant questions.

Not long after we began, I became exasperated with the entire charade. Dr. Harper explained that his aloofness was part and parcel of the way the therapy is meant to work. I told him that our sessions made me feel worse instead of better. He insisted I continue. Such symptoms were the result of bringing to light the painful memories from my childhood, he argued, memories my subconscious mind had done its best to suppress. I had no idea what he was talking about. He couldn't even prescribe sleeping pills to help me sleep because relieving my symptoms would prevent me from gaining insight into the primal conflicts that were at the root of my troubles.

The insights he was looking for eluded me, but I couldn't help but come away with a thorough grounding in the orthodoxies of Dr. Sigmund Freud. For example, if I told Dr. Harper how much I detested social dancing, jazz, modern art, and musical comedies, seeing them as no better than commercialized sex, he would parrot Freud's dictum "Fear is the wish." This meant that I was repressing my sexual impulses and that was what was causing my nervous condition. I often heard Daddy criticize the narrow-minded thinking of the Larchmont Catholics, but I found that these Freudians were more rigidly doctrinaire than any Catholic.

I took a copy of a famed work on Islamic jurisprudence to one session, reading aloud the Islamic laws regarding the proper relationship between men and women. Then I began to describe what my idea of an Islamic utopia would be like. First off, I said, Arabic would be the official language. I wouldn't make the mistake of outlawing Western dress, I told Dr. Harper, but no one would want to wear it. Instead men would don the traditional dress of Saudi Arabia and women would be completely veiled. The sexes would be strictly segregated, attending separate schools. There would be no courtship, only arranged marriages.

In addition to these constraints on social life, there would be no tables or chairs or beds in the homes, and people would eat with their fingers instead of forks and knives. Pork, alcohol, and drugs would be outlawed. There would be no machines or factories, just small shops where traditional craftsmen made everything. In large extended families, the very old, the mentally afflicted, and the handicapped would be lovingly looked after. There would be no need for mental hospitals or old age homes. Everyone would say their prayers five times a day and observe the month-long fast of Ramadan intent in their every action to please God and attain salvation. In such a society everyone would be compassionate and just rather than wholly focused on the accumulation of riches and material comforts. There would be no race prejudice. I told Dr. Harper that I would like to devote the rest of my life to making this dream come true.

This wasn't the kind of dream Dr. Harper wanted to hear about because he broke his own rule to interrupt me. Why are you avoiding confronting your root problem, your fear of men? As if he hadn't heard a word I had said. Why at the age of nineteen are you still a virgin? You live like a nun, he said, in a tone of accusation. If I had had a gun at that moment, Betty, I'm sure I would have shot him.

Instead I took off my shoe and shattered the glass-fronted bookshelves in which he proudly displayed his volumes of *The Complete Works of Sigmund Freud.* I pulled out his issues of the *Journal of the American Psychoanalytic Association* and tore them in half. Only when he shouted at me did I return to my senses and of course I apologized. He was really rather nice about it. Naturally Dr. Harper found in my behavior a confirmation of all his theories.

I can't help but feel that Freud's estimation of what it means to be human is incredibly depressing. In his view, the highest expressions of art and religion all get boiled down to one's base animal instincts. At the same time, Betty, I had been reading Marmaduke Pickthall's translation of the Qur'an. I found this work deeply truthful and inevitably totally at odds with Freud. But if I don't accept Freud's theories and act accordingly, I am told that I am at fault. Should I be so arrogant as to question the validity of his doctrines, I am supposed to be in denial. This passed for medical treatment, for science, for logic.

What never ceases to amaze me is the fact that in all my time under his care, going to his White Plains office five times a week, Dr. Harper never took any interest in my real problems. Instead, he is intent on identifying problems that have never even occurred to me. Ones Dr. Freud insists have to be there. Among the problems I face that seem far more pressing is the question of my future. I have always given a great deal of thought to what I wanted to be when I grew up. Unlike you, Betty, I never had the slightest desire to be a housewife.

On your suggestion, not long after I left the University of Rochester, I wrote to Margaret Mead about becoming an anthropologist. She told me that I had first to finish my degree and then plan to spend several years living among savage tribes of the Amazon or New Guinea. As I was only interested in the highly developed and literate civilizations of Asia, the idea of living among headhunters and cannibals was unappealing. Still, I applied and was accepted to New York University.

Then, last June, a year after I matriculated, I was asked not to return in the fall. Mother probably told you what happened. The dean of women suggested I resume my studies when Dr. Harper could attest to my complete recovery. I wasn't asked to withdraw because of poor grades, Betty. I was an exceptionally diligent student and my work was never late. But for his final lecture the professor in my course "The History of Russia and the Near East" decided to extol the virtues of Turkey's president, Kemal Ataturk. He cited Ataturk's enlightened secular reforms and denounced Islam as backward and medieval.

Of course I know now I should have taken issue with his remarks in a more respectful manner. Instead I argued with him in front of the whole class. And then when the chair of the sociology department expressed her hope that within a generation the entire world would embrace Western values, that modern technology would soon erase cultural difference and the traditional civilizations of the East would be eclipsed, it was the same story. Both professors had called Dr. Harper to complain. I knew then I would never get my college degree.

So how can I support myself? As a child, I wanted to be an artist. So I took a course with George Grosz at the Art Students League at Cooper Union. Though he was a very good teacher, encouraging even the most mediocre talents, I soon realized I painted to please only myself, not the art market, and so I was unlikely to make a living painting. I had also explored the possibility of procuring a pilot's license and, as I always had a number of ideas, becoming an inventor. Unfortunately, I lack the skills for these professions. I like reading history books, but you can't do anything with that but teach. I know I wouldn't be able to tolerate a single day of the monotonous routine of an office or assembly line. The summer after I graduated from Mamaroneck High School, I worked at the plastics factory, making tiny plastic crucifixes in different colors. It was impossible for me to stand on my feet all day.

But Dr. Harper only wants to talk about my virginity. Naturally I find the prospect of dating nerve-racking. How do you draw the line between experience with boys and going all the way? I know you managed just fine and Walter is a respectable husband, but I can't quite seem to. Mother would be furious with me if I lost my virginity. The only prudent solution for me seems not to risk it, which leads to Mother's accusation that I am a prig. With every year that passes and every cousin's engagement party, I despair of ever getting married. So this is another of my dilemmas.

Finally, living at home is growing increasingly difficult. I had proposed moving to Aunt Helen's more spacious house in White Plains, as I often stay with her when Mother and Daddy go off on holiday. Sometimes, too, when their bridge parties go on until late, with twenty or thirty guests drinking cocktails and smoking and keeping me from sleeping, I go to Aunt Helen's to get some rest. But Aunt Helen pointed out that our cousin Jim also likes to throw parties. Jim and his friends dance with wild abandon, playing Elvis Presley records at top volume until early in the morning. I couldn't well expect her to keep her son's friends away, she says. It would cause strife in the family and Jim would end up resenting me. "Just as your mother and father now do," she added pointedly.

I should tell you that this past summer and fall I became utterly absorbed in following the Suez Crisis in the Middle East. Every morning before Mother and Daddy woke up I would go to the door of the apartment to retrieve the *New York Times*. I read every single page, feeling as if my own fate hung in the balance of the contest between Israel and Egypt playing out in its pages. After Nasser bought weapons from communist Russia and proceeded to nationalize the Suez Canal, there was pandemonium in Israel, England, and France. In advance of the presidential elections, the Democrats were falling all over each other in defense of Israel, calling for arms and troops to force the Arab states to recognize Israel and sign peace treaties.

Then the Israelis invaded the Gaza Strip and marched on Suez across the Sinai Peninsula and all hell broke loose. Every afternoon, I listened to the hearings at the UN General Assembly on the radio. The Israeli delegate ranted on and on with his propaganda about how the Palestinians welcomed the Israeli occupation of Gaza. The Israeli army was the harbinger of peace, prosperity, freedom, and enlightenment, he proclaimed. Not even during the 1948 Palestine war had there been such a furor over the Middle East as there was last summer. Only President Eisenhower had refused to buckle, demanding that Israel quit Gaza and the Sinai or face the possibility of the withdrawal of American financial support. Money is the only thing the Zionists understand.

This month the morning headlines brought more of the same. The New York rabbis are in a lather over the forced migration of Jews from Egypt to Israel. From the photos on the front page of the *Times*, it seems to me that these Jews are better dressed and far more prosperous than their fellow Egyptians. If the Suez crisis has now made Jews unwelcome in Egypt, the Zionists have only themselves to blame. More Zionists are protesting King Saud's state visit to the city. To humiliate him, they staged a slave market in front of the Saudi embassy. A *Times* editorial, meanwhile, lavishes praise on General Moshe Dayan as a brilliant military leader who "has been fighting the Arabs since he was twelve years old."

Then this morning, hidden away in the back pages of the paper where only I would think to look, I found a different sort of story. United Nations officials had visited Rafah and Khan Younis on the Gaza Strip and found evidence of a massacre by Israeli troops. Over one thousand innocent civilians have been murdered following the Israeli seizure of these villages in Palestine. I tore out of my room and found Mother and Daddy at the breakfast table drinking coffee.

Look at that! I shouted, throwing the paper down and scattering the silverware to the floor. The Israelis are no better than the Nazis. They are doing everything the Nazis did! I hope the Egyptians defeat every last one of them.

Enough! Daddy shouted. You stop that at once! You're making our lives so intolerable we can't live here in peace!

I lost complete control of myself, Betty, before retreating to my room to write you this letter. I wonder what will become of me. I can't bear even thinking about it.

Larchmont Acres Apartments, Apt 223-C
Mamaroneck, NY

December 1956

In the wake of the outburst I wrote you about in my last letter, Daddy arranged for me to see the most famous psychiatrist in New York City, Dr. Lawrence Kubie. Finding him somewhat sympathetic, I asked him if he would take me on as his patient, since things didn't seem to be improving under Dr. Harper's care. He shook his head gravely and said he would have no better success. He promised to speak to Mother and Daddy to discuss alternatives.

Not two weeks later, Betty, I intercepted his letter to Daddy and carefully pried it open. What I read nearly made me faint. Dr. Kubie wrote that there was nothing to be done but to admit me to a mental institution as soon as possible. If I remained at home, my condition, schizophrenia—catatonic type—would only worsen, he said.

It is a sinister label, schizophrenia. I went to the medicine cabinet and contemplated Daddy's bottle of Seconal. Couldn't I free us all from the prospect of this new misery? But then I remembered what the suras had said about suicide and the hellfire that would surely find me if I went through with it. For the first time ever, I prayed to Allah. Without realizing it, I found myself gluing the envelope shut and putting the letter back on Daddy's desk under a pile of bills.

Dr. Lawrence Kubie would have approved of Dr. Harper's curt interrogation of Peggy on the matter of her unyielding virginity. It was Kubie's belief that, where a physician can afford to have a pacifying bedside manner, the psychoanalyst must be merciless in forcing a patient to face her neurosis. This might involve simply holding up a mirror so that the patient can reflect honestly on her life. Or it might mean the analyst will be obliged to break through a patient's stubborn resistance through what Dr. Kubie termed "the principle of deprivation."

As outlined in his book *Practical and Theoretical Aspects of Psychoanalysis,* deprivation is accomplished first by removing those emotional crutches on which a patient's peace of mind might depend. Then a patient is placed in exactly those situations that will most predictably arouse great fear, anxiety, or anger: "Sometimes, deprivation will be so important to a patient's progress that an analyst must intervene in his daily life and deny him his traditional sources of satisfaction, so as to force the patient into a state of active need." Withholding reading material or denying the patient any contact with her family were among his suggestions. Institutionalization was clearly another.

Kubie saw the analyst's job as strengthening a patient to the point where she will face and accept the whole truth about her illness. Yet reading his book, I felt Kubie's method had less to do with strengthening the patient than with weakening her, much as a warden will force a captive's dependency. Armed with the "whole truth," the analyst conveniently becomes its unquestioned and sole arbiter, the final judge of what might be considered normal. In Dr. Harper's view for Margaret to be a virgin at nineteen was abnormal. Faced with a patient who insisted that whatever was wrong or different about her was the result of her refusal to be co-opted by Western cultural mores, he threw up his hands.

Nor did the impact of larger historical events on the individual psyche carry much weight in Dr. Kubie's or Dr. Harper's worldview. Margaret's daily scouring of the back pages of the *New York Times,* where the rumors of Jewish concentration camps had first appeared, signaled a permanent state of unease and vigilance. The massacres on the Gaza Strip simply confirmed her fears of the new crime under way in the world, hushed up or disbelieved much as the previous one had been. In all these ways, Dr. Kubie's final diagnosis of schizophrenia perhaps conveyed more about the failure of his analytic imagination than about Margaret Marcus's true condition.

In her 1969 work "A Manifesto of the Islamic Movement," Maryam Jameelah took on the broken promise of Western civilization, from the Greeks to Sigmund Freud. The Greeks initiated man's fatal rift with God, she wrote, by insisting that a man's honor depended not on his beliefs but on his actions: morality and theology bore no relation to one another. The humanist philosophers of the Renaissance put their faith in the unfettered expression of human creativity to deliver earthly paradise. In the sixteenth century Francis Bacon was convinced that science held the key to human happiness and would eventually reign supreme over superstition and religious dogma. Once religion was abolished, the apostles of the French Enlightenment foresaw not only heavenly bliss but also the disappearance of bigotry, fanaticism, and tyranny. Once the workers of the world united, Marx held, social injustice would be replaced by a workers' paradise. When his turn came, Freud argued that it was sexual repression that led to conflict and that complete freedom from inhibition was the panacea for all that ailed mankind.

Margaret viewed all these utopian dreams with a skepticism born of personal experience. "All that was good, true, and beautiful" she found in Islam alone: "If anyone chooses to ask me how I came to know this, I can only reply that my personal life experience was sufficient to convince me." Other religions might be partially true, but Islam contained the whole truth, providing its adherents "with a complete, comprehensive way of life in which the relation of the individual to the social and the material to the spiritual were balanced into a perfect harmony." If her embrace of Islam came at the expense of turning away from her own history, away from the social conventions of suburban America and the many contributions of Western science to human welfare, so be it. She wanted out. Like those sixties revolutionaries who followed her, she saw her refusal to compromise as evidence of the purity of her intentions, the power of her raging dissent. "My quest was always for absolutes," she wrote.

Thus Margaret's radical views alone did not constitute evidence of insanity. In the 1952 edition of *The Diagnostic and Statistical Manual of Mental Disorders* published by the American Psychiatric Association Mental Health Service, schizophrenia was divided into several subcategories or "reactions." These terms replaced what was formerly known simply as dementia praecox, providing a diagnostic umbrella under which a variety of behavioral and intellectual quirks might be classified. The list of schizophrenic behaviors included the tendency to retreat from reality, bizarre behavior, disturbances in stream of thought, delusions and hallucinations, and regressive behavior. Patients were classified according to the behaviors they manifested.

Sigmund Freud had lumped the schizophrenic with the psychotic, placing both beyond the pale of his analytic arts. While Carl Jung had worked with schizophrenics, hoping to discover universal truths from them, he concluded sadly that they existed in a waking dream, but a dream that could not be analyzed. According to S. P. Fullinwider's *Technicians of the Finite,* an account of the treatment of schizophrenia in postwar America, a number of prominent analysts on these shores promptly stepped into the breach.

In typical psychoanalytic encounters, patients project their primal emotions onto their analysts. There these emotions can be considered and coolly analyzed. American analysts began noting that something about the schizophrenic patient seemed to reverse this dynamic. Psychiatrists who had described the schizophrenic as entirely lacking in empathy, capable of savage cunning, began to wonder if it was their own cunning or savagery they were describing. The best-trained analysts noted how schizophrenic patients were able to zero in on their emotional weak points and summon at will the furies of anxiety, fear, rage, lust, and conflict that lurked within their professional breasts. Another psychiatrist told of having seen himself as a monster in the eyes of his patient. To his dismay, he promptly began behaving like one.

Was Maryam Jameelah a schizophrenic? I couldn't say. But I couldn't help reading into this description of doctors and their patients an uncanny portrayal of the relationship between America and the Muslim world: a catastrophic folie à deux in which both sides brought out the monster in each other. There was a rote quality to some of Maryam's writing that suggested to me a closed thought process much like that of her classically trained analyst. Perhaps if Dr. Harper had been more established in his practice, he wouldn't have let himself get so rattled. Perhaps, too, if Dr. Kubie had been able to bear the challenge to his own paradigm, some accommodation short of a mental institution could have been reached. Still, it seems odd that neither her doctors nor her parents had any language to address what appears to have been as much a spiritual crisis as a family one.

Muhammad Asad, the author of Peggy's beloved memoir *The*

Road to Mecca, once made reference to the work of an early Qur'anic scholar who interpreted the word *ruh,* commonly translated from the Arabic as the word for "soul," to mean the divine spark, the shock that gives life to dead hearts. No one around Margaret Marcus seemed able to accommodate the idea of a soul. No one credited her unfashionable need to believe in God or an afterlife. They all expected that a conventional, productive life, filled with those pleasures and comforts a wealthy country might provide, was sufficient cure for what ailed her. At times, her parents and doctors behaved as if the mere notion of a life lived by a strict religious code was a personal affront. It was hard not to feel that each of them, in different ways, had attacked Margaret with the same pitilessness with which she had taken on Dr. Harper's glass-fronted bookshelves.

Nichols Cottage
New York Psychiatric Institute
White Plains, NY

August 1957

Neither Daddy nor Mother said anything about Dr. Kubie's letter. From then on, Betty, I stopped going out, even to the library. I wanted only to sleep, to read Arabic poetry and Marmaduke Pickthall's translation of the Qur'an. I neither wanted to see Mother and Daddy nor wanted them to see me. Sometimes, in the evenings, I overheard them talking with Aunt Helen in the drawing room. I would go to the door and listen.

Dr. Harper warned us to expect this, Daddy said.

She has become a human vegetable, Mother said quietly.

Coming out of my daily session with Dr. Harper not long after this, Betty, I was astonished to see Daddy and Mother waiting for me by the reception desk. My surprise was cut short by apprehension. What are you doing here? I asked suspiciously. Why aren't you both at work?

Wouldn't you like to take a drive in the country? Daddy had said in a sugary voice, doing his best to ignore my agitation. I didn't *in the least* want to take a drive. I wanted to go home. I wanted to return to my bedroom and lock the door.

There was nothing to worry about, Daddy told me.

I wasn't taken in for one minute; I knew exactly what they were up to. Yet however much I wanted Daddy to know he wasn't fooling me, I couldn't actually bear to tell him that. I was afraid that if I said it out loud, it would cause my most dreaded fear to come true. In the time that had passed since that day when Dr. Kubie's letter had arrived, I had allowed myself to hope that nothing would come of it. But the drive in the country had lasted no more than ten minutes before the car pulled up in front of the mental hospital. It was my absolute worst fear.

I would be staying for just a few weeks, Daddy promised in a futile effort to calm me, to undergo some tests and treatments. There was nothing to be ashamed of, he said.

I turned on him wildly. There was no point in keeping quiet. I no longer believed anything he told me but I wanted him to admit it would be years, if ever, before I was released. All he could say was that it was the best place for me. The best place!

After an interview with the hospital director, I signed myself in to avoid the degradation of involuntary commitment. I was assigned to Nichols Cottage, a fancy name for the ward for disturbed patients and, I soon learned, the lowest rung of the long ladder out.

Every time they visit, Betty, I beg them to allow me to come home. I swear I'll be good. But Daddy is adamant. I have to do everything the doctors and nurses tell me to so that I will get well, he says. If you truly love me, I say to Mother, you will get me out of this place. But Daddy cuts me off. I am here for my own good and because they only want what is best for me. He reminds me of how impossible the situation at home had become, for all of us. Until they left for a six-week holiday in Trinidad and Tobago, each visit has ended with everyone in tears.

I am denied any rest during the day, even if I haven't slept a wink the night before. I am kept to a strict and unvarying schedule, scolded for minute infractions like a naughty child. Books and writing materials are forbidden. I can't get over the idea that though my captivity is as rigidly enforced as in any prison, I am expected to be grateful. If I don't at least pretend I love it here, that I harbor no ill will toward my wardens, my doctors will decree that I require more time in their care. This makes no sense whatsoever. What sane person would enjoy a mental hospital, no matter how fancy it was? Not even a prisoner is expected to be grateful to his jailer.

We rise at seven and a nurse watches while we take baths, watches us while we get dressed in clothes they have chosen for us. Breakfast is served promptly at eight, in a fancy dining room set with white tablecloths. In the walled courtyard where there is a small lawn and some trees I read the *New York Times* until it is time for the gym. Patients on the convalescent wards are allowed full use of the grounds and have access to tennis courts and a golf green, but the offerings for Nichols Cottage inmates are limited to badminton and Ping-Pong. Twice-weekly "hydrotherapy" takes place in a room that looks like an exclusive beauty salon. There we receive water massage and then get packed off to occupational therapy. Between woodwork and basket weaving and ceramics, I have made a number of nice things for the apartment that I hope will go some way toward replacing all the things I broke. In the evenings we have our only free time before lights-out.

We are always under surveillance. The jangling of keys locking and unlocking doors and cupboards sets my teeth on edge. As the months go by, the world outside has begun to take on a dreamlike quality. Only the *Times* keeps me grounded in the awareness that it is life in the hospital that is unreal. Even painting, something I have always enjoyed, has lost its meaning. It has become just one more way to keep us occupied, to distract us from the paralysis of our lives. Those too afflicted to understand that any attempt to escape is pointless find themselves returned in handcuffs to solitary confinement.

Of course Mother and Daddy say they want me to get well, but though they would deny it bitterly, the truth is they can no longer stand my company. It is hard for me to acknowledge just how much trouble I have caused in the four years since my nervous breakdown. The conflicts over lifestyle and values have made the Larchmont Acres apartment a battlefield. When I am not overcome with self-pity, I try to view Daddy's decision objectively. What if I had a daughter who made my life miserable? Could I honestly say I wouldn't do the same thing? No.

When the time came for my staff conference, I dressed in my very best clothes, fixed my hair, and followed the student nurse to the committee room. The hospital director met me at the door and seated me at the head of a long raised table. After my case was presented to the hospital's staff of psychiatrists, the questioning began. Why hadn't I tried to earn a promotion to a convalescent ward? I said that I preferred to stay behind at Nichols Cottage. There was security in knowing that I could fall no further, I explained. At Nichols there were no demands made of me, no expectations I might disappoint. I pleaded with them to free me. My only desire was to be released to find my place in society and do something productive with my life, I told them.

None of them looked me in the eye. They didn't even seem to register what I had to say, occupying themselves with taking notes on those pads of paper they were never without and talking to each other in low voices. Two weeks later, still waiting to hear what would happen to me, I had a serious breakdown and was packed off to an isolation cell. I don't know how long I was there. Then I was taken to the treatment room.

Patients are sent to the treatment room to be force-fed. There are a number of girls who look like Nazi concentration camp survivors because they have basically stopped eating. There was one girl who told me she had gone on a fad diet she'd read about in a women's magazine while she was at a fancy Florida resort. Ever since then she'd tried to stop losing weight, but she couldn't. When I first met her she weighed fifty-nine pounds and all her teeth had rotted away. Twice a day she would lie next to me on the table while the tube was stuffed down her throat. I always clean my dinner plate.

Electroshock is another therapy taking place in the treatment room. There is no more terrifying prospect than electroshock, which, like forced feedings, is done in full view. For some unknown reason, though Daddy signed the release forms, I have yet to receive shock treatment. Instead, for twelve to fifteen hours a day I am tightly wrapped in icy cloths and left on a table unable to move anything but my toes and fingers. They call this hydrotherapy.

An annual bulletin of the Westchester Division of New York Hospital from the 1950s claimed that 80 percent of the patients treated there were discharged within a year of admission. The glossy photographs accompanying the mission statement show impeccably kept grounds dotted with relaxed-looking clientele. The hospital was reminiscent of Larchmont mansions with sweeping views of Long Island Sound.

In letters she managed to smuggle out to Betty, Peggy described a procession of good-looking, lively, and intelligent girls from privileged families who, for a period at least, joined her at Nichols Cottage. She had known girls like them at Mamaroneck High School, had watched them from a distance. She even met a girl at the hospital who had been in her class at Ethical Culture. They weren't the kind of girls who had sought out her friendship in school, but at Nichols Cottage the usual class hierarchies and religious tensions were held in abeyance until the hospital's ward system, rewarding obedience with perks and promises of promotion, kicked in.

Margaret described how, after being treated with electroshock or a forced feeding, such a girl might begin her progress through the ward system, playing by the rules, finishing the food on her plate, smiling for the nurses, and taking her medications. And the day would come when she would be discharged. A big car would come up the drive, bringing her parents, and after hugs and hand-shaking they would set off. And if this girl's illness went into permanent remission, the hospital would take credit. Either way, another girl, equally good-looking, equally privileged and starving to death, would soon take her place.

Reflecting on her fifteen-month stay at the New York Psychiatric Institute from her quiet sunny room in the Paagal Khanaah, Peggy wrote her parents that such remissions were essentially inexplicable, answering only to the vagaries of mental illness, and as likely to happen outside the hospital as in it. They certainly couldn't be ascribed to the therapeutic wonders of basket weaving. The restorative effects of electroshock and insulin therapies, she insisted, were at best temporary. Even a steadfast belief in God, she admitted, wouldn't make a difference in a patient's prognosis. Of all the treatment options, however, she felt the sessions of endless psychoanalysis had to be the most futile.

Because Margaret was never promoted to Ward 8, she saw firsthand that the chance of complete remission was small. She calculated that two out of three girls would be back in the hospital before the year was out to go through the entire rigmarole again. In Nichols Cottage she learned that many of her fellow patients had already spent years cycling in and out of mental institutions. She also knew that this would continue until their families could no longer afford to pay the bill. Once the money was gone, these girls would inevitably end up on the back wards of a state institution. Even as her own fate remained unclear, Peggy had felt sorry for them.

Reading Peggy's descriptions of her psychiatric hospital stay, I found something unnerving about the enthusiasm for psychiatry in postwar America. Perhaps it was the flip side of the drill to conform. Why the sudden need to know the exact parameters of normal? It was as if the entire nation had acquired the insecurity of a sharp-eyed social climber, alert for any challenge to American domestic bliss, any evidence of foreignness, or simple eccentricity. Margaret Marcus was not the sole misfit in the 1950s asylum. Artists, poets, homosexuals, communists, and unhappy housewives joined her.

Like them, Margaret found it impossible to comply with those little understandings, those slippery accommodations that made the world she was born into run smoothly. The success story America had been telling itself as the richest nation in the history of the world never rang true, focused as misfits tend to be on the unspoken lies, the rank hypocrisies and the inequities of power. Within a decade the voices of the housewives and homosexuals and political dissidents would begin to be heard. These voices would demand more freedoms; they aimed to escape the straitjacket of society, not fit themselves for a new one. But like those wayward girls who sought perfection in their bodies, Margaret sought perfection in the world. She dreamed of a regime as rigidly determined and rulebound with rewards and punishments as the hospital she had been in such a hurry to leave.

Freud's theories held sway in American psychiatry not because they were effective at treating her afflictions, Maryam would write later, but because they fit so perfectly with a materialist worldview. In such a world a person has no essential dignity, has no certainty about right and wrong. In such a world people were free to do whatever they wanted, unrestrained by fears of what would happen in the hereafter. It was enough to simply enjoy good health, good food, the love of family and friends, and partake of those abundant amusements that distract everyone from serious questions.

In Western Civilization Condemned by Itself, Maryam quoted Carl Jung writing in *Memories, Dreams, Reflections:* "I have no judgment about myself and my life. There is nothing I am quite sure about. I have no definite convictions, not about anything really. I know only that I was born and exist and it seems to me that I have been carried along." Maryam couldn't understand how anyone might want to adopt such an empty outlook; she wanted moral judgments and certainty. But Jung wasn't describing an empty outlook, merely a wistful and inconclusive one. Furthermore, he ends his reflection with an unquestioned conviction, if not a statement of belief: "I exist on the foundation of something I do not know." Perhaps by this he meant his faith in a common humanity, or perhaps his idea of the collective unconscious. Whatever that foundation was, however one defined it, it seemed to me both an unquestionable fact and an unconditional one.

More than most, Jung seemed to grasp that in a wholly secular and materialist society, where human beings were too easily treated like moving parts in a great machinery, everyone was brutalized, but no one more than the most invisible and thoughtful. Was a mental institution the only place for them? If there was such a thing as a holy spark, a *ruh,* how long would it stay lit if there was no one there to look for it, or even guess that it was there?

When Margaret first learned she would be transferred to the Hudson River State Hospital, the prospect of even the briefest glimpse of the free world outside, of a ride in a car, was a matter of such immense excitement that I first thought her letter to Betty was describing her journey home. Herbert and Myra had spent all their money on a private hospital only to be told on June 9, 1958, that it had all been wasted. Margaret's stay had been a tremendous mistake, the director told them. Westchester only wanted patients with bright prognoses; chronic schizophrenia did not respond to the available treatment options, they said, as if Dr. Kubie's diagnosis had been kept secret from them.

Despite starting the journey on this grim note, Herbert Marcus did his best to see to it that his daughter's trip to the public asylum in Poughkeepsie was as upbeat as possible. He and Myra took Peggy to the finest hotel in town for dinner and told her she could order whatever she liked. From her extensive descriptions of holiday meals in her letters to her grandparents, it was inescapably clear that Peggy had a healthy appetite. That evening she ordered chicken soup, a mammoth steak, and a side of peas and potatoes. A serving of butter pecan ice cream and a large glass of milk capped off the meal. Reading Peggy's rapturous description of this menu, I was unaccountably moved. It was the most affecting evocation of a meat and potatoes dinner I could conceive of.

Hudson River State Hospital, now derelict, was once a sprawling Civil War–era collection of buildings that overlooked the Hudson River. Its massive main entrance was topped by an ungainly-looking clock tower. During Margaret's stay the grounds were littered with garbage and in the evening bats flew about the turreted rooftops. However haunted and rundown in appearance it was, Peggy nonetheless found it a strangely comforting place. It was more an asylum than a prison or psychiatric institution. Most of the wards were unlocked, and not long before her arrival the hospital administration had discontinued the practice of lobotomies and insulin shock treatments.

After signing the papers, Peggy was fetched by an attendant in a blue-and-white uniform to be strip-searched, showered, and dressed in a shapeless hospital smock. Then, like a prisoner, she was photographed and fingerprinted. Finally, she was parked in the reception area of the admission ward with about forty other patients. This was Ward C. There were scattered chairs filled with senile old people and along the wall stood wild-looking adolescents whom she immediately identified as juvenile delinquents, dope addicts, and sexually promiscuous girls. After a few days' observation she was given an honor card that enabled her to explore the grounds of the hospital unattended. There was no ward system of promotions, no basket weaving, no fears that she could fall any further.

The language here is inevitably that of inmates and prisons, Peggy wrote Betty. Everyone asks how long you have been here, when you expect to get out, and whether your time has been "hard" or not. But the question that worried everyone was never broached: "Can I make it on the outside?" It wasn't until Margaret was transferred to the main building, which housed the chronic patients, that she realized how desperate a question this could become. It was only then that she began to miss the air of hopefulness that sustained the new arrivals in Ward C.

There was a woman in the chronic ward who had been an inmate for fifty years and hadn't had a visitor since 1910. And then there were the girls who were too friendly and simpleminded to make it on the outside. But most depressing of all for Margaret was the long bench filled with women with vacant faces, never looking at one another, never making conversation, but simply lost in their own private hell.

And if the mental hospital alone wasn't a sufficiently dismal fate, for chronic patients who could not be trusted outside unsupervised, a poor diet, close quarters, and badly ventilated rooms conspired to raise the specter of contracting tuberculosis and being moved into the tuberculosis ward. Margaret wrote at length about the desperate conditions of these patients, as if to find something in her own lot to be grateful for.

In contrast to Hudson River State, she found that the private ward of the Paagal Khanaah had a great deal to recommend it. With three ayahs at her beck and call, Maryam was treated like a kind of royalty. Even Janet Hanneman, the Peace Corps nurse, would undertake small errands for her. Still inclined to favor the Muslim way of doing things, Maryam held that it made no difference if you were the daughter of a feudal zamindar or an illiterate

Punjabi peasant; every patient at the Paagal Khanaah was treated with kindness. Maryam, of course, was neither the daughter of a zamindar nor a peasant. In the Lahore madhouse, however, there was social cachet in being an American, and she seemed to accept as her due the privileges and protection that came with this.

As the Margaret Mead of Nichols Cottage, Peggy had once silently calculated the likelihood of relapse of her former ward mates. She observed young girls undergo the savage rituals of treatment without blinking. At the Paagal Khanaah she now took it upon herself to confer with the medical director over the paranoid delusions of a fellow patient. She inquired about the prospects of babies born to mothers in the public wards. (Dr. Rashid did his best, she reported, but most of them died.) Similarly, just as she had at Hudson River State, at the Paagal Khanaah she managed to gain access to her case file (at Hudson State she read everyone else's as well). Peggy never hesitated to find a way around the rules, either because she could not resist the pull of her questions or because she was simply nosy. Of course the same thing might be said of a biographer, burrowing away in boxes and old letters.

Maryam made the most of her experience in mental institutions when she came to write "A Manifesto of the Islamic Movement" in 1969. In this document she encouraged Muslims who persisted in seeing America as a model society to visit its asylums and witness the lives of the lost souls hidden there. It was not only the senile and aged who found themselves rejected and abandoned by their families, but also thousands of others who had been "left to die, herded naked and incontinent like cattle."

"Schizophrenia is the scourge of the twentieth century," Maryam quoted one unnamed psychiatrist as saying. The diagnosis was not hers alone, she seemed to think, but part of a larger, more existential contagion: "Schizophrenia is no longer limited to isolated individuals but the entire social order has become contaminated . . . wherever modernization and urbanization are taking place." Qutb had made a similar observation, describing the "hideous schizophrenia" of modern life, a disease Europe had inflicted on the cultures of the colonized. The remedy for being torn between Islamic values and Western ways, between devout faith and crushing doubt, spiritual values and material longings, remained the same, Maryam insisted. Pakistan must not waver. Islam was an "all embracing system of absolute transcendental morality" that promised "salvation of the individual personality" along with much else. Ten years after she left the Paagal Khanaah, Maryam suggested that she had at last found the salvation that would forever elude all those who chose any other path. She was no longer a divided woman.

Whatever Maryam Jameelah might say, clinical schizophrenia has never been proven contagious. Yet there were other conditions at Hudson State that, like tuberculosis, did appear to be. The crimes of the recent war had infected not only those who had committed them but also those who had suffered them, thereby creating a distinct pathology. Like the majority of the professional staff, the psychiatrist who had been assigned to Margaret Marcus had been trained in Europe before the war. As she was not licensed to open a private practice in America, Dr. Cohen, like many other refugees, was relegated to treating the patients of public institutions.

Hudson River State Hospital
Poughkeepsie, NY

April 1959

I wasn't in the least surprised to learn that Dr. Cohen is a survivor of Hitler's camps. One might think that such an experience would have granted her a certain degree of compassion but that is far from the case. She is more like a prison guard than a doctor and I am not alone in finding her sicker than any of the one thousand inmates whose treatment she is responsible for. Look at how your hands are shaking, she says to me with a look of contempt, look at how you have neglected your personal appearance. I can't imagine how you think you are ready to go home looking the way you do. She tried to have me assigned to the laundry, where the work begins at eight in the morning and ends at six in the evening. There you are made to stand over steaming vats of wet clothes, putting them through the mangle machine until you are ready to keel over. Unpaid labor is considered "therapy" here.

Work will set you free.

I am counting the days until Easter, when I am due to have a month-long trial visit at home. I wish you believed in God, Betty, because then I would ask you to pray that Daddy won't send me back here.

Like a politically fragile country that persists in acquiescing to one strongman after another, Margaret Marcus seemed to live in fear of what she was capable of if she was left to her own devices. In a letter to the Mawlana Mawdudi, written close to her departure for Pakistan, Maryam admitted to having "made mistakes in my life" and "done some foolish things." She provided no details. Perhaps Margaret's condition was simply a response to a culture that refused to rein in her desires or curb her ferocious temper. When it came to sorting out what it meant to be good, Margaret Marcus could not find the single template she required. Only by embracing the notion of a powerful and all-seeing God, nurturing a constant awareness of His gaze, would she be kept in line. Here was her moral guidance.

Writers on Islam, including Mawdudi, make constant reference to the idea that Islam is not a religion, but a way of living in harmony with God and His laws. Those who veer from the Right Path risk hell in the afterlife and maladjustment in the present.

Mawdudi wanted the same clear destiny for Pakistan as he wanted for every Muslim, as if he, too, didn't trust what would become of his country if it chose another, more open-ended path. Given the bloody circumstances under which Pakistan came into being, I couldn't begrudge him the necessity of this security.

As the date of Margaret's month-long trial release came close, the uncertainty and temptations of freedom, however eagerly awaited, must also have been terrifying, particularly if Peggy had begun to believe her fate in the hereafter hung in the balance. Would she make it on the outside? Would she be good? Yet the day finally arrived in the spring of 1959, when a long white envelope from Hudson River State Hospital appeared in the apartment mailbox at Larchmont Acres. It was addressed to Miss Margaret Marcus:

> Upon the written recommendation of your father, your discharge is hereby confirmed. You must try not to harbor too many grievances against us. The pressure of our patients is so great and our resources are very limited. Our knowledge is even more inadequate. We can only do our best with what we have in hand.

Years later Maryam would remember the exact wording. It was like a benediction.

CHAPTER 6

The Convert

Go clear out your heart's chamber.
Make it ready to be the dwelling place of the Beloved.
When you depart, He will come in.
And to you, with self discarded, He will unveil His beauty.
Mahmud Shabistari

Herbert Marcus was intent on keeping his daughter out of the apartment while he and Myra were at work. While it was all well and good for Peggy to do volunteer work at the Westchester Association for Mental Illness, he was impatient for her to settle on a suitable livelihood. This was his constant refrain, Margaret complained to Betty. When she protested, insisting that for that to happen she would have to change into an entirely different person, Herbert lost his temper. She was just lazy! All she thought about was Islam!

And before Margaret knew what was happening, her father was threatening to call an ambulance and have her sent back to the state hospital. Weeping, she would run into her room and slam the door. Afterward, Herbert would knock softly and offer his apologies. The door would open and Margaret would reciprocate. He would suggest that she take a typing course at the Vocational Guidance and Rehabilitation Center in White Plains.

You may find it easier to be accepted in an office, he said.

I'll try, Daddy.

That's my good girl.

For the rest of 1959 Margaret tried to land a position as a secretary, going from office to office and filling out job applications. Without a degree or any work experience, she found that prospective employers were not interested, even if she lied about her age to evade awkward questions about the missing years. She imagined that every interviewer she spoke with had no trouble seeing through her stories, and that only made her more nervous. She resigned herself to typing up the papers and master's theses of international students whose grasp of English was shaky. They seemed to appreciate her expertise and were happy to talk with her about the lives they left behind. Unfortunately, demand for a typist was unpredictable; she was not close to making a living.

On the pretext of looking for a job, Margaret gradually began spending more time in the city, going to the Oriental Division of the New York Public Library, where Mr. Parr helped her find the books she sought. He also brought to her attention *Muslim Digest,* where she would publish her first essays on Islam. After reading *Islam at the Crossroads* by Muhammad Asad, the Jewish convert whose book *The Road to Mecca* had made such a deep impression on her, Margaret began to articulate the kernel of her argument against modern America.

Without some framework of belief, Margaret imagined that America would eventually face a general cultural collapse. Having personally witnessed the havoc Western secular values had wrought upon Christianity and Judaism, she felt obliged to warn Western-educated and English-speaking Muslims that Islam would very likely share the same fate unless they took heed. Margaret was certain that Islam would prove a better vehicle for the dream of social justice, equality, and communal harmony that America and

Israel had so clearly reneged upon. More keenly than anyone else, she had seen how the manicured lawns and pruned landscapes of her suburban childhood could not obscure the ethnic rivalries, religious hatreds, and petty racisms that seethed beneath its smug surface. Nor did it shelter her from the stinging ridicule she had suffered as a stout and stubborn little girl who could not control her temper. One of the first essays she sent off was a paper she'd written at New York University, a glowing appreciation of Sayyid Qutb's work *Social Justice in Islam*.

Maryam would also ascribe the high incidence of mental illness, juvenile delinquency, promiscuity, perversion, children born out of wedlock, and obscenity in the arts and entertainment to the destructive inroads materialism had made into the American mainstream. As for technological progress, medical breakthroughs, and loss of sexual inhibition, she felt these developments had debased rather than liberated the Western world. The obsession with economic prosperity had enslaved both men and women. Out-of-control technology had expanded the reach of America's destructive powers. Education was deemed desirable not to enhance human potential but because it created better workers. The campaign to eradicate mental illness, too, arose not from any sympathy for the afflicted but so that no one's potential to contribute to the GNP would be untapped. Even the appropriate number of babies per family was subject to a cost-benefit analysis. This was the end result of scientific rationalism: a predisposition to surrender awareness of the sacred in manic pursuit of the wholly mercenary.

Underlying these arguments there were echoes of Margaret's arguments with her father over her refusal or inability to become financially independent. And there were more intimate but still unspoken calculations. Peggy's paralyzing childhood fear of death had forced her to ponder the most profound questions of existence for hours on end. When she grew older she compared the sacred texts of Christianity, Judaism, and Islam for their teachings on the hereafter. Of all these faiths, only Islam provided her the clear assurance that her efforts to live a pious life would be justly rewarded.

Similarly, Islam embraced all, not only without regard for birth, skin color, and nationality, but also without regard for private affliction. Indeed, the protection of the weak by the strong is valued above all else. Whatever tribute Islam might exact in return for the promise of heaven and its protective embrace, Margaret was prepared to pay it. Finally, Islam had made the Arabs a great people. Might it ennoble her as well? Provide her the hard and fast practical advice on how to go about the infinitely mysterious, riotously confusing task of finding her place in the world?

Eventually, Margaret Marcus found her way to the Islamic Propagation Center of America, housed in a run-down storefront in Brooklyn Heights. Shaikh Daoud Ahmad Faisal told her he was a pure Moroccan Arab, but Margaret was skeptical; he looked, spoke, and acted like any black man from the Deep South. Margaret judged his Arabic wanting as well. His West Indian wife, Khadija Faisal, introduced Peggy to cricket and taught her how to recite her five daily prayers. While Shaikh Faisal swanned around the Syrian neighborhood in elaborate Arab costume, boasting about his plans for a network of madrasas and colleges, Sharia courts, and halal shops on Atlantic Avenue, Khadija quietly took in young black men who had fallen behind on their rent.

Yet despite her doubts about him, it was Shaikh Daoud Ahmad Faisal who finally convinced Margaret Marcus to submit to God, to obey His commands as set forth in the Holy Qur'an, and to sacrifice her life in this world for the life in the hereafter. Despairing at the news of her daughter's conversion, Myra Marcus consulted a rabbi, though by then it had been years since she and Herbert had gone to temple. The rabbi reassured Myra that Islam was a close kin to Judaism. Consoled, Myra told her daughter, who now called herself Maryam, "You will always be Peggy to me."

Margaret had always imagined that her aunt Helen was more open and sympathetic to her embrace of Islam than her parents ever were. Her aunt had even treated her to occasional meals at Lebanese restaurants. Then one afternoon Aunt Helen dropped by the apartment and Margaret was astonished to discover how long she could talk about the plans for her daughter's wedding. She described in excruciating detail the trips to the city to decide between several competing venues. She shared the minutiae of shopping for the perfect fur coat among the hundreds to be found in Manhattan's most exclusive Fifth Avenue department stores. Finally, the fine points of the cocktail reception her parents were going to host in honor of her cousin required further deliberations. An entire afternoon passed in this way.

But it was when her aunt brought out a copy of the official newsletter of the Women's Zionist Organization and tried to interest her niece in Hadassah's fascinating humanitarian work that Margaret realized she was entirely alone. Despite all the time they had spent together when her parents were on holiday, all those occasions on which Margaret had described her strong feelings about the Arab cause, it was clear none of this had actually registered. Aunt Helen would listen like the fond and doting aunt she was, but her attention would wander. In the end she was no different from her parents or Betty. Not one of them could fathom what Shaikh Daoud Ahmad Faisal and Khadija meant to her. Suddenly she seemed to see them all from a great distance.

It was only a matter of time before Margaret and her father had their final argument. One evening she found Herbert at his desk writing out a check for two hundred dollars to the United Jewish Appeal. When she protested, her mother defended him, insisting that the money would be used strictly to help resettle destitute war orphans in Israel. She couldn't imagine that her parents really still believed that propaganda. They must have known in their hearts where the money was really headed.

It will be used to kill and dispossess Arabs! she shouted.

Her father ordered her to her room. When she emerged some time later, tear-streaked and tentative, he told her it was time for her to leave home. He could no longer live with her in peace. Her mother said nothing.

By the summer of 1961 she had found a room at the Martha Washington Hotel, a women's residence on East Twenty-ninth Street. Her rent and living expenses were still covered by her father, but her existence was no less lonely than before. Though the publication of her writings on Islam had begun to give her life a focus, it appeared that her conversion changed nothing about the outward circumstances of her life. More and more, Margaret came to believe that she would be condemned to live as a misfit in a society she would always hate. Though she couldn't imagine where she would ever find the courage to emigrate, she began to correspond with figures across the Muslim world.

Peggy's list of her correspondents included "mature Arab Muslim leaders deemed reactionary fanatics by the *New York Times.*" The mission of *al-ikhwan al-Muslimin,* the Society of Muslim Brotherhood, founded by Hassan al-Banna in Cairo, had first inspired her. He and Sayyid Qutb were deeply involved in questions of an Islamic social and political order. But al-Banna had been assassinated and, in the wake of an attempt on President Nasser's life, his society was outlawed. Qutb responded to Margaret's overtures through his sister Amina, but he was in prison. So Egypt was out.

Then there was Algeria. Shaykh Muhammad Bashir Ibrahimi, leader of the insurgency against France and a member of the Islamic clergy, had written her a long letter in elegant French about the unspeakable conditions in his country. But he was living in exile in Saudi Arabia. Qutb's younger brother, Mohammed, along with many other members of the Society of Muslim Brotherhood, was too. He acknowledged neither Margaret's letter nor the essays she sent. That ruled out Saudi Arabia.

Less than a year after she moved into the Martha Washington, the day came when her father reached the end of his patience. He and Myra wanted to retire and travel around the world. They would give up their lease on the Larchmont Acres apartment, sell the furniture and household belongings, and embark on a world tour, relieved of all civic and family responsibilities. Even if Peggy had wanted to accompany them, Herbert refused to have her along. Furthermore, once they left the country, he told her, he would no longer contribute to her support. She would be on her own.

It had been three years since her release from the Hudson River State Hospital, Maryam wrote Mawlana Mawdudi that spring, a year into their correspondence. If she didn't find work soon, she would be reduced to joining the welfare rolls or face the prospect of lifelong commitment. She held out no hope for rehabilitation and saw that without her parents there to support her, she was lost. While Pakistan was neither an Arab nor a true Islamic state, it did offer a community of fellow Muslims. In the bosom of the Mawdudi family, under the direct thumb of the Mawlana's rule, how could she go wrong?

"After declining your kind invitation for so long," she wrote to Abul Ala Mawdudi, "would it be too late to accept it now?"

Paagal Khanaah
Jail Road
Lahore

Late July 1963

Long after his return from Mecca at the end of May, the Mawlana finally visited me. During the six weeks of my residence here, I had managed to settle into a routine, but my fear of the Mawlana Mawdudi and the Jamaat-e-Islami was not diminished by his sudden appearance at the hospital. The Mawlana was elaborately proper and polite, but reserved to the point of coldness. Subsequent visits brought no change in his manner and he soon stopped coming altogether, greatly increasing my apprehensions.

Accompanying him to the hospital was a bearded man he introduced as Mohammad Yusuf Khan. Mawdudi insisted that I had once been a guest in his home, but as I had no memory of him, I viewed him glumly as yet another of the Mawlana's Jamaati henchmen. When Mawdudi's visits stopped, Mohammad Yusuf Khan continued to come, often bringing candy, bottles of sweet syrup, and presents. This only heightened my suspicions.

I raised my concerns with Dr. Rashid and asked that this man no longer be allowed to see me. When he agreed, I changed my mind. Instead I asked that I never be left alone with him. Subsequently, whenever Mohammad Yusuf Khan arrived, I would accept his gifts but scarcely said a word to him. The more presents he brought me, the more iced drinks and sweets, the more suspicious I became. Sometimes he came twice a day with food. I didn't feel I had done anything to deserve such attentiveness from a stranger.

Then after several months of uncertainty over my fate, Shaheer Niazi, the journalist from Karachi whom I'd all but forgotten about, suddenly appeared, having tracked me down by traveling to Pattoki and speaking with Baijan and Appa. I was surprised to discover that he was a small wrinkled man dressed in white pyjamas. From his letters I had an entirely different view of him. Niazi brought alarming news; he had it on good authority that the Mawlana had a plan to have his accomplices take me to a remote village and have me put to death. Once again my life was thrown into turmoil.

It gave me absolutely no consolation to learn that my fears had been justified and that my life was in danger. Niazi explained that he could help me only if I renounced Mawdudi's guardianship in writing. With this letter the hospital would have no choice but to release me. Once freed, I would be a welcome guest at Niazi's family home in Karachi until he could arrange a place for me to live independently. Without hesitation, I wrote the letter. He took it and told me he would return the next day to finalize the details of my release.

After he left I wrote letters to everybody I knew, warning them that the Mawlana was not who he appeared to be. I put in everything Shaheer Niazi told me and declared my intention to sever all ties with Mawdudi and the Jamaat-e-Islami. I had my ayah smuggle the letters out since I knew Dr. Rashid would just add them to my file. The next morning Shaheer Niazi returned and told me to pack up all my possessions and ready myself to leave. After completion of the paperwork, he promised to return at nightfall so that by early evening we could be on our way to Karachi. By lunchtime I was ready to go and sat down to wait for his return.

But Shaheer Niazi didn't show up that night or the next. I waited in my room, my bags packed, wide awake and beside myself with fear. Two weeks went by. There was no word from anyone. The Mawlana was silent. Mohammad Yusuf Khan stopped coming with his sweet drinks. I became increasingly distraught. Finally I received Mother's letter informing me that, according to the American consulate, the journalist I had contacted was notoriously unprincipled and Dr. Rashid would not allow me to be released to his care. Furthermore, since I had renounced Mawlana Mawdudi's guardianship, I would not be allowed to remain in Pakistan. Instead, I would be flown back to New York at my own expense.

"If you don't have any American clothes," Mother wrote, "do ask Janet. I'm sure she will be happy to lend you some of hers. And very soon, darling, we'll meet you at the airport in New York. From there we will take you directly to Hudson River State Hospital."

Paagal Khanaah
Jail Road
Lahore
PAKISTAN

Early August 1963

After I received your letter, Mother, I suffered a complete collapse. But then, as is my habit, I approached the question of how I had reached this personal crisis in a methodical and conscientious manner. I applied my mind, heart, and soul to discover whether my fate was to return to America or remain in Pakistan. To do this I had to look more closely at certain unpleasant facts I had previously slighted or overlooked entirely. I will now write you what really happened to me upon my arrival in Lahore.

From the very first, it was clear that the Mawdudi family had been deeply disappointed in me. The feeling was mutual. I didn't convey this disappointment in my letters, even when you begged me for news of myself, because I didn't want you to worry. And maybe I also thought that if I didn't write it down, if I gave it some time, it wouldn't actually be true. I had invested too much in the idea that I would find a home here, that all my difficulties would be resolved.

First of all, Mawdudi's daughters, who I had hoped would become my sisters, were *very* critical of me. Asma chided me for talking too much. She accused me of disrupting their studies and monopolizing their father. But I *enjoy* talking. You are much too free with our siblings, she told me. That is why Ayesha and Khalid are so fresh with you. Until you learn to be reserved as a well-bred Pakistani woman should be, no one will respect you.

Several days into my stay, when I realized that Begum Mawdudi and Asma and Humaira were avoiding me, I braved confronting the Mawlana to find out what was wrong. Without a word, he beckoned me into his study. His family found my behavior so odd they were completely terrified, he told me. I couldn't begin to imagine what made them so fearful. What did they say I had done? I asked in all innocence.

It seemed that when I was still sharing a room with Humaira I had talked in my sleep all night long. And when I was moved to the book-lined hallway outside the Mawlana's study, they could still hear me holding long conversations with myself, interrupted by weeping.

I had no memory of any of this, Daddy, but when I faced the

dread prospect of being returned to America, the Mawlana's words came back to me. From the day of my arrival, he had never tried to hide his disappointment. Rather than finding the charming and brilliant personality of my letters, he was faced with a young woman whose nerves had been shattered by a long ship journey and her treatment at the hands of a hostile captain and crew. The Mawlana was not terribly patient or understanding. He was cold and authoritarian and frightening. He wasn't interested in talking with me about Islam.

Sitting at his desk, the Mawlana went on to lecture me about my bad behavior at the home of his wife's brother. Do you remember those tea parties I told you about? At one I got into an argument with a young Canadian convert who had called Mawdudi a reactionary fanatic. When another man entered the fray with equally anti-Islamic ideas, I grew so incensed I nearly hit him, not even wondering who he was. The Mawlana informed me that the young man was his nephew.

Mawdudi told me in no uncertain terms that I had absolutely disgraced him and his family. Formerly he had had many productive exchanges of views with his nephew and this Canadian convert, but my behavior had put an end to that. Both now refused to come to the house because of my presence here. Well, from that moment on I realized that Mawdudi family unity and solidarity were valued above the teachings of the Prophet and that NO CRITICISM FROM AN OUTSIDER WOULD BE TOLERATED.

It seemed that the harder I worked to please the Mawlana, the more he upbraided me. He would send me notes, drawing attention to my continuing misbehavior. My overfamiliarity with the servants was inappropriate, he said. I wasted the time of my Urdu teacher by talking about my personal problems.

When I discovered those photos of Hindu temple dancers, sexy Indian movie stars, and, to my utter shock and consternation, a painting of Jesus Christ in Muhammad Farooq's room, I thought that the Mawlana should certainly know what his son was up to. But instead of expressing gratitude when I brought these publications to his study, the Mawlana told me I was meddling. He conceded only that none of this trash belonged in a good Muslim home, but he could not entirely prevent the outside world from intruding. "I am doing my best to reform my sons gradually. If I bend the stick too quickly, it will break," he said. When Muhammad Farooq emerged from the Mawlana's study, he angrily accused me of spying on him for his father. And he wasn't the only one who accused me of this.

I was so lonely I began to unburden myself to occasional visitors. When I ventured to complain about how severe Mawdudi was with me, the Mawlana could barely contain his outrage.

I wrote you that it was the suspension of martial law that had occasioned my move to Pattoki. With the four-year-old ban on Jamaat-e-Islami suspended, I explained, Mawdudi was able to return to his political activities, planning trips to Africa and Saudi Arabia to make common cause with the Muslim Brothers in exile and to collect funding from his patron, King Saud. But this wasn't the whole truth. My stay in Pattoki was arranged because no one in Mawdudi's family could bear me any longer.

In the end, Maryam must have felt, what purpose did it serve for her to revisit her past, to determine where, exactly, everything had gone wrong. There were no answers to her present predicament there, however hard she searched for them. If her home was no longer with her father and mother, with her guardian the Mawlana Mawdudi or the evil Shaheer Niazi, where did she belong? In the Paagal Khanaah? In Hudson River State Hospital? These were the questions that now haunted her. Her father had washed his hands of her. Mawdudi had betrayed his promises. All that remained was her faith. The Mawlana had once assured her that she had found the right and only path to God. And each time she traced the logic that led her to convert, it always seemed like the sanest and most hopeful decision she had ever made. Even in her most desperate days.

And what of Mawdudi? What were his thoughts about the fate of his protégée and ward? Why had he invited her to Pakistan? Why was he prepared to let her go?

After the Prophet, a retiring and contemplative man, received the first of his divine revelations, a community gathered around him in Mecca. Many of them were destitute. As the rich and powerful members of his former tribe, the Quraish, watched Muhammad move among these lowly men, they could not believe that God would put those from a poor station above them. The Quraish saw their wealth as a mark of God's favor. When Muhammad, following Abraham, denounced the false gods the Quraish worshipped, directing all to submit to one God alone, this too unnerved them. Abraham was their patriarch; they were his proud descendants. As more and more people joined Muhammad, the Quraish grew defensive, lashing out at Muhammad and his followers. Eventually the Prophet and his companions were forced to flee to Medina to escape the persecution that grew out of the Quraish fears that they were on the wrong path.

Settled in Medina, the Prophet made room for the stream of benighted refugees from Mecca who followed him there. In Medina, too, the Prophet continued to receive divine revelations. In Mecca the suras had defined core beliefs; in Medina the suras began to address the challenge of just and compassionate rule. As the Muslim community at Medina grew larger and more powerful, the Prophet began to actively defend his community from Quraish incursions. To those who surrendered, he was merciful. Those who fought on he killed outright, enslaving their women and children.

In the shadow cast by the story of Muhammad's persecution, exile, and redemption, Mawdudi had imagined he saw not only the lineaments of a true Islamic state, but also the model for his own life and actions. In one of his last letters to Maryam in New York, Mawdudi explained his invitation in this way. In asking her to join his family, he followed the example of the Prophet, who had welcomed refugees from persecution. He welcomed Maryam's hunger to join him in building a new world of liberty and equality, justice and peace, on the template provided by the life of the Prophet and the Holy Qur'an. He imagined that she and the man he would find for her to marry would be part of his journey.

Perhaps out of a sense of delicacy or courtliness, Mawdudi left unsaid certain things. Maybe he couldn't imagine what kind of father would refuse to support a daughter until she was married. Or maybe he simply couldn't conceive of a society in which a husband and wife might leave their home to travel the world like vagabonds without providing for the daughter they left behind. It was certainly beyond his imagining that Herbert and Myra Marcus would let their daughter venture unaccompanied on a freighter halfway around the world, easy prey for the depraved appetites of men. I supposed, too, that it hadn't surprised him that Maryam had been traumatized by the journey, by the threats of the captain and crew. It simply confirmed his conviction that family ties and responsibilities meant little in the West; individual freedom and the pursuit of private pleasure trumped all else. Perhaps Mawlana Mawdudi's sole concern was simply to provide for Maryam Jameelah the protection and guidance and support her own father refused her.

For the Mawlana Mawdudi was also a parent. During the years of his imprisonment, without a father to give them the firm hand they required, his three youngest boys, among them Maryam's favorite, Haider Farooq, had fallen under the influence of his wife's wealthy and Westernized brothers. Not only could Mawdudi not free Pakistan from the spell of the West, his own family seemed resistant to his strictures. Had the Mawlana also thought to himself: Who better to enlighten my children and other Pakistani youth than a convert? Who better to dispel the enchantment with the West than a Westerner? "I hope they learn a lesson from your example," he had written Margaret, on receiving news of her formal conversion.

Despite America's many shortcomings, the Mawlana was not insensible to its glamour and exoticism. Like India, America had once been an English colony. Mawdudi would have admired the vigor with which the American revolutionaries had cast out the English and, in a short time, had made their country a force to be reckoned with. The many examples of American ingenuity simply astonished him: cars, airplanes, the Westinghouse refrigerator that graced his living room, the flush toilet, telephone, air conditioner, and gas stove he would soon acquire. When Neil Armstrong landed on the moon in the summer of 1969, the Mawlana Abul Ala Mawdudi would send him a personal telegram of congratulations.

Though this would come as an unwelcome surprise to a protégée who couldn't leave modernity and scientific technology far enough behind, there was nothing Mawdudi wanted more than to bring the Muslim community into this shiny and sparkling world. It never ceased to amaze him that the American government did not see in his project of Islamic revival a natural ally in its fight against the godless communists.

Eventually, of course, they would.

In Maryam Jameelah's final letter to the Mawlana Mawdudi before she left New York, there had been a note of unease, as if she were trying to prepare him for the possibility that she might not be exactly as he imagined. Maryam began the letter by telling Mawdudi of a comment made by the director of the World Federation of Islamic Missions regarding a certain convert to Islam. "Must be a mental case," he was overheard saying. At first she was shocked, Maryam said, but having given the matter further thought, she decided there was wisdom in his remark.

Considering the perfect contentment of her mother and father,

her well-adjusted and attractive sister, her prosperous aunts, uncles, and cousins, what sense would it make for them to exchange the familiar comforts of the West for an alien and uncomfortable Islamic life? They lacked any motivation to do so. Conversely, had she been a girl more "favorably endowed by nature," there would have been no reason to make such a radical break. Otherwise, what cause would she have to doubt the essential goodness of American society? What would have distinguished her life from that of her sister or parents?

By the end of her letter, Peggy seemed to find her own answer to the questions she posed. What she had once considered the curse of her existence, her sense of being a misfit, she was now obliged to view as a mysterious blessing. Didn't the Qur'an instruct her not to covet those gifts "Allah has bestowed more freely on others" (4:32)? Perhaps she had done some foolish things, but she was now convinced that Islam was exactly the medicine she required, for Allah was forgiving and merciful.

The Mawlana no doubt approved of her conclusion, as he did not address any of her questions in his reply. He had already made it clear that Margaret's maladjustment was a natural consequence of the incompatibility of Islam and the West. Her temperament and taste, her ideas, habits, and conduct, were all fundamentally different from the peculiar and sinful mores of the society she found herself in. In his mind, she was lucky to have been spared even more serious damage. In a metaphor that clearly pleased him, the Mawlana had described her as an equatorial sapling struggling to survive in an Arctic climate. Her spinsterhood was due to similar incongruities, he insisted. By the time he received her final letter, Mawdudi was more focused on what Maryam would need to bring with her and how she might prepare herself for the challenges that awaited her in Lahore.

One year later, as Maryam's fate was being decided, the disappointment of all those hopes that had accompanied her on her journey to Pakistan resembled nothing as much as a comedy of manners. Despite Maryam's frank portrayal of her troubled history, Mawdudi had been too blinded by his assumptions about the West to hear her. After her arrival he must have asked himself: how could he possibly have known from her brilliant writings that this young woman was so deeply adrift? Had he been a more thoughtful man, he might have known that there are no simple calculations about human nature. To cap it all off, just when he had begun making preparations for her release from the hospital, suddenly he heard that she had the temerity to publicly denounce *him*, to question *his* integrity.

Mawdudi had once thought Maryam only required a husband to settle her nerves. But who would marry her now? Once more the whole city was talking about his mad protégée. Questions were being raised both in public and behind his back about the soundness of his judgment. He deeply regretted having invited her to live with his family and having volunteered to be her guardian.

As for Peggy, in her long letter from the Paagal Khanaah, she kept returning to the thought that she would never have accepted Mawdudi's offer to live with his family if she hadn't felt that her life in America was absolutely ruinous. Islam forbade suicide, but wasn't the living death of the asylum nearly the same thing? Her decision to travel to Pakistan was as sane as the logic that had brought her to Islam. What greater proof could there be than the fact that Allah had saved her life the day she stood in front of her father's medicine cabinet?

Yes, Peggy conceded to her parents, she had written intemperately about the Mawlana. On reflection she thought that perhaps the conclusions she drew about his intentions were unsound. He had never intended to kill her. At the time, she had thought it would be better to write down her worst fears than to let such suspicions fester. Bringing her letter to a close, Peggy informed her parents that she had decided to put aside her petty grievances. She would not let them overwhelm her better judgment. Like a good

Muslim, she would resign her fate to Allah. And she would write Mawdudi one last time, begging his forgiveness.

In her favorite childhood game of make-believe Margaret had always taken the part of the handsome but tight-lipped Arab chieftain. Her best friend, Barbara Kenny, playacted the role of a Proper Victorian Lady whose explorer husband had died of thirst in the Syrian Desert, leaving her at the mercy of the elements. In the confines of her parents' two-bedroom apartment, Margaret would throw the protesting, ungrateful Barbara over the back of a camel and cart her off to a tent, a neat contraption of blankets and dining room chairs. Barbara was directed to affect haughty airs, to complain about the heat and the filthy ignorant Arabs. Eventually, faced with this Arab's implacable, fierce nobility, Barbara would finally submit to his proposals. The script rarely changed; Margaret never tired of it.

In her appeal to the Mawlana Mawdudi, Maryam wrote that she now realized that Shaheer Niazi was an evil man who did not have her interests at heart. She recognized all the trouble she had caused him and Begum Mawdudi. She begged him to once again take up his guardianship of her. She gave the letter to Dr. Rashid and asked him to see that the Mawlana received it.

Margaret's tight-lipped Arab chieftain would not have hesitated. It was the code of his desert tribe to shelter the destitute, confer bounty on honored guests, and rescue a woman in distress, no matter how rude or uncivilized her behavior. But several days went by without any word from anyone on Maryam's fate. Maryam became terrified that at any minute the nondescript man from the American consulate would pull up in his long black car to take her to the airport.

The Mawlana might easily have washed his hands of Maryam Jameelah. But he didn't. He had saved her from permanent commitment and given her another chance to make a life, a not insignificant gift and perhaps a greater and more profound indictment of the West than anything to be found in his books. I didn't have to travel to Pakistan to learn this. The evidence is there in the archive and in the long string of books Maryam Jameelah published out of Lahore.

And so it was no surprise when Maryam, returning to her room one night in early July, found two bottles of syrup and a box of sweets on her bedside table. Mawdudi's emissary, Mohammad Yusuf Khan, had returned. The following day Dr. Rashid handed her a three-page letter from the Mawlana.

If Maryam accepted that he had done his utmost for her. If she promised not to disturb his family or his work. If she ceased in her calumnies and tirades of propaganda against him. If she could totally and completely clear her mind of further concoctions and defamations that might even slightly tar his reputation. And if she completely accepted that he had taken the risk of inviting her to Pakistan out of a simple feeling of Islamic fraternity and fatherliness, then he, Mawlana Abul Ala Mawdudi, would resume his guardianship and put the past behind him. As soon as Dr. Rashid approved her release, he would find her a safe lodging in a private home where she might live independently, running her own kitchen according to her taste. She would support herself to the extent that she was able. "The rest will be borne by me," the Mawlana wrote. "If you require any female servant, that too can be arranged. Please let me know if you accept these arrangements or not."

Maryam Jameelah gratefully and gracefully accepted his terms.

---

c/o Mohammad Yusuf Khan
15/49 Sant Nagar
Lahore
PAKISTAN

Mid-August 1963

On his very next visit to the hospital, Mohammad Yusuf Khan brought not only more presents, but also his wife, sisters, and a gaggle of young children. We spent the month of July going on excursions to the Shalimar Gardens and to the bazaars for all those items I would need to set up housekeeping. It was he who found me the room I moved into from the hospital at noon on August 2, 1963. I became the tenant of a school inspector and her three children. It was just five minutes from there to Mohammad Yusuf Khan's home in Sant Nagar. If I got lonely, he said, I could just throw on a burqa and visit them.

As soon as I entered the Khan home, I realized that the Mawlana had been right. I had been there once before, soon after my arrival in Lahore. There had been a big tea party, and unlike at the dozens of tea parties held by Begum Mawdudi's brothers where I got into so many arguments, in the home of Mohammad Yusuf Khan I had been warmly welcomed. When I returned to his home last week, his aged mother, his aunts, his sisters, and his nieces all knew my name. From then on I took my meals there or at the homes of his sisters who lived nearby. When I finally dared ask Mohammad Yusuf Khan why he was being so nice to me, he said that while Mawdudi remained my guardian, he had delegated the day-to-day responsibility for my care to him.

Less than a week after I settled in to my new lodgings, Begum Mawdudi invited me to come to the Zaildar Park house in Icchra for tea. It was August 8, 1963. Mohammad Yusuf Khan arrived to pick me up. I was very nervous. I wanted to be on my best behavior. I imagine I was somewhat distracted. And so I wasn't sure I had heard him properly when Mohammad Yusuf Khan asked me a question. He looked at me expectantly but I couldn't seem to find the right words. So he asked again. Will you marry me?

But . . . you are already married. You have children. You love your wife, don't you?

I love her very much but in Islam a man can have up to four wives and I want to marry you, too.

How can you want to marry me? You know with the condition

I suffer from, it isn't going to be easy for you. I don't want to be a burden on anybody.

You know that Mawlana Mawdudi has told me to take care of you and since there is nobody else except me to provide for you now, what will the neighborhood think to see me entering your room alone every day? From the moral point of view, this is good neither for you nor for me, but if you will marry me, I assure you, everything will be all right.

But what about your wife and her family? Surely they will object to your taking a second wife.

Don't worry about that, he said. This is my responsibility. Will you marry me?

I will ask Mawlana Mawdudi's advice, I told him. If he says I should, then I will.

The man who proposed to take Maryam Jameelah as his second wife was a man whose life, like hers, had been divided in two by exile. Mohammad Yusuf Khan was a Pathan whose ancestors, also known as Pashtuns, had traveled east from Afghanistan to settle in Jullundur in the Indian state of Punjab. There they became powerful feudal landlords. Behind a high wall and a gate locked at night, the residents of the Pathan quarter proved as proudly resistant to the inroads of British influence as they were to the neighboring Sikhs and Hindus. At the slightest sign of puberty, their daughters were veiled and thereafter ventured out of the house only on a litter, hidden behind curtains.

In 1947 Khan and his family fled India for their lives, abandoning their land, belongings, and comfortable life to join the mass migration of Muslims to Pakistan, just as the Hindus and Sikhs left the Pakistan territories for India. Over 7 million traveled in both directions. Trains arrived at their destinations spilling blood and mutilated corpses; refugee camps were attacked, women were raped; massacres of Hindus and Sikhs were answered by massacres of Muslims. Estimates of the number of those killed range from 200,000 to 1.5 million, inexplicably and evenly divided between Muslims and non-Muslims.

Like the subcontinent, the Punjab itself had been divided. Lahore became the capital city of Pakistan's Punjab and Chandigarh the capital of India's Punjab; the largest population exchange took place in this one region. In this exodus the Khans were no longer Pathans and zamindars; they were simply Muslims and refugees. Some of their clan went to Faisalabad, others to Multan, still others to Lahore. Sikhs moved into the grand homes they left behind. For many years tales of how perfect and harmonious life had been in Jullundur would color the struggle to survive in Lahore.

Mohammad Yusuf Khan began his two-hundred-mile journey to Pakistan a vigorous youth of twenty and ended up in a refugee camp not far from Lahore. Broken by malaria, dysentery, exhaustion, and misery, he would spend over a year recovering. It was in the refugee camps that he was first exposed to the work of the Jamaat-e-Islami. Once Pakistan became a reality, Mawdudi's party had thrown itself into the work of caring for and resettling those displaced by the upheaval of Partition.

The ramshackle house in the old Hindu quarter of Sant Nagar where Maryam first visited Khan's family was the house Mohammad Yusuf eventually appropriated after its Hindu owners abandoned it. Khan and his extended clan of brothers and sisters and in-laws broke up a house meant for one family into a tenement-like warren of little rooms bereft of plumbing, running water, and electricity.

Not long after they settled in, the former owners returned, as if such a thing were possible. By then the entire neighborhood had been converted: Hindu shrines into corner mosques, Hindu houses into Muslim ones. Despite Khan's offer to compensate them, they broke down and wept to see what had become of their home, the memory of which had made exile bearable. They returned to India inconsolable.

In Lahore, Mohammad Yusuf Khan's two sources of income were intimately linked with the Jamaat-e-Islami. In the early years a good portion of the Jamaat's revenues came from the publication of the Mawlana's works and from selling skins of the sacrificial goats donated to the party during Ramadan. While the party was banned, Khan oversaw the publication of the *Weekly Shahab,* the distribution of the Mawlana Mawdudi's books, and the collection of goatskins. Like Mian Tufail Muhammad, Khan had been fined and arrested in the wake of the protests over the Family Laws Ordinance. He had published the full text of the ulema's opposition in his weekly. He served nine months and was released just before Maryam arrived in Lahore. While he was in prison, his wife Shafiqa had to sell all her gold jewelry to keep herself and their children from starving.

Pathans rarely married outside their clan; Khan's father had arranged the match with Shafiqa, his cousin. As if to replace the sense of family and cohesion he had lost in the migration to Pakistan, Khan was intent on having as many children as possible. Shafiqa had borne him five, one for each year of their marriage. Four survived. Khan's regard for Mawdudi was such that he hoped to have at least as many children as he had and had even taken to naming his sons and daughters after the Mawlana's. In her first letter describing Khan's home, Maryam had marveled at the infectious energy of the women, contrasting it with the sickly lassitude of their babies. It was as if Mohammad Yusuf Khan was intent on challenging Allah to provide for them, no matter how many babies arrived or how precarious their existence.

c/o Mohammad Yusuf Khan
15/49 Sant Nagar
Lahore
PAKISTAN

Mid-August 1963

On the afternoon of my visit to the Mawdudi home, I took pains to be quiet and well mannered, chastened by the chance to make amends with Begum Mawdudi and her children. The visit went so smoothly that I was invited to stay for dinner. At the dinner table, however, as soon as I opened my mouth the Mawlana began immediately to scold me, launching into his familiar tirade. He complained of my tiresome talk. How he had to commit me to the madhouse, and how when I received Mother's letter I had thrown such a hysterical fit that even the American consul was all for putting me on the first plane home. When he looked at me with the cold fury I knew all too well, I realized I was no longer quite as frightened of him as I once had been.

I have never known a person like you, so completely sane in your writings but then to see you . . .

I interrupted. Mohammad Yusuf Khan has asked to marry me. Please tell me what you think I should do.

The Mawlana looked silently at his plate, his head sunk into his shoulders and his beard draping his chest like a napkin. He frowned. I waited.

Given that you are as you are, I hesitate to take the responsibility of recommending you to anybody. And if after marriage you do not improve, then what? Here is a man of the very best character who is willing to carry the burden. He looked at me with fury and exasperation. Why do you then refuse him?

He paused and looked around the table, suddenly aware of his children's astonished stares. Sixteen-year-old Haider, eighteen-year-old Husain, and eleven-year-old Khalid were completely engrossed.

Anyhow, you should have spoken to me about this only in private. This is not the place or the time to discuss such matters. Mawdudi looked at his children's expectant faces.

Perhaps the children didn't understand me, he added hopefully. They hardly know English.

The table erupted.

Mother, I can only guess at your surprise when you received word of my marriage. Do you remember how often you would complain that if I didn't go out on dates with boys, I would never gain any experience? How you had despaired at my marriage prospects. It wasn't that I didn't want to get married. I just could never figure out how to draw the line. I sacrificed a "mixed" social life to maintain my virtue.

But I am now home with my Khan Sahib, my co-wife Shafiqa, her children and aging mother, and many other relations. Only horse-driven tongas, donkey carts, and the occasional water buffalo find it possible to navigate the streets of our little neighborhood in a rundown part of Lahore. In my chair by the window in my room I can watch the life on the street passing by, secure in the knowledge that while I might know the face of every beggar, street vendor, and child who passes beneath my window, I am myself unseen. After a long search, I have found my place and I will never exchange it for any other. You no longer have to worry about me. I believe I am going to be very happy now.

Inshallah.

PART III

THE CONCRETE LIBRARY

If you go outside your self
You will be under the veil of unity.
And if you go beyond the why and the when
You will leave your self
For the without of why and when

Mas'ud-e-Bakk

CHAPTER 7

The Renegade

In December 2007 I arrived in Pakistan to find Lahore aflutter with demonstrations against the government. In an effort to keep his hold on power, General Pervez Musharraf, the most recent of Pakistan's unelected military leaders, had fired the Supreme Court's chief justice the previous March, setting the entire legal community against him. The prospect of the coming elections and the recent return from exile of Pakistan's former prime minister, Benazir Bhutto, added to the air of possibility, uncertainty, and unrest. Massive cheering crowds had met her plane's arrival on October 18. Yet as her motorcade left the airport, two explosions set off by suicide bombers killed 136 of her followers, including 50 members of the private security detail ringing her vehicle. Hundreds more were injured. Bhutto survived unscathed but shaken.

From that moment, the hope for a peaceful return to democratic rule, along with whatever power-sharing arrangement Bhutto had made with General Musharraf, began to unravel. On November 3, the general had declared a state of emergency, suspending the constitution. Though he cited the rise of religious extremism as part of his rationale for the imposition of emergency rule, he also released from prison a number of Taliban insurgents.

This raised the question of who was calling the shots, the military or those in the ranks of Pakistan's secret service, the ISI, whose agents were known to have ties with al-Qaeda and the Taliban. Bhutto named four individuals in the ISI who she believed had orchestrated the attempt to assassinate her. A week before my arrival, she filed her nomination papers for the January parliamentary elections, escalating tensions still further.

Despite widespread arrests and accounts of police brutality, public opposition to the firing of the chief justice was courageous and unflagging, more exuberant than angry. The city's lawyers suspended court appearances and organized peaceful street protests. Joined by students and activists, the Lahore crowds numbered about a thousand. This comprised the city's sum total of what the newspapers referred to as "civil society." Nonetheless, the Lahore lawyers, distinct and elegant in their black suits and white shirts, seemed to be everywhere, weaving their way through crowded sidewalks and traffic-stalled streets like clerics in a holy city.

In their call for an independent judiciary and an end to military rule, the Lahore lawyers were supported by the Jamaat-e-Islami. No one seemed to note or remark upon the oddness of this alliance. Musharraf suppressed the Jamaat-e-Islami along with every other opposition party, just as General Ayub Khan had once done. The Jamaatis found themselves in the same cells as members of the secularly inclined civil society, represented by the same lawyers. Yet if they acknowledged each other at all, it was with deep distrust.

I stayed in a private home in the gated and heavily guarded suburb of Gulberg. Gulberg figured in Maryam's letters as the "Park Avenue" of Lahore. My hosts were among the most powerful voices of the independent media, which had also been subject to Musharraf's crackdown. Occasionally BB, as Benazir Bhutto was familiarly known, would call to solicit advice about putting together a government and trade gossip about her political opponents.

My hosts kept Bhutto at arm's length, focused more on the lawyers' protests than on the coming election. In the afternoons, they hosted strategy sessions over tea and cake. One woman sighed resignedly when she mentioned that friends from London had canceled their holiday plans to visit. A recent *Newsweek* cover story had described Pakistan as the most dangerous nation in the world. "Of course it's perfectly safe," she added quickly, putting down her cup of tea. "It is just hard to explain that to Westerners." In the evenings we rode in chauffeured cars, accompanied by a guard and his Kalashnikov.

Though I had spent twenty years traveling between India and America, it was my first visit to Pakistan. Instead of the two-week tourist visa I had requested, I was given a five-year multiple entry visa for "family visit," which happened to match the visa I had for India. When I questioned this, the consular official waved me off with a smile. Similarly, the officer at the Lahore airport immigration desk had tapped the little round camera taking my photograph and said, ruefully, "a gift from America." There were many such reminders of the special relationship between America and Pakistan. Indian officials I found rather more . . . officious.

One evening I accompanied my hosts to a wedding reception. The event took place in a fancy hotel owned by the bride's father. We arrived after 1:00 a.m.; people were still waiting for the food to be served. Behind a beaded curtain a belly dancer snaked and swayed on a tiny elevated stage while guests milled around. The women were festively dressed and generously accessorized. It wasn't that much different from a fancy Delhi wedding reception, though there it would be Bollywood dancing, and the wedding party might well join in.

A few of the wedding guests were recently released from house arrest; many had marched with the lawyers. One businesswoman indicated that one of the reasons she marched was just this, raising her cigarette and drink. I looked around: only the belly dancer wore a headscarf. Was this what a secular rule of law amounted to? Cigarettes, illicit alcohol, and dancing girls? No wonder the ranks of civil society were so thin and in need of hired guns. Such a limited notion of individual freedom would mean little to those who had difficulty putting food on the table. I recalled Mawdudi's warning to the students at Lahore Law School almost exactly sixty years before: Pakistan's secular and Westernized elite would hijack Pakistan for their own ends.

Not all had. A few days later a legendary civil rights lawyer visited the house in Gulberg. For years her life had been a succession of death threats, jail terms, and beatings. Her manner bore the scars of her vigilance on behalf of values that might be better described as humanist than exclusively Western or secular. In her law practice she defended the least powerful from the clearcut and unjust incursions of Sharia laws upon secular ones—a blind rape victim accused of fornication, a Christian boy accused of blasphemy—but tyranny in all its forms haunted her. That day, recently released from house arrest, she had stormed the gates of the shuttered courthouse, a flock of lawyers behind her, pulling at the chains as if her tiny arms might break them.

It was this woman who provided me the telephone number of Haider Farooq Mawdudi: Haider Farooq, who, alone of Mawdudi's nine children, had befriended Maryam on her arrival in Pakistan. In civil society circles he was regularly referred to as a "renegade."

I didn't think to ask what they meant by that.

I first began to suspect that Maryam Jameelah had lived to see the September 11 attacks when I came upon the illustrations for *Ahmad Khalil: A Biography of a Palestinian Refugee* in her archive. Maryam Jameelah described *Ahmad Khalil* as a novel she began at the age of fifteen and worked on for ten years. It was part of her efforts to counter Zionist propagandist fiction like Leon Uris's blockbuster melodrama *Exodus* and Arthur Koestler's *Thieves in the Night*. If the British raj was Mawdudi's bête noire, from 1949 onward the

Zionists were Maryam's. Quoting Theodor Herzl's diaries, Maryam had noted the parallels between Herzl's stated Zionist mission and European imperialism in Asia and Africa: "We should in Palestine form a portion of the rampart of Europe against Asia," Herzl wrote, "an outpost of civilization as opposed to barbarism."

Yet in the copy of the novel she left behind in the library, Maryam struck a far more humble note. The first draft and initial illustrations for the book, she wrote, were finished when she was trying to find her way out of a nervous breakdown and the dark years of hospitalization that followed. As much as she aspired to write a work of literature, Maryam reluctantly admitted that the book was fatally encumbered by her agenda. Yet of all the books she would write, *Ahmad Khalil* remained her favorite.

Ahmad Khalil is a peasant whose Job-like life embodies the suffering and nobility of the Palestinian fellaheen. For his ancestral village Margaret chose the real settlement of Iraq al-Manshiya, a village on the eastern edge of the Gaza Strip. Within days of signing an armistice agreement, with Egypt guaranteeing villagers the right to remain in their homes, in March 1949, the local Israeli garrison, acting under orders of "intimidation without end," drove its Arab residents from the land.

Margaret turned fifteen two months later. In the novel she began that year, Ahmad Khalil would kill five Israelis during the siege of his village before being arrested. His prison guard, still bearing the tattoo that marked him as a recent survivor of a Polish concentration camp, becomes his tormentor. It was hard not to see in this turn of events the specter of Dr. Cohen, Margaret's psychiatrist at Hudson River State Hospital. The first draft of *Ahmad Khalil* was completed there.

In the course of the novel Khalil endures every indignity, every possible twist of misfortune. As a child he witnesses the death of his mother at the hands of Israeli soldiers. As an old man, living in exile in Mecca, he sees his own son lose his faith and, after oil is discovered on the Arabian Peninsula, embrace the mantra of Westernized progress. Yet Khalil learns to accept his fate with stoic resignation to the will of Allah. "Every minute of our lives we are being tested," Maryam writes elsewhere, "and the suffering and misfortune we endure on this earth is not the decisive calamity but only part of the testing." The story of Ahmad Khalil was clearly Margaret's and Maryam's, one she would spend her whole life writing and revising, drawing and redrawing, even after the novel was finally published in Lahore.

Maryam Jameelah's archive contains three boxes of drawings and paintings. The first box contains the disassembled portfolio she had left with Mr. Parr as she prepared to depart for Pakistan. Her cover note cites the Egyptian hieroglyphs at the Metropolitan Museum of Art, Diego Rivera's murals, and the drawings of Käthe Kollwitz among the influences on her art. The paintings, done in vivid pastels, consist largely of portraits and scenes from village life in Palestine. There are portraits of men in brightly striped jellabiya reading Arabic newspapers. There are weavers, boys learning the Qur'an, fathers bathing their children, mothers tenderly trying to nurse babies with distended stomachs, and drawings of villagers blinded by trachoma.

A second box contains a smartly bound volume of work, labeled with gold embossed type: "My Artwork from Childhood to Maturity, Larchmont 1938–1957." Some of the work in this volume, bound in Pakistan, can indeed be dated to her earliest childhood and young adulthood. It is the kind of art only a mother could cherish and had undoubtedly been returned to Maryam in the wake of Myra's death. Other drawings in this volume, all scenes from *Ahmad Khalil,* were labeled "additional illustrations made in Lahore" and dated 1969–1989. That Maryam had quietly returned to drawing in Pakistan may explain why she had mislabeled the volume and sent it to the Manuscripts and Archives Division. There it would be beyond the purview of a disapproving husband.

But it is the third box, the largest among them, that contains unbound oversize pencil drawings of even more recent vintage. Here the characters of the novel—Ahmad Khalil, his cousins, wife, and children, his Israeli guard—are all identified by name inscribed near their images. With one exception, all these drawings are captioned with quotations from the Qur'an, as if Maryam imagined that holy inscriptions might protect her from Allah's anger at her transgression. The figures in these drawings crowd each other on the rough paper, their faces drawn with sadness, resignation, or rage. She clearly had no access to paint; I wondered how she managed to get the paper and how she managed to send the drawings to the library without her husband's knowledge.

"From persecuted to persecutor, one of the darkest aspects of human nature," Maryam wrote below the picture of the imprisoned Ahmad Khalil watched over by his prison guard, bearing a concentration camp tattoo. In her novel Maryam had captured the irony of the cruelties and injustices inflicted upon the Arab refugees by Jews who were only recently prisoners and refugees themselves.

The last drawing in the box is titled "Exodus: May 14, 1948." It shows Ahmad Khalil in mourning for his murdered family and his village, grasping a long knife dripping with blood, as Iraq al-Manshiya explodes into flames behind him.

Underneath runs a new legend, not from the Qur'an. Instead, the caption conveys how persecution, retribution, and the notion of two civilizations in a fight to the death can circle around each other indefinitely, like a perpetual motion machine:

Western civilization is superior to Islamic civilization, we fellow Europeans must conquer and westernize these backward Arabs . . .

—*Italian Prime Minister Silvio Berlusconi, September 11, 2001*

Upon reading that, I sat down to write a letter to Maryam Jameelah. I sent it to her care of her publisher and husband, Mohammad Yusuf Khan.

---

c/o Mohammad Yusuf Khan
15/49 Sant Nagar
Lahore
PAKISTAN

April 2007

I was overjoyed to receive your beautiful letter of March 24 and to be assured that my manuscripts and artwork are preserved and appreciated. My late parents, being Jewish and Zionist sympathizers, regarded my drawings of Arabs as merely products of a disordered mind. From 1988 to 2001 I started drawing again, more than fifty additional illustrations for my fictional Ahmad Khalil. I hope now to have conveyed the Palestinian tragedy in pictures by drawing scenes from his life from birth to death. My artwork is intended to convey the same message as my writings. I would be honored and delighted to meet you whenever you find it convenient to come to Lahore. I go outside very rarely and am almost always at home. Awaiting your earliest response with all best wishes . . .

Behind the front door of the house in Icchra the Mawlana's library of Urdu, Persian, English, and Arabic books is encased in concrete. That was the rumor. The Mawlana himself is buried in an unmarked grave at the back. I had also been told the Mawlana's house was no longer the headquarters of the Jamaat-e-Islami. Just before his death in 1979, Mawdudi's party moved its offices to a

Lahore suburb called Mansoorah. In Mansoorah today everyone wears Jamaati clothes, shops at Jamaati shops, and sends their children to Jamaati madrasas where they recite the Qur'an and study Mawdudi's books all day long. The compound at Mansoorah is also rumored to be a martyr factory: for each one of their militants killed fighting for the Taliban, Jamaat-e-Islami leaders are said to receive 60,000 rupees. Of this, 20,000 rupees are passed along to the family.

After the Mawlana's death, there had been an unseemly struggle over where he would be buried: in Mansoorah or in the Icchra backyard. The party elders had long nursed a suspicion that Begum Mawdudi exerted an unholy influence over their leader. Her family had made its fortune as prominent Delhi moneylenders, and usury was a serious offense in the eyes of Islam. Yet in 1937, when Mawdudi first met her, he had been immediately taken by his distant cousin's independent spirit. This was, perhaps, the carefree mark of money. His wife's family wealth had freed him to devote his time to the mission of a Muslim reawakening and, most precious of all, his books. For a time, the Begum proved to be a tad heedless when it came to the rules of purdah, often eschewing the full burqa covering for a mere headscarf. When Maryam asked her why she was not more observant in this matter, Begum Mawdudi suggested that she was unworthy of her husband's great patience.

A judge eventually decided the disposition of the estate by dividing the house and book royalties between the widow and the political party Mawdudi left behind. To guarantee that nothing went missing, I suppose, the Mawlana's library was entombed. If it is true, the idea that his books had survived the fraught 1947 journey to Lahore only to end up rotting under damp cement seemed emblematic of how much had gone wrong in Pakistan's brief history. Though the Mawlana had little patience for poetry, he would have been heir to the collections of ghazals passed down from his grandfathers. His maternal grandfather was a close friend of the great Urdu poet Mirza Asadullah Ghalib. I was sorry to learn that

I wouldn't be able to see what remained of the wall of Persian, Urdu, Arabic, and English books that had so impressed Maryam during her sleepless nights in Icchra so many years before.

There is a newspaper photograph of Mawlana Abul Ala Mawdudi in one of the boxes of the Jameelah archive. In the photograph the Mawlana holds a delicate teacup. His beard is the required length of one and a half fists. Even his hair is combed and styled according to Sunnah practice. But his face contrives to wear no expression at all. Perhaps Mawdudi had walled himself off from the photographer out of his belief that the making of graven images was forbidden. One biographer surmised that his superior affect arose from the loneliness of his youth. I imagined that his sense of propriety was such that he could not look anyone in the eye, even a camera. What had Maryam seen when she first laid eyes upon him?

Though Margaret's heart had first fixed on the Arab world, it was Mawdudi who read her work and who offered her both personal guidance and a refuge. In a letter to her sister a year before she left the United States and subsequently published in *Quest for the Truth*, Peggy refers to Mawdudi as her most faithful correspondent. In her archive, his replies to her letters were bound in a separate volume. Yet Margaret turned only reluctantly toward Pakistan, and tried to console herself by asserting there was nothing special about the Arabs. What virtues they had, Islam had bestowed. "Qutb is a great admirer of you and specially recommended your books to me," she wrote Mawlana Abul Ala Mawdudi.

What had she wanted or expected from him? After her nerve-racking days at sea, she might have needed reassurance that Mawdudi was the compassionate and thoughtful man of his letters. Did she see simply an aloof old man, hobbled by infirmity? Yet what could Maryam really know of him? I asked this question equally of myself. Mawlana Abul Ala Mawdudi and the world he was part of seem as inaccessible as his library. He too is veiled, by differences in culture, belief, and language, distances of time and geography, and not least by the hot glare of recent history.

Mawdudi had come of age at precisely that moment when the struggle for Indian independence became a mass movement. In those years he was clean-shaven and wore Western clothes, signaling his disaffection with his father's faith and his own modernity. As a young teenager he had translated a popular Egyptian book called *The New Woman* into Urdu. The book was a vehement condemnation of purdah. He was seventeen and editing a Delhi newspaper when Gandhi's strategy of noncooperation electrified the subcontinent. For a brief period Gandhi managed to forge Muslim-Hindu unity over an unlikely cause: the fate of the Turkish caliphate. Though the Hindus had no investment in the matter, as Mustapha Kemal Ataturk laid siege to the Ottoman Empire, Hindus nonetheless joined Muslim leaders in a quixotic call for the British to defend the institution. Yet when a lone Muslim assassinated a right-wing Hindu leader for denigrating the Prophet, clashes between the two communities broke out. Rioting Muslims set fire to a police station in a village in Uttar Pradesh with the policemen locked inside. Hindu leaders returned to maligning Islam as inherently violent.

To Mawdudi's dismay, Gandhi, fearful of the escalating violence, suspended the noncooperation movement. The alliance between Hindus and Muslims fell apart. By the time Ataturk dissolved the caliphate in 1924, the cause that had united them was dead and the path was opened for the Muslim League to lobby the British to carve its own, wholly Muslim state from the subcontinent. The league's leader, the immaculately tailored Jinnah, had never seen the point of the caliphate. And Gandhi's native getup and ascetic ways had always set his teeth on edge.

During these years Mawdudi was deep into reading entire libraries of Western philosophy, science, sociology, economics, and political theory. In the midst of the political tumult and disappointment surrounding the suspension of Gandhi's movement,

Mawdudi returned to Islam as if he were returning to an old friend. He matriculated at the renowned seminary attached to the Fatihpuri mosque in Delhi. Technically, a seminary degree would enable him to take the title of *alim*.

But he had seen how the traditional clergy had groomed themselves under their British overlords, fiddling over hermeneutics until they could no longer distinguish between the sparkling clarity of the original Qur'an and Hadith and subsequent medieval corruptions. His writings conveyed a consistent tone of intellectual disdain toward those who were his teachers. Mawdudi would eventually take up the title of *mawlana* to highlight his independent cast of mind and thereby provide a bridge between the past and the future of Islam. But the title he cherished most was that of convert.

The fact that both sides of his family could trace their descent from the Prophet was, he implied, incidental. That his namesake was a Sufi saint who had spread the faith of Islam across India was beside the point. Instead, Mawdudi fancied he saw something of his own path in Margaret Marcus's. In reply to her first letter, he had written, "I studied your life-sketch with great care and interest. As I read it I came to realize how an open and unbiased mind can find access to the Right Path provided it makes a sincere and steady effort. The story of your sufferings, tribulations and mental anguish contained nothing unexpected for me." Like Margaret, Mawdudi held that his own embrace of Islam followed a dark night of the soul, an existential crisis that lifted only when he returned to the Qur'an: "I affirmed my faith after contemplation and reflections. I pondered whether there was another faith that promised more for the welfare of mankind. I applied my mind, heart, and soul to the question." If one approached Islam with the requisite open mind and heart, as this young American woman clearly had, the Right Path would be revealed.

Subsequently, Mawdudi seemed more comfortable pronouncing certainties than showing how he arrived at them. His engagement with Western philosophers became primarily adversarial, more of a defensive gesture than an open-ended inquiry. He appropriated concepts he judged "Western" by renaming them "modern," as if his right hand didn't know what his left was doing. He viewed technological breakthroughs as easily acquired tools for his cause rather than as products inextricably embedded in the materialist worldview Maryam railed against. Similarly, he admired Marx not for his critique of capitalism but simply for having conscripted the masses in a worldwide movement and for having the boldness to insist the world was heading in the direction he willed it to.

His relentless drive was perhaps a means to keep uncertainties at bay, as if in his race to extract a new social contract from the Qur'an and the Hadith he couldn't afford to reflect too long on their manifold ambiguities. If these works didn't have the exact solutions he needed, he didn't hesitate to provide them or at least suggest they would soon be forthcoming. The ulema were often dismayed at his improvisations with classical Arabic, feeling he stretched the traditionally understood definitions to accommodate more modern vocabularies. Many were uncomfortable with Mawdudi's scholarship and questioned the depth of his engagement with the issues surrounding Islamic jurisprudence and Qur'anic interpretation. Others doubted his grasp of Islamic history. Sometimes, in response to criticism, he accused his critics of intentional misreading and made the required clarifications. Equally often he let even the most glaring contradictions stand, as if to challenge those "mischief mongers" who sought to question his authority.

Mawdudi's first major work was an early and influential series of essays on Islamic jihad, first published in book form in 1930, when he was twenty-seven. For centuries *jihad* has been a deeply contested word. Most plainly, *jihad* is the Arabic word for "struggle." In an Islamic context, however, *jihad* refers to a particular religious duty and this is where it becomes complicated.

Generations of Qur'anic commentators have sought to establish the exact nature of this duty. For some *jihad* refers purely to the quiet daily struggle to affirm one's faith in word and action. For others *jihad* mandates a more vocal struggle against an unjust or un-Islamic political order or an assiduous effort to spread the word of Islam. Maryam and Mawdudi engaged in both these forms of jihad. But military struggle has also fallen under the rubric of jihad, sparking debates over even finer distinctions. Is military jihad solely "defensive" or, as generations of Orientalists have insisted, does it mean that Muslims must spread the word of Islam, enlarging its domain on Earth by any means necessary? This was the debate that Mawdudi hoped to join in the 1930 book, *Al-Jihad fil Islam,* as well as his 1939 speech, "Jihad in Islam." In both works he described his mission as a response to those who portrayed Islam as intrinsically violent.

Though "Jihad in Islam" is readily available on the Internet, *Al-Jihad fil Islam* has never been completely translated into English. Mawdudi prefaced "Jihad in Islam" by describing an imaginary painting with a familiar Orientalist motif: hordes of bearded savages with fiery eyes holding swords to the necks of infidels. This image, captioned "The History of This Nation Is a Tale of Bloodshed," was as familiar as it was indelible. Mawdudi mocked and parroted those ulema who, under the thumb of the English, sought to underplay more militant notions of jihad: "Sir, what do we know of war and slaughter. We are pacifist preachers like the mendicants and religious divines. . . . What concern have we with sabers! Now 'Jihad' only refers to waging war with the tongue and the pen. To fire cannons and shoot with guns is the privilege of your honor's government and wagging tongues and scratching with pens is our pleasure."

I imagined that Mawdudi's caricature of the ulema betrayed something of his disillusionment with Gandhi's decision to suspend his campaign of resistance. For a young man in a hurry, this would have smacked of defeatism and weakness, if not cowardice.

That Gandhi had also publicly rebuked the Muslim community for its recourse to violence no doubt added to his disillusionment. A sympathetic account of Gandhi's thought had been the subject of his first book, confiscated by British authorities before it could be published. More than any other thinker, Gandhi shared Mawdudi's reservations about imposing an overlay of Western ideas of liberalism and democracy on India. His vision of an Indian state was rooted in the indigenous arrangements—inseparably spiritual, economic, and political—of traditional village life. Mawdudi's subsequent turn away from Gandhi was premature, tragic yet not necessarily inevitable.

Instead, Mawdudi turned back to the Orientalist painting of the fanatical hordes and asked the question that would forever set him apart: who is the artist? He looked past the canvas to unmask the face of the foreigner at the easel. And then, in an inspired rhetorical flourish, he took up a brush himself. Mawdudi had a flair for painting a picture in words, suggesting a secret flamboyance. His own painting depicted a vast army of imperialist thieves, bristling with deadly weapons. Behind them lurked smartly dressed white-suited officials holding out pens and paper. These were the men who vowed to protect Muslims from tyrants, to guarantee their rights, he pointed out. These were the men who, in the midst of their fine speeches about freedom, never for a moment ceased their plunder.

There was an unmistakable note of respect in Mawdudi's description of how completely the West had bypassed the Muslim world in scientific discovery and invention. And the brushes and pens of the West, he allowed, were no less ingenious than their swords. When Muslims finally awakened, he wrote, Christian Europe ruled over them with both sword and pen, making them foreigners in their own land. It was past time to contest the lurid history of Islam the West had written, Mawdudi insisted. It was time for a full awakening.

The historical failings of Muslims were inconsequential when they were weighed against the human cost of five centuries of Western domination. Yet such was the West's skill at depicting the gory history of Islam that its own crimes had long been obscured. Muslims had been fooled into shame and apology, Mawdudi held, when it was the West that had been shameless. No part of this planet has been spared the bloodbaths resulting from their wars, he pointed out, wars fought not for God but for Mammon. The year he gave this speech, 1939, Western civilization was on the brink of another godless bloodbath, one that would be accompanied by inconceivable barbarism. Muslims would be fools no longer, Mawdudi pronounced.

But what form would wisdom take?

Gandhi, assessing the power of the empire he confronted, had turned to nonviolence not simply as a political tactic, but as an expression of deeply held beliefs. Mawdudi, dazzled by a storied Mughal past and a vision of the Prophet as righteous leader, turned to war. In *Al-Jihad fil Islam,* he sketches a brief history of how Western powers defined the laws of war. Until the seventeenth century there was no provision for amnesty; to surrender was to be killed. Until the twentieth century, no country had to even make a declaration of war before starting one. The First World War involved no higher principle than a fight over the spoils of weaker nations. International laws governing the conduct of war were broken at whim. What kind of civilization was this? Mawdudi asked. What kind of moral example was being upheld?

According to Mawdudi, Islam provided a far nobler model for war. Islam steered a middle course between the extreme pacifism of Buddhism and the wholesale slaughtering of the secular state. Drawing on the Qur'an, Mawdudi outlined the conditions in which military jihad was justified. It might be used to right wrongs against the Muslim community, to regain land or possessions that had been unjustly taken from them. But Sharia also dictated that wars be fought only for "the cause of Allah," never to exact retribution, to prove oneself brave, for material gain, or to preserve national honor. Similarly, divine law dictated that no combatant should be killed in a surprise attack, set on fire, or tortured to death. Jihad was not permissible against a country with which the Muslim state has a signed treaty. Prisoners of war could never be killed, only enslaved. Following Sharia in the conduct of war was a moral and political obligation, he insisted. By confining his discussion of Islamic warfare to this ideal, Mawdudi neatly skirted the way wars had actually been fought by Muslim conquerors. Undoubtedly these wars were no less high-minded and no less lawless than any other. Sharia has proved as easy to set aside as the Geneva Conventions.

Yet the more deeply Mawdudi immersed himself in the holy laws governing war and peace, the more central a militant notion of jihad became to his vision of how Islam might be renewed. After sketching the precise circumstances in which jihad is justified, Mawdudi suddenly reverted to broad and careless brushstrokes. Jihad might also be used against infidels who "are preventing the truth of God from prevailing." Others would follow his lead. In 1951, soon after he returned to Egypt after studies in America, Sayyid Qutb encountered Mawdudi's treatise on jihad for the first time. To define jihad as primarily, in a military sense, defensive was to embrace intellectual and spiritual defeat, Qutb soon wrote.

After Pakistan became a state, Mawdudi would insist that he disdained "direct action." He raised no secret militias; his swords and rented veils remained figures of speech. As the leader of an opposition party, targeted by Pakistan's unelected and lawless leadership, he developed a deep respect for law and order. His political activism was carried out openly and peacefully. In November 1962 he issued the following statement:

> After years of study and thinking, I have come to the firm
> conclusion that respect for Law is indispensable to the very

existence of civilized [society] and if any movement destroys this respect [even] once, it becomes virtually impossible [for society] to restore it. . . . Similarly, underground work suffers from such inherent defects [that] make those who resort to it a great menace to the society. . . . Thus, whatever I have done I have always done openly within the boundaries of the law and existing Constitution, so much so that I have never violated even those laws which I have fought hard to oppose. . . . I have tried to change them through lawful and constitutional means.

Was there then a role for a militant jihad once a true Islamic republic has been achieved? In "Jihad in Islam," Mawdudi wrote that once Pakistan had implemented the Islamic system he had in mind it would fall to the state to ensure that once a person becomes a Muslim, he follow Islamic laws to the letter. Force would be used only as a last resort. If such a person committed apostasy, the "sword of law" descended. The same would be true for "communities on the wrong path." Mawdudi would later identify the Ahmadiyyas as one such community. Similarly, the Islamic Republic of Pakistan should seek to export its system to other countries around the world, to whatever extent possible. To achieve this, it was imperative that the Islamic state have complete access to and understanding of the most up-to-date military technology: tanks, airplanes, and so on.

This was both menacing and puzzling; like something written in code. Which was it, the sword or the law? In his last sermon at Mecca, the Prophet Muhammad related how Allah had explicitly cautioned him: "Remind them, for you are but an admonisher, / You are not at all a warden over them. / But who is adverse and disbelieves, / Allah will punish him with direst punishment. / Lo! unto Us is their return / And Ours is their reckoning." (88:21–26). Yet Mawdudi, conflating Muhammad's role as a military leader with that of fiery prophet, seemed to override this with another sleight of hand. In the third edition of *Al-Jihad fil Islam,* published the year Maryam arrived in Lahore, Mawdudi made his own translation of the last four lines: "But after the failure of admonishing, when the Caller to Islam took the sword in his hand, and said 'Beware! All kinds of distinctions and blood and wealth are under my feet today.'"

In all the major translations of the Qur'an, the sword of punishment is Allah's alone to wield. Yet here Mawdudi seemed to take the sword from Allah's hand and pass it to the Prophet, using the euphemism "Caller to Islam." Jihad as Mawdudi now conceived it not only mirrored imperial conquest but ended up looking very much like the Orientalist painting he had begun his 1939 speech trying to discredit. The leader of the Ahmadiyya Muslim community, a man who had been declared a non-Muslim by Mawdudi, understood all too well what Mawdudi was calling for. He despaired upon reading the 1930 work on jihad: "I tremble after reading this writing.... These are not words but merciless stones." It is possible that the Mawlana also came to reject this appropriation; in the English translation of *Towards Understanding the Qur'an,* the more traditional interpretation of the verse is quoted.

Al-Jihad fil Islam had begun as a simple virus of an idea, a rereading of the genetic code of an entire faith that, several decades on, had mutated into something far more virulent and less susceptible to negotiation. We were all now witnesses to the worldwide contagion. Mawdudi's proposed jihad would not stop once the Indian subcontinent had rid itself of its British overlord or when Pakistan became a proper Islamic republic. "Islam requires the earth," he proclaimed in 1939, "not just a portion, but the whole planet."

For many months I had struggled to summon the man who wrote these words from the frisson of alarm he inspired. Mawdudi was thirty-six and had only recently (and reluctantly) begun to sport a beard. He was the father of two young sons, newly arrived in Lahore after the holy community he founded in the northernmost reach of the Punjab had foundered. India was not yet in his past, Pakistan was eight years in the future, and the British Empire still ruled. Yet his utopian belief that Islam was destined to annihilate all tyrannical and evil systems in the world was undimmed.

There was, nonetheless, something familiar about Mawdudi's worldview. The more I considered him, the more he grew to resemble a twentieth-century avatar of America's own forefathers, those doleful and anxious seventeenth-century dissenters for whom it was an offense to smile. They too saw in the struggle with Satan at large in the world, an echo of the civil strife in their hearts. Permanent and total warfare was also their favorite metaphor. A self-imposed exile from worldliness, sacred readings, and ceaseless self-scrutiny were the means to excise the impurities of their hearts and minds. Those beyond redemption—adulterers, thieves, wayward women—might be whipped, be branded with a hot iron, have their ears cut off, or be hung from the scaffold in public executions. The Puritans saw the conquest of their own souls and those of their community sufficient territory for their rule. Once that wilderness was tamed, however, their descendants would discover that they, too, had a manifest destiny to exorcise the sins of the world.

In his later writings and speeches Mawdudi shifted to those moral and political "jihads" that would eventually bring about an Islamic renaissance and a new world order. To throw off intellectual slavery, to cast off infidel clothing, would require men of thought and vision. Yet the means to achieve this renaissance were as obscure and abstract as the means to embark on military jihad. Where were the poets? Where were the academies, the political institutions, the sources of patronage? What arts and sciences would be practiced? Despite Mawdudi's lifelong efforts, despite the reading rooms and madrasas, the Jamaat-e-Islami never produced the required men of thought and vision.

A speech given in 1945 seemed to foreshadow this failure. Impatient with the repetition of vague exhortations and abstractions, sounding more and more like a voice in the wilderness, Mawdudi suddenly seemed to hit on an allegory that conveyed his urgency and impatience.

The world, he said, was like a train hurtling down a track. Passengers on this train are willing and unwilling hostages to the direction in which it is heading. Getting off the train is not an option, nor is returning to a time before trains. Those who would prefer to travel in the opposite direction might, at most, turn their face toward it. Yet this will not alter the train's trajectory. They will find themselves getting further and further from their desired destination. If the direction of the world is to be changed, Mawdudi concluded, some believers in God should rise to the occasion and wrest control of the train.

And that, I now realized, is what happened. Those who rose to the occasion were not pious men of thought and vision, however certain their belief in God. In wresting control of the train, they did not first exhaust the tools of reason and debate. They did not even deliberate long over their holy texts to assure themselves that the means they chose had the blessings of Allah and Sharia. And while they had not yet succeeded in changing the world's course, it was plain to see that Pakistan, with the fate of the subcontinent in its arsenals, was now heading in an ominous direction.

On my way to meet Haider Farooq Mawdudi, I had to stop numerous times to ask directions from harried-looking men carrying home sacks of vegetables. The car I traveled in, like my thoughts about the Mawlana Mawdudi, seemed to circle endlessly, turning down every tiny street in Icchra in search of 5-A Zaildar Park. After the death of his mother, Begum Mahmudah Mawdudi, Haider Farooq had taken over half of his father's house. He now lived there with his wife and three children.

As the car turned left and right, backed up, reversed course, and followed one pointed finger after another, I wondered if the books of the Mawlana's library might be preserved beneath their concrete blanket. Was the Qur'an that had opened his eyes still intact? Or had book beetles managed to tunnel their way in to ingest its contents? White ants would not distinguish the imported titles, the freighted Marx, the godless Voltaire, from indigenous fare. Western or Islamic, sacred or profane, it was all the same to them. Yet whatever titles survived would tell a far truer account of the complicated journey Mawdudi had taken through life than I would ever manage. I was certain of one thing. However roundabout the Mawlana's journey, the path of those who followed him was as profound a betrayal of their God as it was of Mawdudi himself. While they took from him his unassailable sense of certainty, they drew on too few books, in too few libraries.

When the car finally turned into the drive, the fluorescent streetlights gave the half boarded up, half occupied house a desolate and funereal air. Despite the steady stream of income from the Saudis and its martyr factory in Mansoorah, the Jamaat-e-Islami had never relinquished its claim to half of Mawdudi's house, the legacy of the man buried behind it, and the unreadable books inside it. As I stepped out of the car, a side door opened and a soft-spoken youth gestured for me to come in. Behind him a tall bearded man gave me a wordless and stone-faced greeting, indicating I should sit on a distant chair. This was Haider Farooq Mawdudi, the renegade.

Looking around the gloomy parlor, I wondered if someone had forgotten to turn on the lights. I had barely seated myself when Haider Farooq announced that his son, Ali, would translate what he had to say on the subject of Maryam Jameelah. But first he wanted to show me something.

Avoiding my eyes, he handed me a photocopy of a photograph of a mutton-chopped gentleman in a high starched collar, wide-lapeled waistcoat and suit, standing aside a table. His hand gripped the top edge of a book as if he planned to bang it down like a gavel. It was titled "Lord Macaulay's Address to the British Parliament, 2 February 1835." Beside the photograph were the words of the address:

> I have travelled across the length and breadth of India and I have not seen one person who is a beggar, who is a thief, such wealth I have seen in this country, such high moral values, people of such caliber, that I do not think we would ever conquer this country, unless we break the very backbone of this nation, which is her spiritual and cultural heritage, and, therefore, I propose that we replace her old and ancient education system, her culture, for if the Indians think that all that is foreign and English is good and greater than their own, they will lose their self esteem, their native culture and they will become what we want them, a truly dominated nation.

Even now, fifty years past independence, the greed and cynicism of the British still haunted the Mawdudi house. At a loss as to how to respond, I kept quiet.

In the course of the interview that followed, Haider Farooq would become impatient with Ali's translation. He would interrupt, correct him, and put what was said in starker and more brutal terms. My questions were brushed off with an equally dismissive and curt wave of his hand. It was as if I'd disturbed a wasp's nest. It was hard to believe this man once nurtured a fondness for stray kittens.

Ali Mawdudi didn't seem at all fazed by his father's interruptions. In contrast to Haider Farooq's intensely felt Urdu, the Mawlana's grandson spoke English with a rather laid-back cowboy accent, punctuating and softening his father's angry declarations with the leitmotif "basically, what he is saying is . . ." At one point I asked Ali if he had been educated in America. He glanced at me and looked away. I work for a call center, he replied tone-lessly, soliciting funds for American charities. It was the only question I would be allowed to ask for some time.

Instead, Haider Farooq Mawdudi embarked on a long mono-logue in which he explained the circumstances that had led to Maryam's correspondence with his father. He described his fa-ther's first impressions of her and her impression of him. The situation that had led to her exile in Pattoki was addressed, as were the reasons for her removal and commitment to the Paagal Khanaah. Finally Ali seemed to pause and look at his father. He turned to me.

Your husband is Muslim?

I had been busy noting all the curious and profound ways in which Haider Farooq's version of events differed from Maryam's. It took me a moment to respond.

No, I said. Ali continued his translation.

As the evening wore on, I felt like I was becoming increasingly mired in a game of Mother, May I? Every time I found an open-ing to ask a question, Haider Farooq would sense my impatience and proceed down a road he knew I had no interest in traveling. In fact, it was quite often in a direction that took me further and fur-ther away from where I thought I would be. By the time I realized this, I had completely forgotten the question I'd wanted to ask. I left his house stunned.

When I returned to Gulberg that night, I looked up Lord Macaulay's 1835 address to the British Parliament. Macaulay had mandated that under British rule India would adopt English over Sanskrit or Arabic as the medium of higher education. The quote, I learned, was a fabrication, and a fairly well known one at that. Ironically, its origins had been traced to a publication of Indian Hindu fundamentalists. Thomas Babington Macaulay hadn't even been in England in 1835.

CHAPTER 8

A War Between and Within

"Haven't you met her yet?" Haider Farooq had thundered. I had been wondering if someone was going to turn on a few more lights. The room was terribly dark; I could barely make out his features.

"Isn't it clear there is something wrong with her?! Even the most anti-Western Islamists would see why the West got rid of her!"

Once again Ali stepped in to translate his father's intemperance into a lower key. "The way Maryam was talking, he said, it was pretty aggressive. From her eyes you could guess, from her eyes you could tell, she was crazy. She would look right at you. Basically, what my father is saying is, someone who is mentally not well, mentally ill, that person doesn't have one direction. He might go in one direction one day and in another direction another. She couldn't be a true Muslim if she was insane."

"You played Ping-Pong with her," I said, with a note of accusation in my voice that sounded inane. I was trying to find the sweet-tempered boy he once had been in the merciless and unforgiving man he had become. I was losing hope. Haider Farooq interrupted his son to answer me directly in English.

"Yes, I was the only supporter of her in my house. My whole family was against her. They said she was a bad woman, and told my father to throw her out of the house, send her to the madhouse."

187

"But your father didn't."

"No, my father, he was in shock!"

He looked away. Ali resumed translating.

"When she first met him, the shock was mutual. She basically thought he was a young man and instead she found out he was an old guy. She said she needed a razor to shave her legs. He couldn't follow her English so she lifted her shalwar and she bared her leg!"

I was aware of Mawdudi's strong views on "the feminine urge to display." In *Purdah and the Status of Women*, he didn't mention shaved legs, only makeup, fancy hairdos, gauzy and bright clothes. Though such things were frowned upon, they were not legislated against. "No law can be made to check and control this tendency, as it springs from the woman's own heart," he cautioned. Only thorough self-scrutiny can reveal whether such displays are filled with "hidden evil desire." I was certain Maryam's motives were innocent, but I couldn't begin to imagine the Mawlana's response to a naked female calf. Nakedness of any sort (including one's own) was "the breeding place for the germs of indecency and obscenity."

"After Mawlana Mawdudi recovered from the insult," Ali continued, "he arranged for Maryam to go and live with this rich landlord in Pattoki who would adopt her and pass all his property on to her. And again she was under the impression that this man would be a young guy and she would marry him."

"But Maryam had refused her many suitors, she had resigned herself to not marrying in Pattoki," I protested, struggling to get a word in. The idea that Maryam had set her cap on marrying Mawdudi before arriving in Pakistan, only to pivot to settle on the prospect of marrying Baijan one month later, was hard to swallow. Peggy had led her parents to believe she hadn't taken her many suitors seriously, but according to Haider Farooq, she thought of little else but marriage.

Had Maryam arrived at her decision not to marry because she was fearful of marrying a complete stranger, as I had supposed, or, as Haider Farooq insisted, because her suitors, on meeting her, could see that underneath that burqa was a crazy person? Perhaps they decided she was crazy simply because she looked them in the eye, just as she had Mawdudi. It was unforgivable for an unmarried woman to look a man in the eye, even through a burqa. Adultery, Mawdudi believed, first springs from "the evil look." I imagined, too, that Maryam didn't strike a demure and silent pose. She would have wanted to talk. That would be another strike against her.

"No, I am telling you. When she got there she was very upset about the fact that the wealthy landlord too was an old man. She beat up his wife. They came to Lahore to complain to Mawdudi. They were really upset, they were crying. That is why the Mawlana committed her."

I dismissed the desperate-to-be-wed and wife-beating home wrecker that Haider Farooq imagined Maryam to be as nothing more than a kind of bizarre cultural mistranslation. Though Maryam obviously had a temper, I hardly thought she was as dangerous as he made out.

It was only when Haider began talking about Maryam's engagement to Mohammad Yusuf Khan that my sense of certainty was thrown entirely off; I felt like a carpenter who, while he is dutifully milling old boards, sees his saw bite on a hidden nail, sending splinters flying in all directions. Only then did it occur to me that I had made the same mistake his father had made. From a series of letters, I had conjured an entire being. I imagined I knew Maryam Jameelah.

There was pandemonium, Ali said. Mohammad Yusuf Khan's first wife had arrived at the house in Icchra, children and mother-in-law in tow, deeply upset that her husband had taken a second wife. She begged Begum Mawdudi to do something. The Mawlana was furious. "I give you something to work on and you just mess it up," he yelled at Mohammad Yusuf Khan. "How dare you have done this thing!"

As a way of explaining his actions, Khan told Mawdudi that the marriage was Maryam's idea. She kept saying this English word, *marriage,* over and over, he protested. He didn't know what it meant; he had to ask someone.

Mohammad Yusuf Khan did not speak a word of English, Ali Farooq explained; he was a simple Pathan. When he learned what the word meant, he went back to Maryam to confirm that she wanted to get married. Maryam took that as a proposal.

I burst out laughing. He was joking, no? When I glanced at Haider Farooq, he looked positively murderous.

Ali continued relentlessly. "Mawdudi felt obligated to Mohammad Yusuf Khan because he had gone to prison on behalf of the Jamaat-e-Islami. He gave him odd jobs to do to help him support his large family." In Haider's telling, Mawdudi found out that Mohammad Yusuf Khan had taken Maryam out of the asylum only when Maryam showed up at Mawdudi's door in a wedding dress, beaming and triumphant, with Khan at her side and his furious wife behind them.

Mawdudi registered a kidnapping case against Khan and brought a suit against the hospital, Haider Farooq told me. He believed that, as Maryam's guardian, he alone had the authority to sign for her release. Eventually, he dropped the case. According to Haider Farooq, he banned them both from ever crossing his threshold again.

I was flummoxed. I had assumed that Mohammad Yusuf Khan married Maryam Jameelah as a loyal party worker, to help his beloved leader out of a difficult spot. Like marrying the boss's daughter, I had supposed. But if he didn't marry her to curry favor, but in fact married her without Mawdudi's permission and at the risk of his displeasure, why had he done it? A number of possibilities presented themselves. I settled on one and turned to Haider Farooq. Had he married her for love? I felt ridiculous immediately. Even Peggy had never mentioned anything like love.

"Why?" Haider Farooq asked, a note of rising disbelief in

his voice, as if I were the most foolish woman he had ever come across. A torrent of Urdu ensued, and his eyes flashed in my direction. I felt pinned to the chair. Ali translated a gentler version. "Because Yusuf Khan imagined that he could make a lot of money off her books," he said laconically. "Get his children into the U.S. and live over there, start educating over there. That was the only reason. Nothing like love."

Oh, I thought. I watched the narrative edifice Maryam had constructed with her twenty-four letters home begin to weave back and forth, threatening complete collapse. For whose benefit, I wondered, had she narrated her happy ending, replete with a comically glowering Mawdudi at the supper table and a coyly written scene of her deflowering? Had she written this to allay her parents' fears about her welfare or to establish her triumph? Was it meant as a piece of entertainment or of propaganda?

Putting aside my confusion, I asked Haider Farooq to explain why he thought his father had invited Margaret Marcus to live with his family as his adopted daughter. This was a more fundamental question. For the first time since I stepped through the door there was silence, broken by the sudden arrival of Haider's wife. She turned on the light, offered me a plate of samosas, and retreated to the kitchen. When Haider Farooq answered, his voice was low.

"Because he felt sorry for her," Ali said. "Maryam wrote him that to get her off Islam her parents got her admitted to a mental hospital. She was from a Jew family and her parents were forcing her to get married. Basically, he is saying Mawdudi wanted to rescue her from a marriage to a non-Muslim."

"I've read the letters; she doesn't say anything like that in the original letters." I found my feet. The letters might not be reliable, but by now I could practically recite them.

"He is saying that he doesn't think you have read all of the letters, those letters that he is talking about."

"Where are they?" More letters, I thought bleakly.

"He is saying these letters are there but they basically can never be published."

"She has them?"

"No, we have them."

I followed Maryam Jameelah up a narrow cement staircase to the second floor, my attention fixed on the hiss made by her cheap sandals every time her foot hit the stairs. She had the side-to-side gait of an arthritic. I had arrived at the house unannounced the day before to arrange an interview. Maryam immediately recalled all the personal details I had included in the letter I sent eight months before. She recited them to me.

Maryam still lived with Mohammad Yusuf Khan in the old Hindu neighborhood of Sant Nagar. She shared the house with two stepsons, and their wives and children. Shafiqa had died in 1995, having raised nine children. Of Maryam's own surviving children, her youngest son (named after Haider Farooq) now lived in Chattanooga, Tennessee, where he owned a combination gas station and food mart. Her second son was in Pennsylvania. Her two daughters were still in Pakistan, but only one lived close enough to take her to the doctor. This was the only time Maryam ever left the house.

Instead, it appeared that Maryam Jameelah spent most of her time alone in her second-floor bedroom, where we were now headed for our interview. Here, under the harsh glare of tube lighting, she lived surrounded by eight locked steel almirahs containing her library. Inside the almirahs were countless books and the bound volumes of letters from her family. Here too were more newspaper clippings about her. Ancient copies of *National Geographic* and Time Life encyclopedias supplied by her mother over the years to fuel Maryam's argument against the West were also stored in the almirahs. The only place to sit was on her unmade bed.

From the various bound volumes of family letters Maryam proceeded to pull out hidden photographs of her children and grandchildren to show me. Her husband didn't approve of photographs, although, like Mawdudi, he sometimes sat for them with a disapproving expression on his face. It was a sin to have them, Maryam admitted, a sin to even look at them. But she couldn't help herself. Above her bed she pointed out an air conditioner, bought with the small inheritance she received on her father's death. She would like to do without such modern conveniences, she said, but during the summer her room is like an oven.

Maryam began our first conversation by describing to me the illnesses and deaths of her many longtime correspondents. Her voice was strangely high pitched and keening. Betty had moved into a nursing home without sending her the address, Maryam wailed. It had been years since she had heard from her. As she talked, she rocked her upper body, she flapped her hands; she couldn't sit still. When she was agitated, she slapped her forehead. Her brows were arrowed steeply over her eyes, like a cartoon of anger. She wore a cheap acrylic sweater over layers of clothes against the cold.

Maryam ticked off the medications she had taken over the years, Thorazine and olanzapine among them, and spoke frankly about her illness. Because of her "nervousness," her husband and Shafiqa had looked after her babies; she didn't even nurse them. "I don't know anyone else who would have done that," she said, as if they had had a choice. Nor had she ever learned to cook. There were no canned or packaged foods in Pakistan; everything had to be made from scratch, she explained. It was too time-consuming for her, so Shafiqa and the other women of the household did the cooking. She had her books to write.

From one of her almirahs Maryam retrieved a 1953 edition of *Life* magazine with a cover story on the American teenager. Maryam put the magazine on my lap and slapped the front cover, her fingers lingering nervously over it as if she didn't entirely trust me. Girls in fluffy sleeveless gowns sat and stood on a carpeted staircase of an upper-middle-class home, laughing and whispering. Inside the issue was a transcript of a girl gabbing on the phone with her boyfriend. Maryam wanted to make the point that she'd never had any part of such foolishness, but she couldn't seem to take her eyes off the photographs.

It was hard not to wonder if Peggy had once secretly longed for those dresses, those girlish confidences. She must have asked her mother to find and send exactly this issue. Suddenly Maryam snatched the magazine from my lap and returned it to the almirah. She scurried back to the bed.

"I am going to tell you something I have never told anyone," Maryam said. "Not my parents, not my doctors, not my husband or children."

At that point, I'd been in Maryam's bedroom about ten minutes and had scarcely gotten a word in, much less a question. Despite having come all this way, I wasn't sure I was ready to hear whatever it was Maryam wanted to tell me. It hardly mattered; Maryam was ready to talk.

"When I was eight years old," she began, "I was approached by a group of older teenage boys. They tricked me into going with them to the woods behind the Larchmont apartment complex."

She had to find her way home half undressed. It happened again when she was nine with a boy of eleven; he got her down into the basement of the apartment building. Before anything could happen, she said she heard her father calling. She was able to get her clothes back on before he saw anything. Maryam described what had happened as sexual molestation.

"Why didn't you tell anyone?" I asked, thinking of her five-times-a-week sessions with Dr. Harper.

"I was ashamed," she said.

Was Maryam trying to ingratiate herself, involve my sympathies by telling me this dark secret? The fact that it had happened twice, I supposed, increased her credibility. I wondered vaguely if Peggy had taken off her clothes herself, recalling the "foolish mistakes" she'd written Mawdudi about. No sooner did this thought cross my mind than I realized I didn't really want to know. It was all too easy to imagine she had been chosen by these boys because she was overly trusting in the way that lonely and socially awkward children often are. It would explain her morbid fear of dating. For many, it would explain everything. But I was more surprised by my disinterest. I suddenly became aware of my own impatience, my chilly detachment. Armchair analysis was too easy and, when I got right down to it, explained nothing. What did I want from her? I tried to remember.

"I refused requests to write anti-Semitic tracts for the Jamaat," Maryam said out of nowhere, clearly sensing that my mind was wandering. "Whenever I receive books to review that traffic in anti-Semitism, or books that deny the Holocaust, I throw them in the garbage. It wouldn't have mattered if I were a Muslim convert in Germany in 1938. I would have gone to the ovens with the rest of my family. That is what happened to the family of Muhammad Asad, the author of *The Road to Mecca*. He lost everyone." Until Israel, she said, Islam had never been against the Jews. Anti-Semitism was an import from Europe.

I remembered one thing I wanted her to explain. I wanted to know the real reason the Mawlana had committed her to the Paagal Khanaah. I wanted to get that question answered and then leave. For some reason I couldn't wait to get out of that room. I interrupted her. What had happened in Pattoki that had so angered Mawdudi? On hearing the question, Maryam was immediately mournful, rocking back and forth in agitation, slapping her head.

"I hit Appa over the head with a frying pan. . . . She wasn't hurt. She wasn't harmed, but Appa and Baijan couldn't forgive me for that."

I was so completely shocked, I nearly laughed. Peggy's letters had been so filled with expressions of affection for Appa. Haider Farooq had said Maryam had attacked her in a jealous rage. Had he been right?

Why did you do that? How could you do such a thing?

Maryam couldn't or wouldn't remember. She said she was mentally upset.

Khan Sahib had warned her about being too free with her confidences, Maryam told me the next time we met. Khan Sahib was what she called her husband. "You might be an enemy," she said, shooting me a sideways glance, "ready to use my words against me."

Was I? I wasn't sure. For nearly a year I had shifted between fascination and mistrust of this woman, a woman whose core beliefs struck deeply at my own and yet whose critique of the West was both familiar and unerring. Her letters moved and perplexed me. Her books unsettled me, stirred me into another way of looking at the complacent assumptions of my world. In person, however, Maryam seemed less sure of herself than her books had led me to believe. And Khan Sahib was right to be concerned. She was inordinately trusting. Yet her eagerness for company, her obvious loneliness, disarmed me. When I pointed out the inconsistencies or impracticalities of her ideas, when I questioned her about *hudud* and Sharia, Maryam blandly admitted she didn't have all the answers. "Ask the ulema," she said before jumping up to dig something new out of her almirah.

"Do you regret anything you have written?" I finally thought to ask.

"Yes," she said.

In a pamphlet titled "Who Is Maudoodi?" Maryam described her mentor as a "great Mujaddid of the Modern Age," going so far as to suggest that the mystic who had foretold his birth "might have been an angel in disguise." She now regretted this bit of hyperbole. Maryam couldn't think of anything else.

Though Haider Farooq insisted that Maryam's breach with his father was irrevocable, Mohammad Yusuf Khan never stopped working for Mawdudi's party. And once things calmed down, Maryam, with Mawdudi's tacit blessing, made her name as an

Islamic pamphleteer and ideologue. They would exchange books and holiday greetings. Maryam would send her prayers whenever the Mawlana suffered a health crisis; he in turn would mark the arrival of her babies with a note. His last handwritten letter was sent the year before his death and addressed to "my dear daughter in Islam." Though women would never become part of the inner circle of the Jamaat, after Mawdudi's death Maryam was paid to check the English-language proofs of his works. Jamaat officials would ask Maryam to defend the party when it came under criticism from the Western press.

In 1987 Maryam wrote an article reappraising Mawdudi's work. She dug this out of her cupboard for me to read, but kept on talking. She was grateful to Mawdudi for saving her from America, for finding her a husband. I tried to read. After his death, however, as Mawdudi's work was translated into English, she began to realize just how adulterated by modernism, even Orientalism, his idea of Islam was. She cited his description of the Prophet as "the real pioneer of the modern age" with undisguised contempt. She dismissed his desire to harness science and modern technology, which he viewed as "morally neutral," as a utopian fantasy of an Islamic society. In her view, far from being a return to Islam's essential traditions, Mawdudi's vision of Islam was modernism at its very worst.

In fact, Maryam was no longer greatly invested in the dream of a genuine Islamic state in Pakistan or anywhere else.

"I think the best that can be hoped for in the present situation is a liberal government that respects freedom of religion and freedom of expression. Islam needs more saints, not more politicians," Maryam said. I recognized this last line from recent published interviews.

Maryam had not shared her newfound quietism with the readers of her previous books. After her mother's death in 1984, the steady stream of book parcels came to an end and with it the research materials she required. Since the publication of *Quest for the Truth* in 1989, Maryam had limited her writing to book reviews. She hadn't written a word about the war being waged in the name of Islam against America. She hadn't written about the beheading of journalist Daniel Pearl. She hadn't denounced the Taliban or Osama bin Laden. During the government's siege of the Red Mosque in Islamabad in the spring of 2007, the leadership of the Jamaat-e-Islami had voiced support for the embattled jihadists who had barricaded themselves with hostages inside. When they were "martyred" by the army, the Jamaat-e-Islami leaped in to make political hay. But Maryam was quiet. Even her critique of Mawdudi was muted in tone. Though it was published in a Jamaati publication, neither her husband nor his party registered the depth of her renunciation.

"Their English isn't good enough," Maryam confided sotto voce with a distinct note of triumph. Khan Sahib still believed that she was in ideological lockstep with Mawdudi, she said.

"Don't tell him," she said, as if we were now girlfriends in league together.

While I always brought a long list of questions to Maryam's house, I never seemed to get to them. Maryam would begin talking and explaining some key point and it was difficult to interrupt. There was a rehearsed quality to these speeches. She never repeated herself and she spoke in perfect paragraphs. I always knew exactly what was coming because I had read a nearly word for word version of it elsewhere. I found myself impatiently completing her sentences.

Yet it wasn't until later, when I transcribed the interview alone in my room in Gulberg, that I grasped how deeply Maryam Jameelah's affect unsettled me. On the tape I would hear myself acquiesce to Maryam's new line. The devastation wreaked upon the environment by the West was now a subject of deep concern to her. I noticed that every time I tried to probe more deeply, Maryam managed to divert my line of questions by droning on interminably. No sooner would I arrive in Maryam's room than I couldn't wait to leave. And yet as soon as I left, I felt compelled to return, as if I had forgotten something.

I remembered reading a psychiatrist's account of his growing unease during the long hours he spent treating a patient. He would begin to imagine that his patient was cannibalizing him: "I thought of the amoeba ingesting a particle of food—and ingesting me, actually." Merely stepping into her room, he said, was "like going inside her."

Not long before his death Mawlana Mawdudi received a letter from an old Jamaati colleague. Wasi Mazhar Nadwi had been with him when he founded the Jamaat-e-Islami in 1941 but had been expelled from the party in 1976. Mawdudi himself had resigned from active involvement in 1972 for health reasons but also because he had been shattered by his party's failure to capture many seats in the long-awaited 1971 parliamentary elections.

Wasi Mazhar Nadwi wrote: When we created this party, these were our objectives. He proceeded to outline the original mission of Jamaat-e-Islami before concluding: We did not achieve any of them. What exactly did we achieve?

I am aware not only of the failures you have listed in your letter, Mawdudi replied, but also of failures you cannot begin to conceive of. But now that I am an old man, with failing faculties, there is nothing further I can do.

In the 1970s the Mawlana had watched the movement he founded be compromised by Saudi oil money. The student wing of the Jamaat, the Islami Jamiat Talaba, had turned to violence, taking over the student union of Quaid-e-Azam University, policing secular-minded professors, and beating up Western-clad students like a nascent Taliban. Many of these hooligans would go on to take positions of party leadership. According to Ahmad Farooq, his second-oldest son, during this time Mawdudi had watched his closest deputies compromise their Islamic principles out of political expediency. He knew some of them reported on his activities to the government.

Once he fell ill, Mawdudi was at the mercy of ambitious men in the Jamaat he imagined he had trained in selfless submission to Allah. After the 1977 coup brought General Muhammad Zia-ul-Haq to power, the government began to actively court the party. Prime Minister Zulfiqar Ali Bhutto had initially appointed the general, a member of the Jamaat, to the post of army chief to keep the Jamaat happy, but Zia would be Bhutto's undoing. With Zia's coup, the relationship between the Jamaat-e-Islami and the central government became something more insidious and symbiotic. Zia so admired Mawdudi that he distributed copies of the multivolume *Towards Understanding the Qur'an* to his prize soldiers and proposed to include it in the army curriculum. Yet he, too, used the Jamaat for his own ends.

By 1979, the year of Mawdudi's death, the long-simmering ambitions of the Jamaat-e-Islami seemed to gain purchase. In February, to Mawdudi's great pleasure, Zia introduced the most extreme forms of the Islamic penal code. Six months later, at the urging of both Mawdudi and the new amir of the Jamaat, Mian Tufail Muhammad, Bhutto was executed on a trumped-up murder charge. Perhaps this accounted for the chastened tone of Mawdudi's letter to Mazhar Nadwi.

At the end of his life, there was no sign of the moral awakening Mawdudi had once prayed for. There was no sign of the Islamic renaissance he had called for so passionately in his speeches. The political leadership of Pakistan, though now adept at exploiting his party, was no less corrupt, the West no less powerful. At best, Mawdudi concluded in his letter, he would be remembered as yet another in a long line of men who had tried and failed to revitalize Islam. Yet he could not accept that his paradigm might be at fault. He prayed that at least the shell of the Jamaat-e-Islami would remain intact until he was no longer around to worry about it.

Though Mawdudi imagined he had failed, for many he remains the purest embodiment of the most noble and heroic aims of the Muslim faith. His godly voice, his incorruptible dream of an Islamic state, are now in everyone's head, haunting even the most secular-minded citizens of Muslim countries. Faisal Shahzad, the Pakistani-American who parked an explosives-filled Nissan Pathfinder in Times Square in 2010, cited Mawdudi's books in e-mails to friends. There will doubtless be more like him, converts and native-born, who will find in Mawdudi and his ideological heirs a justification for their hatred of the West. But even ordinary law-abiding Muslims can see for themselves how America has colluded with corrupt governments to serve its own ends. In this way their countries are kept weak, their people deprived of a more hopeful future. In short, none of us can escape Mawdudi, even long after his death.

The revolution Mawdudi envisioned finally did take place. By popular referendum, on April 1, 1979, Iran officially became an Islamic republic; the Ayatollah Ruhollah Khomeini its supreme leader. By then the Mawlana had moved to Buffalo, New York, where his son Farooq had settled, for medical treatment. According to Ahmad Farooq, though his father was in pain, both his parents enjoyed their brief time in America. Mawdudi passed away on September 22, 1979, missing the news of the Soviet invasion of Afghanistan just over three months later.

More than the revolution in Iran, this war would become the crucible that would transform the ideological legacy of Maryam Jameelah and Abul Ala Mawdudi. Within weeks of the Soviet invasion, Osama bin Laden made his first visit to Pakistan, ferrying money for the Jamaat from the Saudis. It was not long before CIA money and donated weaponry began pouring into Pakistan. An Afghan branch of the Jamaat-e-Islami had sparked the insurgency that prompted the invasion, but it was American money that funded the full-fledged war that followed.

"Freedom fighters" from Egypt, Iraq, China, Chechnya, Somalia,

Saudi Arabia, Tajikistan, Uzbekistan, Nigeria, Turkmenistan, and India arrived to bring down the "evil empire." The American fight against the godless communists had finally been reframed as Sharia-sanctioned jihad. As Pakistan now became the principal front in the cold war, great numbers of Jamaatis joined the Pakistani intelligence service. In the 1980s and 1990s the Jamaat-e-Islami would become the mother of all jihadi organizations.

"We are not bigots or fanatics," Maryam wrote in her 1969 *Manifesto of the Islamic Movement.* "We make our case for Islam on the basis of calm and logical reason." Yet by 1979 Maryam, too, had reached the end of calm and logical reason. As the Afghan war heated up, Maryam began to relish the talk of jihad. With the death of Mawdudi, perhaps she hoped to claim the title of ideological heir. In cheap, simply written pamphlets devoured by restless teenagers in Kashmir, Islamabad, Tehran, and Brooklyn, Maryam Jameelah began writing accounts of famed mujahidin. Whether their long-ago battles were against British or French imperialists, Zionists or Christian crusaders, each of these mujahidin was shown to be a true Muslim of sterling and gallant character; a "freedom fighter" who had embraced violent jihad as the "highest form of worship."

"Make up your mind to participate in jihad," Maryam quoted the eighteenth-century jihadist Sayyid Ahmad as saying, as he brandished his carbine and matchlock. "Learn the use of weapons for that purpose.... Mystical exercises can never excel the virtues of fighting in the way of Allah. Did not our own Prophet take up arms against the infidels to spread the light of Truth?" "Since we are all destined to die anyhow, is it not better to die as a *Shahid* or martyr ... at the peak of one's mental and physical powers and use-fulness to society? ... We must ... launch an offensive and provide from the Quran and the Sunnah the only remedies that can save mankind from destruction and collective suicide." Attempts to rec-oncile Islam with the man-made philosophies of Voltaire, Darwin, Marx, Freud, and the French existentialists would mean the de-struction of the human race: "Everything they stand for [is] EVIL!"

William James wrote that in "the possibility of violent death [lies] the soul of all romance." Among those members of the student wing of the Jamaat-e-Islami who signed up for the Afghan jihad were the two sons of Maryam Jameelah.

I resolved that my last interview with Maryam would be different. As soon as I sat down, I asked her if she had ever considered how her denunciation of Westernized Muslims and Americans might have inspired the extremists of al-Qaeda or the Taliban. Maryam immediately became agitated, either because she had already worried herself over this question or because she hadn't expected me to ask it. She began to rock.

"I have never preached violence," she said, punctuating her insistence with a high-pitched "oooo, no, no, oooo, no, no." "I wrote only on a *philosophical* plane," she said, with emphasis. "I never incited hatred of Westerners as *individuals*," she said. She wrote admiringly only of those mujahidin and freedom fighters who fought against foreign domination one or two centuries ago, *never* al-Qaeda or the Taliban.

When I pointed out that these distinctions might be lost on some, Maryam was insistent, stubborn. "I never wrote with any of that in mind," she said. "I feel no responsibility." Besides, she added, in the sixties and seventies, when she was publishing, "extremism was not evident."

But violent extremism was evident by then in Egypt, I pointed out. Maryam had taken Wilfred Cantwell Smith to task for unjustly maligning the Muslim Brotherhood. In one essay she quoted a long passage from his *Islam in Modern History*, only to discount it. Smith had written:

All the discontent of men who find the modern world too much for them can in movements such as the Muslim Brotherhood find action and a satisfaction. . . . The burning of Cairo, the assassination of prime ministers, the intimidation of Christians, the vehemence and hatred in their literature—all of this is to be understood in terms of a people who have lost their way, whose heritage has proven unequal to modernity, whose leaders have been dishonest, whose ideals have failed. In this aspect, the new Islamic upsurge is a force not to solve problems but to intoxicate those who can no longer abide the failure to solve them.

Pure slander, Maryam insisted. The Muslim brothers weren't illiterate rabble-rousers; they were well-educated and responsible youth from modern colleges and universities. There was "hardly any truth" in this, she wrote then, as if she couldn't quite come up with a blanket absolution.

I asked again. How could Maryam be sure her writings hadn't played a role in the radicalization of Muslim youth?

"I can't be so sure. I don't know every reader of my books. All I can say is that it was never in my mind. It was never my intention."

Maryam paused and then perked up. Her books were never cited in jihadist publications! And what of her mentors—Sayyid Qutb? Mawlana Mawdudi? Were they responsible or did they, too, only write on a "philosophical plane"?

"These are the writers they cite."

"You created a very convincing picture of the West as an evil place."

Maryam Jameelah didn't hesitate: "I still feel that it is."

"And 9/11? Was it justified?"

"I think it was horrible. I never wrote anything in favor of that sort of thing. And you know the Muslims who were charged with 9/11 were not good Muslims. Before they boarded the plane they were drinking and gambling . . ."

I thought that was squirrelly and cut her off. "By that measure, bin Laden is a good Muslim." Maryam neatly changed tack.

"I don't think anything justifies 9/11. But if the building had been empty, if nobody had been in the World Trade Center at the time of the bombing *[sic]*, it might have been justified. It couldn't have been empty, but if it *were* empty, its destruction would have been justified as a symbol of American finance. Because it was the center of Western civilization and so was the Pentagon."

The destruction would have been justified because it was the center of Western civilization. Was this what I had come to Pakistan to hear?

"But it was horrible because of the many Muslims who were killed in the Trade Center; there were many Muslims working in the Trade Center."

I stopped listening. What began as childish tantrums had, over time, become rages. Maryam's rages, in turn, had grown grandiose until she believed the destruction of the World Trade Center and the Pentagon were appropriate targets for spiritual practice, provided no Muslims were killed.

As I was leaving, I thanked Maryam's stepdaughter-in-law for the tea and samosas she had brought up to the room. Her smile slowed my eagerness to flee: I began to feel myself again. Though she spoke no English, I was suddenly thanking her effusively. It wasn't until I got into the car that I realized how abruptly I had left Maryam's room. I'm not sure I said good-bye.

One week later Benazir Bhutto was assassinated, shattering the fragile atmosphere of hope I had found on my arrival in Pakistan. I was in India when I heard the news. I watched the civil-rights lawyer who had given me Haider Farooq's telephone number weep like a child on television. At the sight of this weeping woman, the nuances of the argument between Islam and the West over modernity, the details of the dueling narratives of Margaret Marcus and Maryam Jameelah, seemed entirely beside the point.

The war had its own life now.

By the time I left Lahore, Haider Farooq and I had reached a kind of truce. I had made him laugh. He told me his father was a misguided man, but a good father. Yet he refused to produce Maryam's original letters. I enlisted intermediaries to beseech him, but to no avail. He held no grudges, he insisted, in case such a thought might have occurred to me. If Maryam disavowed writing them he might change his mind. "Let her deny it," he said.

Did it really matter, I wondered, if Maryam exaggerated the peril she would be in if she remained in America? Wasn't life-long commitment a sufficient calamity? In the meantime, it was enough to have glimpsed the curious boy within the embattled and conflicted son of Mawlana Mawdudi. This, too, was Mawdudi's patrimony.

I didn't return to the reading room for a long time. When I finally went back to the library, I took a closer look at the Mawdudi correspondence to see if I could determine whether letters were missing. Unlike the correspondence with her parents, which consisted entirely of Margaret's letters, both sides were on deposit. On Margaret's side, there were a number of postmarked aerograms to Mawlana Abul Ala Mawdudi. It briefly crossed my mind that Maryam had snuck into Mawdudi's study and pinched them, but it was more likely that Mawdudi had returned the ones he could find to Mohammad Yusuf Khan. By the time the correspondence was published, Mawdudi might have felt responsible for the marriage and Maryam's upkeep. He would have known that a book of her correspondence with him would sell well.

Apart from a few aerograms, however, I now saw that the majority of Maryam's letters to Mawdudi were retyped and paginated like setting copy, either because she didn't have the originals or because she had decided to rewrite them for publication. I hadn't noticed any of this earlier. It would be impossible, I realized, to know when these letters were written or how much they had been altered.

The Mawlana Abul Ala Mawdudi's side of the correspondence was bound separately and prefaced by a cover note describing the letters as "unexpurgated." This volume included obviously authentic letters signed in his hand, on his personal stationery. It even included his letters in Urdu, which his secretary had translated. But here and there were letters that seemed questionable. These were typed on generic Jamaat-e-Islami office stationery, and Mawdudi's printed signature was pasted in. The glue was brown with age.

I compared both the authentic and questionable letters with their published counterparts in *The Correspondence of Maulana Mawdudi and Maryam Jameelah*. I found that Mawdudi's letters to Margaret Marcus as published were clearly edited to obscure the fact that a number of her letters to him were missing. I also caught a few details that Maryam sought to clean up. In one letter Mawdudi cautioned Margaret Marcus that she could not really do justice to the new book she proposed to write without proficiency in Urdu, Persian, Arabic, and Turkish. This was cut. In another, Mawdudi pointed out that the Muslim name she had chosen—Jameel—was a man's name. Maryam retroactively corrected it. I felt as if the entire archive had been rendered suspect. I opened another gray box.

When I had first read the letters collected in the 1989 book *Quest for the Truth: Memoirs of Childhood and Youth in America, 1945–1962: The Story of One Western Convert,* I had been puzzled by a few things. First, there were no accompanying manuscript letters in the archive. Second, Maryam referred to the book as a memoir. A letter to Betty oddly dated November 31, 1949, supposedly written when Peggy was fifteen, had also caught my eye. This was the same letter in which she described Eleanor Roosevelt's speech glorifying the new state of Israel at Mamaroneck High School the previous evening.

I did a search in the back issues of the local paper and discovered that Eleanor Roosevelt's speech wasn't until the following February. The letter hadn't been written on the date indicated. So when was it written? Peggy described Roosevelt's speech as all about the triumph of the state of Israel, an issue on which she was known to be sympathetic. The *Larchmont Times* described the Roosevelt speech as being about the drafting of the Human Rights Proclamation.

And then there was the letter written to Betty from Hudson River State Hospital. On my third or fourth reading I finally noticed that Peggy had begun the letter by describing the stratagem she had taken to mail it: "I had to sneak it out directly to the staff post office box; luckily the clerk didn't suspect I was an inmate."

Had Maryam written all these letters in Pakistan? Did that explain why she had indulged in a meticulous evocation of her childhood: the games of make-believe, the multicourse holiday meals, the Christmas concerts, beautiful dolls and memorable books? There had always been something odd about them, as if she had set out to evoke a lost and more innocent world, like Mohammad Yusuf Khan's tales of Jullundur. Yet for every pleasant memory, there was an ugly one; the cruel bunkmates at camp, indifferent psychologists, bullying teachers, impatient job placement administrators, and enraged Zionists. In the initial twenty-four letters from Pakistan, Maryam had often responded to the family news related in her parents' letters and fretted about those that had gone astray. The American letters acknowledged no family news and expressed no such concerns, I finally realized, because they had never been sent.

I now saw that Maryam had composed these letters as missives to posterity, a Cinderella backstory plotted to foreshadow how her embrace of Islam had rescued her from America. The evils of Western civilization amounted to no more than a stage drop for her private travails. It was as if Peggy never ceased mining the material of her own life to establish certain proof that Islam was the answer to all the riddles it posed.

Before Myra left on her round-the-world cruise, she had sent her daughter's twenty-four letters to Mr. Parr at the New York Public Library, most likely on Peggy's instructions. There they would sit until I came along to unearth them, childishly eager to know what happened next and how it all turned out. I had been a willing party to Margaret's elaborate game of dress-up. By the time these letters made their way to the manuscript vault, Maryam had the consolation that the story of her journey to Pakistan from America, despite its unexpected detour to the madhouse, had the storybook ending she'd dreamed of. But what kind of story did I have?

Dispirited and disillusioned, I had put off reading the two bound volumes of later letters, donated to the library in 1992. Documenting thirty years of marriage, motherhood, and political upheaval, they had never been published. When I finally turned to them it was immediately clear that, like the first twenty-four, they had not been altered or rewritten. Unlike the first twenty-four letters, however, with their evildoers, dramatic dialogue, sudden reversals, and rescues from certain peril, there is little melodrama. The story the later letters tell is no fairy tale. Soon after Maryam posted her twenty-fourth letter, announcing her marriage to Mohammad Yusuf Khan, her Oriental adventure had come to an end and an entirely different story began.

On September 11, 1963, just over a month after her release from the asylum, Maryam Jameelah once again suffered what she called a mental relapse, perhaps brought on by her co-wife's unceasing hostility, perhaps by the realization that she was already pregnant. Over the course of the subsequent twelve months, Maryam Jameelah would suffer from dysentery, malaria, and flu, all the while in the grip of her special illness. That year Herbert and Myra, in the midst of their world travels, made the first of two visits to her, a visit that nearly coincided with their daughter's thirtieth birthday.

Her parents didn't stay long and, according to Maryam, were anxious to leave almost as soon as they arrived. There was little they could do but leave money to pay for a doctor to see her through her pregnancy. Their money also paid for eggs and meat to build up their daughter's strength in her final weeks. These were considered expensive items that Mohammad Yusuf Khan could not afford to provide. When she came to write her parents of subsequent events, in the first of the bound volume letters, Margaret didn't say whether these foods were shared with the rest of the family, or with her equally pregnant co-wife. Ayesha Jameelah was born soon after Margaret's parents left, not long after Shafiqa delivered a baby of her own, her sixth.

Spending large parts of the day in a stupor, Maryam was unable to look after the infant. Instead, she remained in her room, sleeping and rarely emerging. Ayesha Jameelah was left in the care of a teenage niece of Mohammad Yusuf Khan and fed watered-down buffalo milk laced with sugar. The baby would live for four months, lying on a charpoy in the courtyard, sunk in listlessness under a canopy of pink nylon netting to keep off the flies. Her cousins and half siblings gave her intermittent attention before she slipped away.

A nephew awakened Maryam the day her daughter died. "Ayesha is calling for you," he shouted from the transom of her room. In a daze she rose and went down to the courtyard, her legs trembling from fever or fear. There Ayesha lay blue and still beneath a shabby quilt, her ears stuffed with cotton and her jaw bound with a strip of cloth. When Khan Sahib arrived, he showed no sign of emotion but simply stood next to his wife while his niece filled a big bucket of water from the pump and, after washing the baby over the sewage drain, wrapped the small form in a shroud. Men from the Jamaat waited outside to accompany Khan Sahib to the burial site. Maryam watched from behind her curtain as they disappeared from sight down the dark narrow street.

A month later her illness receded and Maryam once again returned to her writing. She reported Ayesha's fate to her parents at the close of a thirteen-page letter, noting that the day of her death coincided with a Supreme Court reversal of another government ban on the Jamaat-e-Islami. She wrote of her daughter's death from malnutrition seemingly without emotion. "I look up at the pink sky," the letter concludes, "soon the Azan from the mosques will call the sun-set prayer, and with a sudden pang of poignancy, I realize that my youth has gone and I have entered into the full ripeness of mature womanhood."

I read these two bound volumes of letters in the hope that I would find answers to the last of my questions. How well did Maryam's pronouncements on the true Islamic way of life serve her as a wife and mother? How well did her frail spirit withstand a life defined not by abstract notions but by whooping cough, typhoid, malaria, smallpox, diphtheria, cholera, polio, malnutrition, unending pregnancies, and the nervous collapses that followed the birth of every baby? I read them to see how Maryam Jameelah explained what had happened to Pakistan over the past forty years. Had she achieved something noteworthy, or had she squandered her life on a dream? If the story didn't end happily, how did it end?

When I finished reading the last letter, I sat down and wrote once again to Maryam Jameelah.

"There is no joy in motherhood for me."

These are your words, Maryam. You wrote them in a moment of weakness at the prospect of bearing your fifth child. You had wanted an IUD; Khan Sahib wouldn't agree to it. Despite ten children with Shafiqa and five with you, the decision to have another child was Allah's to make. How could you argue? Like Mawdudi, you believed that birth control was an invitation to indulge in illicit sex.

Khan Sahib also refused to vaccinate your children. *"Modern industrialization promotes the philosophy that man can banish poverty, disease and ignorance without divine aid."* These are your words. *"Science has made man independent of Allah."* Is your faith that tenuous?

In the same letter where you lament Khan Sahib's stubbornness over birth control and inoculations, you describe a plan to write a book denouncing the women's liberation movement. *"In*

211

Islam . . . [a woman's] success as a person is judged according to her fidelity to her husband and the rearing of worthy children. . . . While men are the actors on the stage of history, the function of women is to be their helpers concealed from public gaze . . . a less exciting and more humble role perhaps, [but] essential for the preservation of our way of life."

Why were you intent on preserving a way of life you never managed to live yourself? You stood on the stage of history and let Shafiqa raise your babies.

"I just can't cope by myself with a new baby: I'll be just as incompetent with my fifth as I was with my first. I don't need to talk anything out: I just need somebody else to take over the care of the baby and do what I will not be able to do."

In your books you extolled an Islamic ideal that proved of no practical use in your own life. Shafiqa made that possible, yet you were consistently critical of her.

"Too many Pakistani women I know have the dirty habit of continuously littering the floors of their homes . . . with garbage and rubbish. Islamic education should teach girls cleanliness and orderliness."

While you complained about the filth and the constant food shortages, Shafiqa endured, not out of the strength of her faith (in this too she was grossly delinquent) but because she did not have the choice.

It is one thing to espouse these views as a sheltered and single American woman. But how could you continue to denounce science, with its "naked atheism and materialism," while you were asking your mother to send you books on infant nutrition? Or while you were pleading with your father to intervene with your husband on the subject of your children's vaccinations for polio, smallpox, and diphtheria?

To whom should your sisters in faith direct their appeals?

Your books on the "perverted 'cultural' values" of the West, you boasted, brought in more income than Khan Sahib's work for the Jamaat-e-Islami. Did you write them for money?

"Feminism is an unnatural, artificial and abnormal product of contemporary social disintegration which in turn is the inevitable result of the rejection of all transcendental, absolute moral and spiritual values. . . . The result will be suicide, not only of a single nation as in the past, but of the entire human race."

"[The women's liberation movement] . . . AIMS TO DESTROY THE ENTIRE INSTITUTION OF MARRIAGE, HOME AND FAMILY."

Tell me, how many people did these American women kill?

How many wars did they start?

How many young men did they flog?

"According to Islamic teachings, life is not a pleasure trip but an examination."

How carefully have you weighed what you have written against how you have lived your life?

Can we talk, as you once did to your parents, about more immediate things than abstract questions of transcendental values? Can we begin with the health, education, and future happiness of our children, the histories we share, the struggles all of us face in trying to live a meaningful life? Can we reach some kind of respectful accommodation?

The past will always be there. It will be pieced together from old books and photographs, taken from gray boxes, locked almirahs, and unreliable memories. But the long walk of history has never been stopped. This walk leaves some behind brokenhearted while others pass them by triumphant, anticipating the next bend in the road. Their stories, like your own, will never be as simple as you would like them to be. They will be complicated.

But this is not complicated. Muslim youth are killing their sisters and brothers, mothers and fathers. This is social disintegration. Young men and women are killing themselves to better kill others. This is perversion. In Lahore, saints' shrines have been locked, pilgrims turned away, out of fears of suicide bombers intent on poisoning the very wellspring of your faith.

Yet now you are quiet.

Now you say, "Ask the ulema."

You drew a savage and titillating portrait of America and of those who didn't practice their Muslim faith exactly the way you wanted them to, yet you disclaim all responsibility for the crimes these youth commit and still conspire to commit every day in Pakistan or New Jersey or Somalia or Malaysia. *"We must always be prepared to wage Jihad . . . [Mujahidin] must be trained in combat." "The Mujahid . . . will not merely oppose* Kufr *but be inwardly and outwardly equipped to establish a true Islamic society according to that of the Holy Prophet Mohammad."*

Your words. The Jamaat-e-Islami no longer needs your books to sell Muslim youth on martyrdom. They have others to do that now.

You told me you had had no opinion one way or another about your sons' decision to go to Afghanistan. Their decision, like that of their brothers today, was entirely their own.

Do not all young people desire proof that they are good in the eyes of God? Don't sons want to make their parents proud? *"[A good Muslim mother] should entertain her young children with the thrilling deeds of the great Muslims past and present and try to inspire them with the desire to emulate these virtues."* Why were all these great Muslims jihadis? Where are the poets and painters and singers?

Did your sons realize that the war they were sent to fight was not the one you and the Jamaat-e-Islami sold them on? Is that why they left Pakistan?

Would you have preferred that they had been martyred in a proxy war of the Americans?

"The Jamaat-e-Islami has become too concerned with politics. Party leaders should reflect more on matters of faith and spiritual purity."

These are your words now.

And these are mine: What is this spiritual purity? When the jihadis come to the door of your house in Sant Nagar, will they find the family living there sufficiently pure? Don't you have an American passport? Don't your children and grandchildren? Will it matter to these men that you have been a Muslim for fifty years, or will someone remind them you were born a Jew?

When will you speak up?

If not now, I asked Maryam Jameelah, when?

> c/o Mohammad Yusuf Khan
> 15/49 Sant Nagar
> Lahore
> PAKISTAN

November 20, 2008

This is to acknowledge safe receipt of your last letter of November 6. As a nonbeliever and non-Muslim, you have the right to express your own views in your forthcoming book. However, at this late stage at the end of my life, I stand by everything I have written and spoken and have no intention of making any change in my views on Mawlana Mawdudi, Islam, or the West. All I ask of you is to send me copies of your book or articles as soon as published. I will preserve them carefully in my files. With regards.

Sincerely,
Maryam Jameelah

CHAPTER 9

The Lifted Veil

"I" and "you" are the veil
Between heaven and earth;
Lift this veil and you will see
No sect and no religion.

When "I" and "You" do not exist
What is mosque? What is synagogue?
What is fire temple?

Mahmud Shabistari

The trap of history, it turns out, cannot easily be unsprung.

When Maryam was not trying to sugarcoat things or concoct some kind of Oriental romance, she was a more unforgiving inquisitor than I would ever be. She would never lose sight of the fact that she might die at any moment and would have to answer for the life she had lived. Her most earnest conversation would never be with me, or with those impressionable youths who had once devoured her books, or even with the Mawlana Mawdudi. This conversation would always be with Herbert and Myra, with her past, and with a (hopefully) compassionate God. It is all too easy to revert to the certainties and judgments life in a powerful state affords us. Maryam was neither oracular or mad, but simply an old woman, filled with fears, living alone in a room with little more than her faith, her library, and letters from her grandchildren for comfort. It was as if a veil had been removed and I could now see her face clearly.

When Margaret Marcus was a young woman, her questions were an endless source of anxiety. Her search for happiness and fulfillment had brought her to Islam. But where had the answers the Qur'an provided gotten her? Not to a perfect society, certainly. Not to an end of questions. Mawdudi, too, was denied a peaceful end. According to his son, Ahmad Farooq, it was a hospital visit from a member of the Jamaat-e-Islami that provoked the heart attack that ended his life. Yet Maryam's faith had consoled her in the acute loneliness of her life in New York and Lahore, in the darkness of her mental breakdowns, in the sorrows and failures of motherhood. Her faith granted her the assurance that evils she had witnessed and injustices she had suffered would not go unpunished. And her community of faith had provided her a loyal husband and a family that accepted her place in it, whatever her afflictions.

Herbert and Myra's love had also sustained her. In the anxious weeks before she left for Pakistan, Margaret Marcus had asked the Mawlana a simple question: how was it that though her parents were unbelievers, they were still good and kind people? This went to the heart not only of the supposed divide between the West and the Muslim world, but also of the divide between believers and nonbelievers. Whatever one's private beliefs, whatever one's particular culture, politics, or set of values, what is more transcendent than the love and concern of a parent for a child?

All that was good in Herbert and Myra was due to the trace of belief that still clung to their hearts, Mawdudi answered. After a generation or so, this trace would inevitably disappear, leaving their children or their children's children open to the worst depravities. I didn't entirely discount this argument. Still, for the umpteenth time I wondered: how did he know this?

"Nay, but they are sure of nothing!" (52:36). The fifty-second sura of the Qur'an was an exasperated debate between Allah and

Muhammad over what to do with those unruly mortals who, after hearing the Prophet recite the suras, decided that without more certain proof of divine inspiration, they couldn't be sure that Muhammad hadn't made them up. He might be a poet or mad. They would take a wait-and-see attitude.

In reply, Allah commanded his Prophet to remind his doubters that he was "neither a soothsayer nor a madman" (52:29). But if these doubters truly suspected Muhammad was crazy, for Muhammad to simply insist that he wasn't would never be a promising line of defense.

Mystified by the Prophet's difficulties getting the Meccan tribes to follow him, Allah was driven to ask His Prophet what he supposed the problem was. "Is it their minds that bid them take this attitude or are they simply people filled with overweening arrogance?" Perhaps they imagine they created themselves out of thin air? Or maybe they had a different "stairway to heaven" (52:33, 35–38)?

Was there a hint of sarcasm here?

Or, Allah continued, did they think that given enough time they would eventually puzzle out the mystery of creation and write down their own illuminating verses (52:41)? Let them try their hand at it! (52:34) Definitely sarcasm. Allah posed His questions as if men were as much a riddle to Him as He was to them.

There was a story in the *Mishkat al-Masabih* that touched on souls undone by questions such as I had been asking. Baghawi's collection of ahadith drew from a number of esteemed traditions, but also included material not found elsewhere, all arranged thematically. In a chapter titled "Evil Promptings," the Prophet got straight to the point. Weary and exasperated with his doubting Thomases, Muhammad had finally settled on an answer that pleased him. Men will continue to pose one question after another, he said. Inevitably someone will ask, "God created all things, but who created God?" This was indeed just the kind of big question that always defeated me. But the Prophet had an answer. He advised that one must simply reply "I believe in God and in His messengers" and be done with it.

There was not a little wisdom in that. Spitting three times on your left side for good measure was also recommended. The devil was behind this last question, the Prophet seemed to suggest, threatening to undo the hard-won understandings that came before it. Not all questions, I hoped, just this last one. That sounded about right.

So, putting aside the problematic notion of an existential rift between Islam and the West, how did I begin to repair the impasse between Maryam and me? In the eighty-sixth verse of the fourth sura, and the sixty-first of the eighth, I found instruction. This was how I understood what I read. When, in the course of battle, the believer hears a greeting of peace, even from someone who might possibly belong to the enemy camp but who, in outward appearance, has peaceful intentions, the believer is required to accept it.

"If they incline towards peace, incline thou to it as well."

And Lo! Allah, the knower, hearer, and seer, takes into account all things.

I wrote Maryam again to say that if I failed to understand her, it was because I lacked sufficient imagination and detachment, not because I was a nonbeliever or kufr. If it was that simple I might have dismissed her out of hand, as she now hoped to dismiss me. Instead, part of the difficulty of the task I had set myself stemmed from the effort required to set aside the many beliefs I did have. I then asked Maryam if I could write her story as if she were writing once again to her family. Having her voice pass through my own, perhaps I might understand her better. I wanted her blessing to use the correspondence in her archive, the doctored and make-believe letters as well as the real ones, to quote and paraphrase and arrange as I saw fit. It was a great deal to ask. She would have to trust me.

For years I had been writing this story as if it were mine alone to tell. Yet only now did I see that the story of how Margaret Marcus became Maryam Jameelah was only half of what there was to tell, and the easy half at that. In a postscript I mentioned that I had tracked down Barbara Kenny and Julia Bustin. I thought she would be pleased to know that they remembered her fondly.

---

c/o Mohammad Yusuf Khan
15/49 Sant Nagar
Lahore
PAKISTAN

March 15, 2009

Thank you for your letter of February 23. Mujahidin must never be confused with "terrorists." All the Mujahidin I have written about were genuine freedom fighters struggling on their native soil against foreign occupation and oppressive imperialism. All of them strictly observed the dictates of lawful jihad to distinguish between combatants and innocent women and children. If I have praised them it is because they deserve it in their thoroughly legitimate struggle. . . .

My most recent article, submitted to an Indian Muslim weekly in Delhi under the title "Muslim Savages," deplores the wholesale destruction of girls' schools and even hospitals, and the banning of female education so far as threatening to throw acid on any woman or girl who ventures outside of her home. . , . Radical extremism is even worse than modernism. I feel quite dismayed that most Pakistanis I know, including my husband, dispute even the existence of al-Qaeda or Taliban and blame all of Pakistan's troubles on a grand conspiracy of America, Israel, and India to destroy Islam/Muslims. Incredible as it may seem to you, most people here think 9/11 was a Zionist plot to give America the pretext it needed to attack Afghanistan and Iraq and control the Muslim world.

I am so happy that you found my childhood playmates alive and well, still remembering me after these many years. Before my parents died, I wrote to them that I was now convinced they loved me and did their best. I no longer held them responsible for any of my mental/emotional difficulties. I felt the need to apologize for all the suffering I inflicted upon them while [I was] growing up. Did you ever find that letter in the library?

Yes, you have my permission to use my letters as you see fit. I think you will be as fair as it is possible for a nonbeliever to be. When [your book is] published, please arrange to have three copies [. . .] sent direct to my address by REGISTERED post if you can possibly afford the expense. It will become a part of my library.

A few weeks later I found her article on the Internet.

"Muslim Savages"
Under the false pretext of Islam, in the northeast territories of Pakistan, female education has been totally banned, more than 170 girls' schools have been destroyed, and numerous CD and barber shops blown up. There have been dire threats to throw acid upon any woman or girl who dares emerge outside her home. All forms of entertainment and cultural activities are now prohibited, a death-sentence invoked for anyone opposing them. Public exhibits of the corpses of offenders are hung from street lampposts. So unbearable is Taliban rule in these areas, everyone who can is leaving. There are now thousands of displaced and destitute people. Under the rule of Taliban, too, terrorism thrives. Youthful suicide bombers, both male and female, prowl everywhere in Pakistan, sowing death and destruction. Among these are those guilty of destroying the Marriott Hotel in Islamabad together with all its many casualties. Without doubt they are re-

sponsible for the recent atrocities in Mumbai. Taliban is notorious for kidnappings and beheading captives, especially foreigners.

Bearing in mind the terrible times in which we live, a genuine Islamic order must express compassion and mercy as it did during our greatest days in the past.

Maryam Jameelah, March 2009

In her most recent letter to me, Maryam asked that I send her two copies of a *National Geographic* book of photographs.

I'm still trying to decide what books I will send instead.

A Note on Methodology

Though I have called this book "a tale," *The Convert* is fundamentally a work of nonfiction. However, unless her words are accompanied by quotation marks and a specific citation, the actual and imaginary letters of Maryam Jameelah do not appear here as she wrote them. As I make clear at the close of the book, I have rewritten and greatly condensed these letters. I have also moved an anecdote or thought from one letter to another, or taken an anecdote or thought from an essay and put it into a letter.

Throughout these reconstituted letters, I have tried to retain Maryam's distinctive voice, one that often came more easily to me than my own. I do not ascribe to her feelings or thoughts that she did not have. I do not make anything up. Some readers might find this simply unorthodox, others may well feel misled. In my defense I can only say that faced with the particular puzzle the letters presented and the moment in history when I found them, I tried to use them, as Maryam Jameelah herself often used them, as a way of making narrative sense of her life and my response to it. The Mawlana Abul Ala Mawdudi letter that opens the book exists both in Urdu and in a rough English translation that I have polished and shortened slightly. This letter and Herbert Marcus's reply (which is unchanged) can, like the rest of the letters I have drawn on here, be found in the Maryam Jameelah collection on deposit at the Manuscripts and Archives Division at the New York Public Library. Maryam's letters to me I've shortened or combined but basically left untouched.

Transliteration is notoriously tricky and I have tried my best to be consistent. As is clear in the endnotes that cite his translated works Mawdudi's name has been rendered in the Roman alphabet in different ways over the years. For the first citation I've used the name as it is spelled on the book's cover; for subsequent citations of that same book, I've used the more up to date Mawdudi. I've followed the *New York Times* in rendering the names of public figures (Ayub Khan, General Zia, Mian Tufail Muhammad) and common Arabic words (madrasa, hajj), but rather than impose consistent spelling of the Arab honorific "Sayyid" on a speaker of Urdu or Persian, I've used "Syed" and "Seyyed," respectively.

Unless otherwise noted, quotations from the Qur'an are from Muhammad Marmaduke Pickthall's *The Meaning of the Glorious Qur'an,* revised and edited into modern standard English by Arafat K. El-Ashi and republished by Amana Publications in 1996. The book's opening epigraph, the part II epigraph, and the account of the Prophet's advice to his questioners in chapter 9 are from A. N. Matthews's 1809 translation of Muhammad ibn 'Abd Allah Kahtib al-Tibrizi's *Mishkat al-Masabih* (Calcutta: printed by T. Hubbard). Two excerpts from poems by Mahmud Shabistari, the thirteenth-century Sufi poet, provide the epigraph for chapters 6 and 9; Mas'ud-e-Bakk, from the Chisti tradition (the same Sufi tradition that Mawdudi's family was from) provides the epigraph to the part III opener. The quotations from Abul Ala Mawdudi's letters to Maryam are drawn on those I found in the archive, rather than from Maryam's published version of those same letters.

Finally, Maryam did not ask to read the manuscript before publication. She trusted, as the reader will have to trust, that I would do my best to remain true to the facts of her life and to my own (perpetually faltering) efforts to imagine and understand.

Notes

PART I: THE MARBLE LIBRARY

Chapter 1: *al-Hijrah*—The Escape

13–14   "Maryam Jameelah's significance . . . across the Muslim world." John L. Esposito, ed. *The Oxford Encyclopedia of the Modern Islamic World* (New York: Oxford University Press, 1995), 60.

14   "Vali Nasr, Mawdudi's biographer . . . was revolutionary." Personal communication with Vali Nasr and Seyyed Hossein Nasr, October 2007.

19   "Islam's borders are bloody . . . superiority of their culture." Samuel Huntington, "The Clash of Civilizations," *Foreign Affairs,* Summer 1993, 31, 40.

19   "any compromise with . . . defeat of the latter." Maryam Jameelah, *Islam Face to Face with the Current Crisis* (Lahore: Mohammad Yusuf Khan & Sons, 1979), 44.

19   "After Copernicus, the western astronomer . . . accident or a mistake." Maryam Jameelah, *Islam versus the West* (Lahore: Sh. Mohammad Ashraf, 1962), 30.

25   "The destruction of the natural environment . . . life on earth." Maryam Jameelah, *The Resurgence of Islam and Our Liberation from the Colonial Yoke* (Lahore: Mohammad Yusuf Khan & Sons, 1980), 28.

25 **For so-called "primitive" peoples, "the impact . . . often their extinction."** Maryam Jameelah, *Westernization and Human Welfare* (Lahore: Mohammad Yusuf Khan, 1976), 81.

25 **American oil companies . . . a proud desert culture.** Jameelah, *The Resurgence of Islam,* 7.

25 **"our political sovereignty is more nominal than real . . . determined to keep it that way."** Maryam Jameelah, *Islam and Modern Man* (Delhi: Crescent Publishing Co., n.d.), 9.

25 **"Orientalism is not a dispassionate, objective . . . culture as obsolete."** Maryam Jameelah, *Islam and Orientalism* (Lahore: Mohammad Yusuf Khan, 1971), 105. See also Maryam Jameelah, *Western Imperialism Menaces Muslims* (Lahore: Mohammad Yusuf Khan, 1978), 30–34.

26 **Quoting Malcolm X . . . traditions and faith.** Jameelah, *Westernization and Human Welfare,* 24–25.

Chapter 2: The Mawlana

35 **When Abul Ala Mawdudi's grandfather . . . English education.** Masudul Hasan, *Sayyid Abul A'ala Mawdudi* (Lahore: Islamic Publications, 1984), 3–4, 7.

36 **Only when the family . . . represent the innocent.** Seyyed Vali Reza Nasr, *Mawdudi and the Making of Islamic Revival* (New York: Oxford, 1996), 10–11.

36 **The rest of his life . . . world as it was.** Syed As'ad Gilani, *'Maududi': Thought and Movement,* trans. Hasan Muizuddin Qazi (Lahore: Farooq Hasan Gilani, 1978), 43.

37 **"a revolutionary ideology and program . . . tenets and ideals."** Text of Abul Ala Mawdudi, "Jihad in Islam," an address delivered on Iqbal Day, April 13, 1939, at the Town Hall in Lahore (Salimiah, Kuwait: IIFSO; Lagos: Ibrash Waqf Foundation, 1980?), 4.

38 **A caliph's life . . . unsparing in the hereafter.** Mawdudi, "Jihad in Islam," 27.

38–39   **In the Islamic Republic of Pakistan . . . enforcement was erratic.** Abul A'la Maududi, *The Islamic Law and Its Introduction in Pakistan,* ed. and trans. Khurshid Ahmad (Lahore: Islamic Publications, 1960), 38–39 fn.

39   **Among the many challenges . . . contemporary constitutional frameworks.** Ibid., 199–200.

39   **All these questions . . . fight for independence?** Ibid., 37–40.

39   **Sayyid Qutb of the Muslim . . . on this basis?** Ali Rahnema, ed., *Pioneers of Islamic Revival* (London: Zed Books, 1994), 91.

40   **Once the fundamental principles . . . in the past.** Mawdudi, *Islamic Law and Its Introduction in Pakistan,* 31.

40   **Naturally, religious minorities . . . would be just.** Mawdudi, "Jihad in Islam," 24–25, and Abul A'la Mawdudi, *Islamic Law and Constitution,* ed. Khurshid Ahmad (Lahore: Islamic Publications, 1969), 141.

40–41   **The Sharia dictates . . . chaste and honest.** Mawdudi, *Islamic Law and Constitution,* 50–51.

41–42   **"unusually deep insight . . . and all the major problems of life."** Abul A'la Maududi, *A Short History of the Revivalist Movement in Islam,* trans. al-Ash'ari (Lahore: Islamic Publications, 1963), 41.

42   **The Jamaat declared itself victorious, but Mawdudi was noticeably restrained.** For a detailed discussion of Mawdudi's role in the struggle over the constitution of Pakistan, see Seyyed Vali Reza Nasr, *The Vanguard of the Islamic Revolution: The Jama'at-I Islami of Pakistan* (Berkeley: University of California Press, 1984), 116–46, 193–94. Nasr's biographical study, *Mawdudi and the Making of the Islamic Revolution,* was also critical to my thinking about Mawdudi, the world he came from, and the evolution of his political philosophy.

42   **Though its treasury . . . the democratic process.** Charles J. Adams, "The Ideology of Mawlana Mawdudi" in *South Asian Politics and Religion,* ed. Donald E. Smith (Princeton, NJ: Princeton University Press, 1966), 376–78. See also Gilani, *'Maududi': Thought and Movement,* 79.

43 **"If the expectation . . . remote and uncertain?"** Mawdudi, *A Short History of the Revivalist Movement*, 43.

43 **It was actually formed . . . along religious lines.** Adams, "Ideology of Mawlana Mawdudi," 375.

44 **The profession of faith . . . military and police.** Mawlana Mawdudi, *Haqiqat-i-Jihad*, 16–17, as quoted in Hazrat Mirza Tahir Ahmad, *Murder in the Name of Allah* (Cambridge: Lutterworth, 1989), 44.

45 **"All these so-called . . . to this fact."** Margaret Marcus to Abul Ala Mawdudi, December 5, 1960, (New York Public Library). See also *Correspondence between Maulana Maudoodi and Maryam Jameelah* (Lahore: Mohammad Yusuf Khan, 1969); I have relied on the "original" letters on deposit in the Jameelah archive in dating and quoting from this correspondence.

45 **"Does not an evil remain . . . sympathy than society?"** Jameelah, *Islam versus the West*, 124.

45 **"Would this [sovereignty] . . . very *raison d'etre*?"** Ibid., 52.

46 **By the time Mawdudi described . . . another way.** Abul Ala Mawdudi to Margaret Marcus, December 16, 1961, NYPL.

46 **It was no exaggeration . . . would be heard.** Ibid.

46 **He also exchanged letters . . . among his correspondents.** Mawdudi had met Qutb's brother Mohammad on a trip to Cairo in 1960 and had received copies of his prison writings. "Each one of us knows the other fully," Mawdudi wrote Margaret Marcus on June 20, 1961, NYPL.

47 **Mawdudi immediately drew up . . . Ayub Khan's government.** Adams, "Ideology of Maulana Mawdudi," 377–79.

47 **"eye-opener for Muslim youth."** Abul Ala Mawdudi to Margaret Marcus, June 20, 1961, NYPL.

54 **"rightful place to accommodate . . . an 'asylum.'"** Gilani, *'Maududi': Thought and Movement*, 58.

54 **Mawdudi also believed . . . "lest [they] should, like Adam himself, be lured into a life of pleasure."** Abul A'la Maududi, *Purdah and the Status of Woman in Islam,* ed. and trans. al-Ashari (Lahore: Islamic Publications, 1972), 10–11.

58 **"There are certain eras . . . born of affliction."** Susan Sontag, *Against Interpretation and Other Essays* (New York: Anchor Books, 1961), 49.

58 **"America is allegedly . . . four million are slain."** Maryam Jameelah, "A Manifesto of the Islamic Movement" (Lahore: Matbaat, El-Maktaba-il-Ilmiyyah, June 1969), 14. Later reprinted and reworked as *Islam Face to Face with the Current Crisis.*

Chapter 3: Doubt

62 **Some of the less . . . Prophet's household.** G. H. A. Juynboll, *Encyclopedia of Canonical Hadith* (Leiden: 2007), xxix.

63 **Reading this, an early scholar . . . not true Muslims.** Ibn Taymiya, Al-Ihtijaj bil-Qadar, in his Rasa'il, Cairo 1323 AH, II, 96–97, as cited in Fazlur Rahman, *Islam* (Garden City, NJ: Doubleday, 1968), 133.

64 **The Mawlana, however, was impatient with medieval hermeneutics.** Adams, "Ideology of Mawlana Mawdudi," 386.

64 **He claimed he could tell . . . the Prophet's intentions.** "I have sensibly understood the Deen by a direct access to the Holy Qur'an and the Sunnah, and not from the exegesis of the present or the past. Therefore in order to know, sensibly, what the Deen expects and demands of me, I shall never try to quote the answer given by certain scholars, or the examples lived by others. I shall only try to ascertain, 'What does the Qur'an say; what did Rasulullhah do?'" Gilani, *'Maududi': Thought and Movement,* 56.

64–65 **While he was in the Holy Land . . . over the precious cloth.** Maryam Jameelah, *Islam in Theory and Practice* (Lahore: Mohammad Yusuf Khan, 1967), 233–34.

65–66 **"She is simply suffering from hysteria . . . like-minded Muslim gentleman."** May 29, 1963, edition of *Nawai Waqt,* as cited in *Tolu-e-Islam,* July 1963.

67–70 **Mawlana Mawdudi has said . . . change our destiny.** *Tolu-e-Islam,* July 1963. I have reworked a very rough translation.

70 **There are even hints . . . this particular view.** Nasr, *Mawdudi and the Making of Islamic Revival,* has a discussion of this work, including Maryam Jameelah, "Who is Maudoodi?" (Lahore: Mohammad Yusuf Khan, 1973), 140.

71 **His unpublished memoirs . . . "true benefactor."** As quoted in Khurshid Ahmad's foreword to Syed Abul 'Ala Maudoodi, *Towards Understanding the Qur'an,* trans. Zafar Ishaq Ansari (Leicester, UK: Islamic Foundation, 1988), vol. I, xii.

72 **"Just as in logic . . . a particular society."** Sayyed Abul ala Maudoodi, *The Process of Islamic Revolution, an Address Given at Aligarh Muslim University* (Lahore: M. Abdul Waheed Khan, 1947), 3.

72 **"Kant, Nietzsche, Hegel, Marx . . . producing thereon huge volumes."** Translator's foreword, *Towards Understanding the Qur'an,* xii.

73 **"drove a quiet, kind-hearted man . . . a world gone astray."** Mawdudi, *Towards Understanding the Qur'an,* 24.

73 **First, as the Qur'an . . . God's commands.** Ibid., 9.

74 **"Nothing is missing . . . no part is vague or wanting."** Mawdudi, *Islamic Law and Constitution,* 197.

74 **Each of the Qur'an's 114 . . . same large questions.** Mawdudi, *Towards Understanding the Qur'an,* 23–24.

74 **There will also be . . . states of mind.** Ibid., 4.

74 **There will be words . . . long in disuse.** See Mawdudi, *Islamic Law and Constitution,* 198. "The Quranic terms relating to constitutional matters, as also those of Hadith and Fiqh, have long been out of use and have by now become incomprehensible. . . . That is why, on hearing

of the constitutional concepts and directives of the Qur'an, even fairly well-read people [are amazed]."

74 **He was simply preserving . . . scholarly obscurantism.** Gilani, *'Maududi': Thought and Movement,* 51.

74–75 **There is room . . . "blocks of wood."** Mawdudi, *Towards Understanding the Qur'an,* 29.

75 **Only those who read . . . similarly damned.** Ibid., 28–30.

75–76 **"spread confusion and disorder . . . all around him."** Abul A'la Maududi, *Towards Understanding Islam,* revised ed., trans. Khurshid Ahmad (Lahore: Islamic Foundation, 1960), 20–22.

76 **For Mawdudi, it was "a principle of creation" that women be docile and acquiescent.** Mawdudi, *Purdah and the Status of Woman in Islam,* 234.

76–77 **Picture making was the first step . . . before coming to Pakistan.** Abul Ala Mawdudi to Maryam Jameelah, March 30, 1962, NYPL, and interview with Maryam Jameelah, December 2007.

77 **In his editorial . . . Islam by force.** *Tolu-e-Islam,* July 1963.

78 **Parwez trotted out . . . precipitated Maryam's mental collapse.** Ibid.

79 **The Paagal Khanaah on Jail Road . . . five hundred women.** "Janet Hanneman: PCV in Pakistan," *The Rotarian,* June 1964, 12–15.

83 **"Nobody who knows me or has seen me has ever or can truthfully ever describe me as 'charming,'" she once commented.** Maryam Jameelah to Herbert and Myra Marcus, February 28, 1977, NYPL.

PART II: *JAHILIYYA*—THE AGE OF BARBARISM AND IGNORANCE

Chapter 5: Paagal Khanaah

116 **"Sometimes, deprivation will be so important . . . into a state of active need."** Lawrence Kubie, *Practical and Theoretical Aspects of*

Psychoanalysis (New York: International Universities Press, 1975), 86–89.

118   **"All that was good, true . . . sufficient to convince me."** Maryam Jameelah, *Why I Embraced Islam* (Delhi: New Crescent Publishing Co., 1997 reprint), 12.

118   **"with a complete, comprehensive way of life . . . into a perfect harmony."** Jameelah, *Islam versus the West,* 7.

118   **"My quest was always for absolutes."** Jameelah, *Why I Embraced Islam,* 11.

118   **The list of schizophrenic behaviors . . . they manifested.** *Diagnostic and Statistical Manual of Mental Disorders:* 1952 edition. "Schizophrenic reaction, catatonic type. These reactions are characterized by conspicuous motor behavior, exhibiting either marked generalized inhibition (stupor, mutism, negativism and waxy flexibility) or excessive motor activity and excitement. The individual may regress to a state of vegetation."

119   **Psychiatrists who once had described . . . began behaving like one.** S. P. Fullinwider, *Technicians of the Finite: The Rise and Decline of the Schizophrenic in American Thought* (Westport, CT: Greenwood Press, 1982), 150.

119–120   **Muhammad Asad . . . gives life to dead hearts.** Muhammad Asad, *The Message of the Qur'an* (Gibraltar: Al-Andalus, 1980), 393.

126–127   **Freud's theories held sway . . . serious questions.** Jameelah, *Why I Embraced Islam,* 11.

130   **"left to die, herded naked and incontinent like cattle."** Jameelah, "A Manifesto of the Islamic Movement," 32.

130   **"Schizophrenia is no longer limited . . . are taking place."** Jameelah, *Westernization and Human Welfare,* 67–68.

130–131   **Qutb had made a similar observation . . . of the colonized.** Paul Berman, "The Philosopher of Islamic Terror," *New York Times Magazine,* March 23, 2003.

131 **"all embracing system . . . salvation of the individual personality."** Jameelah, "A Manifesto of the Islamic Movement," 32.

132 **"made mistakes in my life" and "done some foolish things."** Maryam Jameelah to Abul Ala Mawdudi, April 7, 1962, NYPL.

Chapter 6: The Convert

135 Epigraph from *The Secret Rose Garden of Sa'd ud din Mahmūd Shabistarí*, trans. Florence Lederer (London: John Murray, 1920), 72.

137 **Maryam would also ascribe . . . a cost-benefit analysis.** Jameelah, *Islam Face to Face with the Current Crisis*, 5, 7–10.

141 **"After declining your kind invitation for so long . . . too late to accept it now?"** Maryam Jameelah to Abul Ala Mawdudi, March 22, 1962, NYPL.

149 **"I hope they learn a lesson from your example."** Abul Ala Mawdudi to Maryam Jameelah, June 20, 1961, NYPL.

149 **It never ceased to amaze him . . . fight against the godless communists.** Abul Ala Mawdudi to Maryam Jameelah, April 1, 1961, and May 19, 1961, NYPL.

149–150 **Maryam began the letter by . . . Allah was forgiving and merciful.** Maryam Jameelah to Abul Ala Mawdudi, April 7, 1962, NYPL.

150 **He had already made it clear . . . similar incongruities, he insisted.** Abul Ala Mawdudi to Maryam Jameelah, February 25, 1961, NYPL.

153 **If Maryam accepted . . . "Please let me know if you accept these arrangements or not."** Abul Ala Mawdudi to Maryam Jameelah, July 2, 1963, NYPL.

155–156 **Over 7 million traveled . . . Muslims and non-Muslims.** Jacques Semelin, ed., "The Partition Massacres, 1946–1947," *Online Encyclopedia of Mass Violence.* http://www.massviolence.org/.

156 **Once Pakistan became a reality . . . upheaval of Partition.** Adams, "Ideology of Mawlana Mawdudi," 376.

PART III: THE CONCRETE LIBRARY

Mas'ud-e-Bakk poem from http://www.chishti.ru/shisti_poetry.html

Chapter 7: The Renegade

164 **This comprised the city's sum total . . . referred to as "civil society."** Conversation with Najum Sethi, December 2007.

167 **"We should in Palestine form a portion . . . an outpost of civilization as opposed to barbarism."** Jameelah, *Western Imperialism Menaces Muslims,* 26.

167 **Within days of signing . . . Arab residents from the land.** Benny Morris, *The Birth of the Palestinian Refugee Problem Revisited* (Cambridge: Cambridge University Press, 2004), 521–25.

168 **"Every minute of our lives . . . part of the testing."** Jameelah, *Islam versus the West,* 116.

171 **The compound at Mansoorah . . . passed along to the family.** "An Interview with Haider Farooq Mawdudi," J&K Insights, translated from "Diwar-e-Shahar," August–September 1998, http://www.jammu-kashmir.com.

171 **Her family had made its fortune . . . eyes of Islam.** Nasr, *Mawdudi and the Making of Islamic Revival,* 33–34, 152.

171 **When Maryam asked her . . . husband's great patience.** Interview with Maryam Jameelah, December 2007.

172 **"Qutb is a great admirer of you and specially recommended your books to me."** Margaret Marcus to Abul Ala Mawdudi, May 29, 1961, NYPL.

173 **To Mawdudi's dismay . . . noncooperation movement**. Adams, "Ideology of Mawlana Mawdudi," 373.

173 **During these years . . . economics, and political theory.** See translation of Mawdudi's autobiographical notes, *Khud Nawisht,* in Masudul Hasan, *Sayyid Abul A'ala Mawdudi and His Thought* (Lahore: Islamic Publications, 1984), 2 vols., 24.

174 **"I studied your life-sketch . . . unexpected for me."** Mawlana Mawdudi to Maryam Jameelah, February 25, 1961, NYPL.

174 **"I affirmed my faith . . . soul to the question."** Gilani, *'Maududi': Thought and Movement,* 50–51.

175 **He appropriated concepts . . . his left was doing.** "Now if these books are merely translated they cannot be of much use to us. It is, therefore, imperative that persons having knowledge of modern legal systems should work on all such materials and rearrange them to fulfill the modern requirements." Mawdudi, *Islamic Law and Constitution,* 104.

175 **The ulema were often dismayed . . . doubted his grasp of Islamic history.** Ahmad, *Murder in the Name of Allah,* 28. In chapter 2 of this book the author shows the continuities between the Orientalist representation of Islamic history and Mawdudi's own grasp of it.

175 **Equally often he let . . . question his authority.** Mawdudi, *A Short History of the Revivalist Movement in Islam,* preface to the 4th edition, 4.

176 **"Sir, what do we know . . . pens is our pleasure."** Mawdudi, "Jihad in Islam," 2.

177 **A sympathetic account . . . before it could be published.** This is speculation based on the period in which the book was written. It seems to me too that had it been a critical book, the British would not have censored it.

177 **More than any other thinker . . . traditional village life.** In developing this point I am indebted to Akeel Bilgrami's insightful essay "On Enlightenment and Enchantment," *Critical Inquiry,* Spring 2006.

178-179 **But Sharia also dictated . . . preserve national honor.** Mawdudi, "Jihad in Islam," 8–9.

179 **Similarly, divine law . . . only enslaved.** Hasan, *Sayyid Abul A'ala Maududi and His Thought,* 51–62.

179 **Following Sharia . . . obligation, he insisted.** Dr. Sayez Riaz Ahmad, *Mawlana Mawdudi and the Islamic State* (Lahore: People's Publishing House, 1976), 122.

179   **Yet the more deeply . . . how Islam might be renewed.** Ibid. See discussion of the writing of *Al-Jihad fi'l-Islam* in notes, 64.

179   **"are preventing the truth of God from prevailing."** Ahmad, *Maulana Maududi and the Islamic State,* 123–24, citing *Al-Jihad fi'l-Islam* (Lahore: Islamic Publications, 1962), 48–50.

179   **To define jihad as primarily . . . Qutb soon wrote.** Rahnema, *Pioneers of Islamic Revival,* 84.

179–180   **"After years of study and thinking . . . lawful and constitutional means."** *Nawa-i-Waqt,* November 10, 1962, as quoted in Jameelah, *Islam in Theory and Practice,* 256.

180   **In "Jihad in Islam". . . "communities on the wrong path."** Abul A'la Maududi, *System of Government Under the Holy Prophet* (Lahore: Islamic Publications, 1978), 19-20.

180   **Similarly, the Islamic Republic of Pakistan should seek . . . to whatever extent possible.** "Hence it is imperative for the Muslim Party for reasons of both general welfare of humanity and self-defense that it should not be content with establishing the Islamic System of Government in one territory alone, but to extend the sway of the Islamic System all around as far as its resources can carry it." Mawdudi, "Jihad in Islam," 21.

180   **To achieve this, it was imperative . . . tanks, airplanes, and so on.** Mawdudi, *A Short History of the Revivalist Movement in Islam,* 146–47. Mawdudi seems to equate science with military technology. He never mentions its other contributions to human welfare, for example, medicine, electricity, the internal combustion engine. Instead he defends Islam's appropriation of Western military technology by citing the Prophet's use of the battering ram.

181   **"But after the failure of admonishing . . . under my feet today."** Al-Ghashiya 88:23–26; quoted in *Al-Jihad f'il-Islam,* 3rd edition, 1962, 141–42.

181   **"I tremble after reading this writing . . . not words but merciless stones."** See "A Review of the Pakistani Government's 'White Paper';

Qadiyaniyyat—A Grave Threat to Islam: Replies to Some Allegations," a sermon delivered by Hadrat Mirza Tahir Ahmad, on February 15, 1985, at the Fadl Mosque, London, 30–34. http://www.alislam.org.

181 **"Islam requires the earth . . . the whole planet."** Mawdudi, "Jihad in Islam," 6.

183 **The world, he said . . . wrest control of the train.** This speech, given in April 1945, has been translated twice. I have paraphrased drawing on both versions. Sayyid Abul A'la Mawdudi, *The Islamic Movement: Dynamics of Values, Power, and Change*, ed. Khurram Murad (Leicester, UK: Islamic Foundation, 1984), 72, 77. See also Abul A'la Maududi, *The Moral Foundations of the Islamic Movement* (Lahore: Islamic Publications Ltd., 1976), 8. "The duty of a person who puts faith in the creed of Islam is not confined to ordering his life so far as is possible according to the tenets of Islam, but his faith demands that he should direct all his efforts to the attainment of one purpose only, i.e. that power and authority should be wrested from the hands of the infidels and the wicked and that the Divine code of life be established in the world."

Chapter 8: A War Between and Within

188 **"No law can be made . . . germs of indecency and obscenity."** Mawdudi, *Purdah and the Status of Woman in Islam,* 167–68, 171.

197 **In 1987 Maryam wrote an article reappraising Mawdudi's work.** Maryam Jameelah, "An Appraisal of Some Aspects of Maulana Sayyid Ala Maudoodi's Life and Thought," *Islamic Quarterly* 31, no. 2 (1987).

198 **During the government's siege . . . make political hay.** Joshua T. White, "Vigilante Islamism in Pakistan: Religious Party Responses to the Lal Masjid Crisis," (Washington D.C.: Hudson Institute, November 11, 2008). http://www.currenttrends.org.

199 **"I thought of the amoeba . . . going inside her."** As quoted in Fullinwider, *Technicians of the Finite,* 149.

199 **Not long before his death . . . nothing further I can do.** Interview with Haider Farooq Mawdudi, December 2007.

200 **Once he fell ill ... submission to Allah.** Interview with Ahmad Farooq Mawdudi, September 2008. See also Nasr, *Mawdudi and the Making of the Islamic Revivalism,* 45, for an account of Mawdudi's disillusion with the direction of his party's political struggle.

200 **With Zia's coup ... in the army curriculum.** Nasr, *Vanguard of the Islamic Revolution,* 172.

200 **In February, to Mawdudi's great pleasure . . . Islamic penal code.** A. Rashid Moten, *Islam and Revolution: Contributions of Sayyid Mawdudi* (Kano, Nigeria: Bureau for Islamic Propagation, 1988), 29–30.

200 **Six months later ... trumped-up murder charge.** Nasr, *Vanguard of the Islamic Revolution,* 181, 190.

200 **At best, Mawdudi concluded ... worry about it.** Interview with Haider Farooq Mawdudi, December 2007.

201 **His godly voice ... citizens of Muslim countries.** Misbahul Islam Faruqi, *Introducing Mawdudi* (Karachi: Student Publications Bureau, 1969), 7. As quoted in Sheila McDonough, *Muslim Ethics and Modernity: A Comparative Study of the Ethical Thought of Sayyid Ahmad Khan and Mawlana Mawdudi* (Waterloo, Ontario: Canadian Corporation for Studies in Religion, 1984), 62.

201 **Faisal Shahzad ... e-mails to friends.** "For Times Square Suspect, Long Roots of Discontent," *New York Times,* May 15, 2010.

201 **Osama bin Laden made . . . from the Saudis.** Steve Coll, *Ghost Wars* (Penguin Books, New York, 2004), 86. Twenty years later, Khalid Shaikh Mohammed, the architect of the 2001 attacks and the confessed executioner of journalist Daniel Pearl (during the month Mohammed was waterboarded 183 times), was arrested in the house of a Jamaat party official. Gretchen Peters, "Al Qaeda–Pakistani Ties Deepen," *Christian Science Monitor,* March 6, 2003.

201–202 **"Freedom fighters" from Egypt . . . all jihadi organizations.** See pp. 6–9 and 37–51 of the 1993 Congressional Report "The New Islamist International," detailing the nexus between the ISI and the Jamaat-e-Islami and the role played by the Jamaat in the export of Islamist doctrine and terrorism, particularly to Kashmir, but also to Central Asia, Egypt, Liberia, Lebanon, Algeria, Sudan, India, and Bangladesh.

202 **"We are not bigots . . . calm and logical reason."** This quote also appears in Jameelah's *Islam Face to Face with the Current Crisis,* a reworking of her 1969 manifesto, 43.

202 **In cheap, simply written . . . famed mujahidin.** Conversation with Basharat Peer, April 2009.

202 **"Make up your mind to participate in . . . the light of Truth?"** Maryam Jameelah, *Two Mujahidin of the Recent Past and Their Struggle for Freedom against Foreign Rule* (Delhi: Crescent, n.d.), 9–10.

202 **"Since we are all destined . . . destruction and collective suicide."** Jameelah, *Western Imperialism Menaces Muslims,* 39–40.

202 **"Everything they stand for [is] EVIL!"** Jameelah, "Manifesto of the Islamic Movement," 44.

203 **"the possibility of violent death [lies] the soul of all romance."** William James, *William James: Writings: 1902–1910,* ed. Bruce Kuklick (New York: Library of America, 1988), 1284.

203–204 **"All the discontent of men . . . failure to solve them."** Wilfred Cantwell Smith, *Islam in Modern History* (Princeton, NJ: Princeton University Press, 1957), 163–64.

204 **Pure slander, Maryam insisted . . . with a blanket absolution.** Jameelah, *Islam and Orientalism,* 65–66.

211 *"There is no joy in motherhood for me."* Maryam Jameelah to Herbert and Myra Marcus, June 27, 1972, NYPL.

211 **You had wanted an IUD; Khan Sahib wouldn't agree to it.** Maryam Jameelah to Herbert and Myra Marcus, July 21, 1972, NYPL.

211 **Khan Sahib also refused to vaccinate your children.** Maryam Jameelah to Herbert and Myra Marcus, December 19, 1972, NYPL.

211 *"Modern industrialization promotes . . . man independent of Allah."* Jameelah, *Islam versus the West,* 120–21.

211 **In the same letter where you lament . . . women's liberation movement.** Maryam Jameelah to Herbert and Myra Marcus, December 19, 1972, NYPL.

211–212 *"In Islam . . . [a woman's] success . . . for the preservation of our way of life."* Jameelah, *Islam in Theory and Practice*, 86.

212 *"I just can't cope by myself . . . I will not be able to do."* Maryam Jameelah to Herbert and Myra Marcus, July 21, 1972, NYPL.

212 *"Too many Pakistani women I know . . . teach girls cleanliness and orderliness."* Maryam Jameelah, *Islam and the Muslim Woman Today* (Lahore: Mohammad Yusuf Khan, 1976), 14.

212 **"naked atheism and materialism."** Maryam Jameelah, *Modern Technology and the Dehumanization of Man* (Delhi: Crescent Publishing, n.d.), 59.

212 **Or while you were pleading . . . for polio, smallpox, and diphtheria?** Maryam Jameelah to Herbert and Myra Marcus, December 19, 1972, NYPL.

212 **"perverted 'cultural' values."** Jameelah, *Islam in Theory and Practice*, 86.

213 *"Feminism is an unnatural, artificial . . . of the entire human race."* Jameelah, *Islam and the Muslim Woman Today*, 40, 51.

213 *"[The women's liberation movement] . . . MARRIAGE, HOME AND FAMILY."* Maryam Jameelah to Herbert Marcus, February 1, 1973, NYPL.

213 *"According to Islamic teachings, life is not a pleasure trip but an examination."* Jameelah, *Islam versus the West*, 116.

214 *"We must always be prepared . . . must be trained in combat."* Jameelah, *Resurgence of Islam and Our Liberation from the Colonial Yoke*, 31.

214 *"The Mujahid . . . will not merely oppose . . . of the Holy Prophet Mohammad."* Ibid., 31.

214 *"[A good Muslim mother] should entertain her young children . . . desire to emulate these virtues."* Jameelah, *Islam and the Muslim Woman Today*, 13.

214 *"The Jamaat-e-Islami has become too . . . faith and spiritual purity."* Interview with Maryam Jameelah, December 2007.

Chapter 9: The Lifted Veil

217 Epigraph from *The Secret Rose Garden of Sa'd ud din Mahmud Shabistari*, Lederer, trans., 65.

219 **"Is it their minds . . . filled with overweening arrogance?"** Asad, *Message of the Qur'an*, 249-50 (52:32). I think Asad's translation reads better in this instance. The paraphrases in this section reflect my own reading.

219–220 **Men will continue to pose . . . was also recommended.** Khaṭīb al-Tibrīzī, Muḥammad ibn 'Abd Allāh. *Mishkat al-Masabih* (Calcutta: T. Hubbard, 1809), 20–23.

220 **"If they incline towards peace, incline thou to it as well."** Asad, *Message of the Qur'an*, 249.

Acknowledgments

To write a book is to incur a stack of debts, many of which won't ever be repaid or even properly acknowledged, no matter how many endnotes one appends or perfunctory lists one makes. This book is no different. The sturdy patron at the center of this narrative is undoubtedly The New York Public Library, Astor, Lenox and Tilden Foundations. It is to that grand institution and the many, many remarkable individuals that hold it aloft that I owe not just this book but also a large part of my education and livelihood. In the course of my research for *The Convert* I benefited greatly from the expertise, both bibliographic and linguistic, of those librarians in Shoichi Noma Reading Room of the Asian and Middle Eastern Division (formerly the Oriental Division and now defunct entirely). I would particularly like to thank John M. Lundquist, Gamil Youssef, and Sunita Vaze, but also the long departed "Mr. Parr" who first welcomed Margaret Marcus and, eventually, her archive. The Manuscripts and Archives Division and the Brooke Russell Astor Reading Room where I first encountered the Maryam Jameelah Collection, is also under the library's capacious roof. There I found Assistant Curator Thomas G. Lannon unfailingly cordial, helpful, and enthusiastic. Finally, in 2008–2009 I was the beneficiary of a fellowship at the Dorothy and Lewis B. Cullman Center for Scholars and Writers. This enabled me to research and write this book full-time, providing me not just an office in the library but a remarkable group of fellow writers, each of whom provided constant inspiration from a variety of directions. I would particularly like to thank my fellow Cullman scholar Deborah Cohen for her close reads of an early draft of the manuscript and Akeel Bilgrami for suggesting ways the debate between Islam and the West might be reframed. I will never forget, too, Jean Strouse's comic reflections on the mysterious byways, both psychic and narrative, of the biographical art. I salute all my Cullman brethren, and most particularly, the late Dorothy Cullman, who made this dream of refuge and reflection real.

Now for the breathless, far from complete list of those without whom I could never have managed: Durre S. Ahmed, Negar Azimi, Jonathan and Julie Baker, Katie Dublinski, Jennifer Elliott, John Esposito, Gregory Gibson, Judith Ginsberg, Richard Grinker, Susan Hobson, Adina Hoffman, Mahnaz Ispahani, Lynn Marasco, Mandy McClure, Albert Mobilio, Mira Nair, Geoffrey O'Brien, Ahmed Rashid, Katherine Russell Rich, Elizabeth Rubin, Ranjana Sengupta, Michele Stevenson, Melanie Thernstrom, Salman Toor, and Eliot Weinberger either gave my manuscript honest and close reads, or provided me a comfortable bed, or a pointed conversation at vulnerable points on this expedition. In Lahore I was a houseguest of Najam Sethi and Jugnu Mohsin. In their late night banter, living room discussions over tea, and their patient answers to my all too innocent questions, they and their friends provided a necessary historical context for the events that were then consuming (and continue to consume) their city and country. I am also grateful to Abul Ala Mawdudi's two sons, Ahmad Farooq and Haider Farooq, and his grandson Ali Farooq, as well as to Asma Jehangir for bringing us together. Ali Sethi was my guide to the secret palaces and sacred places of Lahore; I couldn't have had a better one. I would also like to thank my literary agent, David McCormick, and to acknowledge his formidable doggedness on behalf of this book and the roundabout path it took to find a publisher. My editor Ethan Nosowsky helped the manuscript arrive at its final form; I am frankly wary of reckoning the extent of *that* debt. Fiona McCrae, director of Graywolf Press, played the part of benevolent fairy godmother.

Finally and essentially: thank you, Lila, Nayan, and Amitav.

A Graywolf Press Reading Group Guide

THE CONVERT

A TALE OF EXILE AND EXTREMISM

Deborah Baker

The Subject Talks Back

Anyone who has ever written about a living person knows *the wait*. Sometimes you receive a laundry list of grievances. Sometimes word trickles back of rage and feelings of betrayal. There might be a letter from a law firm or simply a punishing silence. When all is said and done, the person you have written about has a kind of hold over your work that a reviewer can only dream of. I'd nearly given up when there it was, wedged between the water bill and a bank statement, an airmail envelope addressed to me. Familiar handwriting, familiar return address in Lahore, Pakistan.

My first book was a biography of an obscure American poet born in 1901. When I approached her in 1989, she was living as a recluse in a Florida citrus grove. Fifty years before, she had not merely renounced her own poetry but everybody else's as well. Through an intermediary, she conveyed to me that I should write a sample chapter (she assigned the topic). If it met with her approval, we would work together on her biography. She could use a secretary, she said. But before I could reply, she fell ill. When she heard I had proceeded without her, she wrote me angrily, calling me "sluttish." Her minions sent me lengthy poison-pen missives, dissecting my character with the calculated cruelty she had once dispensed to her admirers.

She never read a word of what I'd written. The day after I sent the final manuscript to the publisher, she had a heart attack and died, as if my book and her life were paired like Siamese twins and

I had killed her by finishing it. This is the kind of magical thinking that binds the biographer to her subject.

When I first came upon the archive of the Islamic writer Maryam Jameelah, six years after the attacks of September 11 and in the thick of the American wars in Iraq and Afghanistan, I wasn't sure what I had found. From the early 1960s until the mid-eighties, Jameelah had written numerous books and pamphlets, translated into a dozen languages. These books were welcomed all over the Islamic world as the definitive word on the superiority of Islamic values over Western ones. Moreover, in mini-biographies of fabled mujahidin, she urged young Muslims to martyr themselves as "freedom fighters" against the godless infidels of the West and their secular Muslim enablers. Her author photo was that of a shapeless black ghost; not even her eyes could be seen behind the dark folds of her veil.

But the Maryam Jameelah archive also contained letters to her parents, Herbert and Myra Marcus, secular Zionist Jews living in a New York City suburb. For Jameelah had been born Margaret Marcus in White Plains in 1934. In 1962 she had left for Pakistan, never to return to America. She went there to live as the adopted daughter of the founding father of militant, political Islam. Her vivid and titillating portrayal of the moral and cultural depravity of America, I then realized, was drawn from Peggy Marcus's coming-of-age in a postwar suburb, the same one depicted in the best-selling comic memoir *Please Don't Eat the Daisies*. The infidels she condemned were her own people.

Yet unlike the hectoring prose of her books, her letters to her parents were affectionate, funny, and acutely observant. Filled with dramatic incident, dialogue, and surprise developments, there were pages and pages of mesmerizing details about living in purdah under the roof of the aging emir who was the first to call for a twentieth-century global jihad against the west.

I was well into writing her story when I came upon a drawing she'd done dated September 11, 2001, nearly forty years after she had left America. Even then I was not prepared to consider the possibility that Maryam Jameelah might still be alive. Was I obliged to meet her? I had her letters and writings, what more could she add? What need did I have of an old woman with unreliable memories living on the other side of the world?

But if she lived to see the attacks, what did she make of them? Did she watch the city she had once known so well fall to pieces? Had she changed her mind about the evils of the West or did she remain resolute? Could she help me make sense of 9/11 and the war on terror that followed, or would she see me as her sworn enemy? Suddenly, the obscure story of Margaret Marcus and Maryam Jameelah became the means by which I might cut the Gordian knot that bound America and large parts of the Islamic world in enmity.

At one level I knew this was yet another example of magical thinking. But in the long and largely lonely years spent writing a book, all sorts of absurd ideas keep you company. So I wrote a letter to the address of her publisher and Maryam Jameelah promptly wrote back, inviting me to come see her in Pakistan. I arrived six months later, in December 2007, at the height of the state of emergency.

As soon as I stepped into her room, I realized that the woman I had conjured from the letters bore little resemblance to the woman in front of me. While she talked nonstop in a strange keening voice I tried to remember what it was I had wanted from her. Her third-floor bedroom was suffocating; as soon as I arrived, I couldn't wait to leave and no sooner had I left then I realized that I had to go back. This kept up for two weeks. I still can't fully explain what happened to me in that room. But then Benazir Bhutto was assassinated, and with that the nuances of the argument between Islam and America and the details of the dueling narratives of Margaret and Maryam seemed pretty much beside the point. I returned to New York shattered.

Eventually, I reconceived the entire book, stretching the art of biography to accommodate both the facts and the fantasies Maryam and Margaret had spun in those letters to her family. For she, too, had struggled to make sense of the mystery of her life. She had cast and recast the signature events of the twentieth century in a way that made the radical turn she had taken defensible, romantic, even noble. By portraying that struggle both in her words and in my own, I hoped to get beyond the supposed divide between our respective, warring worlds.

And when I tore open that long-awaited letter it seemed at first to promise a kind of truce: "This note is to acknowledge safe receipt of your book parcel from Delhi (India)," she wrote. "I am satisfied with your book as a fair and just detailed appraisal of my life and work." Not a week later, however, the library in which I found her archive also received a letter. In this one, Maryam Jameelah insisted my portrayal of her was filled with falsehoods and unfounded allegations.

Perhaps I had captured only a hint of that woman beneath the veil. Or perhaps fifty years of purdah limited her view of herself and the world she had a hand in making. But somewhere between these two letters lay the unearthly promise of biography: a partly open door, a glimpse of another life. As if all it takes is a moment to look in and wonder.

This essay first appeared on the Paris Review *Daily*

Questions and Topics for Discussion

1) Did you find Maryam Jameelah to be a sympathetic or admirable figure? Why or why not? Were there any parts of Jameelah's tale that you found you could personally relate to?

2) What do you think drew Deborah Baker to Jameelah as a biographical subject? Despite their very different lives, do you think Baker and Jameelah share any value systems or life experiences that make them particularly well matched as biographer and subject? Why do you think Baker chose to bring her own voice and point of view into the narrative of Jameelah's story? How does this differ from other biographical or nonfiction works you've read?

3) Baker points out how mental illness was treated and viewed in the 1950s and 1960s. How do you think Jameelah's life might have unfolded differently if she were a teenager today? How did the revelation of her illness impact your reading of her letters?

4) Does the fact that Jameelah was left alone to write her books, forgoing the traditional chores and dependent roles she and Mawdudi advocated for Muslim women, undermine the substance of her critique of feminism and Western lifestyles?

5) Most of Jameelah's letters in *The Convert* are addressed to her parents. Why do you think she continued to maintain this

connection, which seemed so vital to her existence, despite having renounced her parents' country, culture, and religious beliefs?

6) Baker conducted the majority of her research for *The Convert* at the New York Public Library, where Jameelah's letters are archived. Why do you think Jameelah chose to not only make her letters available to the public, but to entrust them to a Western institution? Why not send her archives to an institution in Pakistan?

7) At the end of *The Convert,* Baker writes, "In her most recent letter to me, Maryam asked that I send her two copies of a *National Geographic* book of photographs. I'm still trying to decide what books I will send instead." What books would you send to Maryam Jameelah, and why?

8) Baker opens *The Convert* with the following epigraphs:

> "If a man passes a door which has no curtain and is not shut and looks in, he has committed no sin."—Muhammed ibn 'Abd Allah Kahtip al-Tibrizi, *Mishkat al-Masabih*

> "Whoever undertakes to write a biography binds himself to lying, to concealment, to hypocrisy, to flummery. . . . Truth is not accessible."—Sigmund Freud

Why do you think Baker chose these epigraphs? Did the revelation that she had rewritten and condensed many of Jameelah's letters change your reading of *The Convert* as a work of nonfiction up until that point? Is there ever such a thing as "pure" nonfiction when it comes to biography and memoir?

9) What do you think motivated Mawdudi to take Jameelah into his home?

10) Does it matter what Jameelah makes of *The Convert?*

© Julienne Schaer

DEBORAH BAKER was born in Charlottesville and is a graduate of the University of Virginia. She is the author of *In Extremis: The Life of Laura Riding,* which was a finalist for a Pulitzer Prize. In 2008 Penguin published her book *A Blue Hand: The Beats in India,* a narrative account of Allen Ginsberg's travels in India. While a Fellow at the Cullman Center for Scholars and Writers at the New York Public Library, she researched and wrote *The Convert.* She is married to Amitav Ghosh, with whom she has two children, and together they divide their time between Goa and Brooklyn.

This book is made possible through a partnership with the College of Saint Benedict, and honors the legacy of S. Mariella Gable, a distinguished teacher at the College.

Previous titles in this series include:

Loverboy by Victoria Redel

The House on Eccles Road by Judith Kitchen

One Vacant Chair by Joe Coomer

The Weatherman by Clint McCown

Collected Poems by Jane Kenyon

Variations on the Theme of an African Dictatorship
by Nuruddin Farah:
Sweet and Sour Milk
Sardines
Close Sesame

Duende by Tracy K. Smith

All of It Singing: New and Selected Poems by Linda Gregg

The Art of Syntax: Rhythm of Thought, Rhythm of Song
by Ellen Bryant Voigt

How to Escape from a Leper Colony by Tiphanie Yanique

One Day I Will Write About This Place by Binyavanga Wainaina

Support for this series has been provided by the Manitou Fund
as part of the Warner Reading Program.

Book design by Rachel Holscher.
Composition by BookMobile Design and Publishing Services,
Minneapolis, Minnesota.
Manufactured by Versa Press on
acid-free 30 percent postconsumer wastepaper.